IF FOUND, please notify and arrange return to owner. This instruction technique book is important for the owner's preparation for the Fundamentals of Instructing Knowledge Test administered by the Federal Aviation Administration. Thank you.

Pilot's Name: _____

Address: _____

City   State   Zip Code

Telephone: (_____) _____

Additional copies of *Fundamentals of Instructing FAA Written Exam* are available from

Gleim Publications, Inc.
P.O. Box 12848, University Station
Gainesville, Florida 32604
(352) 375-0772
(800) 87-GLEIM
FAX: (352) 375-6940
Internet: www.gleim.com

The price is $9.95 (subject to change without notice). Orders must be prepaid. Use the order form on page 148. Shipping and handling charges will be added to telephone orders. Add applicable sales tax to shipments within Florida.

Gleim Publications, Inc. guarantees the immediate refund of all resalable texts returned in 30 days. Shipping and handling charges and software are nonrefundable.

ALSO AVAILABLE FROM GLEIM PUBLICATIONS, INC.

ORDER FORM ON PAGE 148

Private Pilot and Recreational Pilot FAA Written Exam
Private Pilot Practical Test Prep and Flight Maneuvers
Pilot Handbook
Aviation Weather and Weather Services

Advanced Pilot Training Books

Instrument Pilot FAA Written Exam
Instrument Pilot Practical Test Prep and Flight Maneuvers

Commercial Pilot FAA Written Exam
Commercial Pilot Practical Test Prep and Flight Maneuvers

*Flight/Ground Instructor FAA Written Exam**
Flight Instructor Practical Test Prep and Flight Maneuvers

Airline Transport Pilot FAA Written Exam

*Companion book to *Fundamentals of Instructing FAA Written Exam*

REVIEWERS AND CONTRIBUTORS

Barry A. Jones, ATP, CFII, MEI, B.S. in Air Commerce/Flight Technology, Florida Institute of Technology, is our aviation project manager and also a flight instructor and charter pilot with Gulf Atlantic Airways in Gainesville, FL. Mr. Jones drafted answer explanations, incorporated numerous revisions, assisted in assembling the text, and provided technical assistance throughout the project.

Karen A. Louviere, B.A., University of Florida, provided production assistance throughout the project.

Travis A. Moore, M.B.A., University of Florida, is our production coordinator. Mr. Moore coordinated the production staff and assisted in the production of this edition.

Nancy Raughley, B.A., Tift College, is our editor. Ms. Raughley reviewed the manuscript, revised it for readability, and assisted in all phases of production.

John F. Rebstock, B.S., School of Accounting, University of Florida, reviewed portions of the text and composed the page layout.

The many FAA employees who helped, in person or by telephone, primarily in Gainesville, FL; Jacksonville, FL; Orlando, FL; Oklahoma City, OK; and Washington, DC.

The many CFIs, pilots, and student pilots who have provided comments and suggestions about *Fundamentals of Instructing FAA Written Exam* during the past 10 years.

A PERSONAL THANKS

This manual would not have been possible without the extraordinary effort and dedication of Jim Collis, Terry Hall, and Rhonda Powell, who typed the entire manuscript and all revisions, as well as prepared the camera-ready pages.

The author also appreciates the proofreading and production assistance of Adam Cohen, Chad Houghton, Mark Moore, and Larry Pfeffer.

Finally, I appreciate the encouragement, support, and tolerance of my family throughout this project.

Groundwood Paper and Highlighters -- This book is printed on high quality groundwood paper. It is lightweight and easy-to-recycle. We recommend that you purchase a highlighter specifically designed to be non-bleed-through (e.g., Avery *Glidestick* ™) at your local office supply store.

SIXTH EDITION

FUNDAMENTALS OF INSTRUCTING

FAA WRITTEN EXAM

for the FAA Computer-Based Pilot Knowledge Test

by Irvin N. Gleim, Ph.D., CFII

**with the assistance of
Barry A. Jones, ATP, CFII, MEI**

ABOUT THE AUTHOR

Irvin N. Gleim earned his private pilot certificate in 1965 from the Institute of Aviation at the University of Illinois, where he subsequently received his Ph.D. He is a commercial pilot and flight instructor (instrument) with multiengine and seaplane ratings, and is a member of the Aircraft Owners and Pilots Association, American Bonanza Society, Civil Air Patrol, Experimental Aircraft Association, and Seaplane Pilots Association. He is also author of Practical Test Prep and Flight Maneuvers books for the private, instrument, commercial, and flight instructor certificates/ratings, and study guides for the private/recreational, instrument, commercial, flight/ground instructor, fundamentals of instructing, and airline transport pilot FAA pilot knowledge tests. Two additional pilot training books are *Pilot Handbook* and *Aviation Weather and Weather Services*.

Dr. Gleim has also written articles for professional accounting and business law journals, and is the author of widely used review manuals for the CIA exam (Certified Internal Auditor), the CMA exam (Certified Management Accountant), and the CPA exam (Certified Public Accountant). He is Professor Emeritus, Fisher School of Accounting, University of Florida, and is a CIA, CMA, and CPA.

Gleim Publications, Inc.
P.O. Box 12848 • University Station
Gainesville, Florida 32604

(352) 375-0772
(800) 87-GLEIM
FAX: (352) 375-6940

Internet: www.gleim.com
E-mail: admin@gleim.com

ISSN 1078-2087
ISBN 0-917539-55-9
Fifth Printing: August 1997

This is the fifth printing of the sixth edition of *Fundamentals of Instructing FAA Written Exam*.

Please e-mail update@gleim.com with FOI 6-5 in the subject or text. You will receive our current update as a reply.

EXAMPLE:

To:	update@gleim.com
From:	your e-mail address
Subject:	FOI 6-5

HELP !!

This is the Sixth Edition, designed specifically for pilots who aspire to the flight instructor certificate and/or ground instructor certificate. Please send any corrections and suggestions for subsequent editions to the author, c/o Gleim Publications, Inc. The last page in this book has been reserved for you to make comments and suggestions. It can be torn out and mailed to Gleim Publications, Inc.

A companion volume, *Flight/Ground Instructor FAA Written Exam,* is available as is *Flight Instructor Practical Test Prep and Flight Maneuvers*, which focuses on the FAA practical test, just as this book focuses on the FAA pilot knowledge test. Save time, money, and frustration -- order both books today! See the order form on page 148. Please bring these books to the attention of flight instructors, fixed-base operators, and others with a potential interest in acquiring their flight instructor certificates. Wide distribution of these books and increased interest in flying depend on your assistance and good word. Thank you.

NOTE: ANSWER DISCREPANCIES and UPDATES

Our answers have been carefully researched and reviewed. Inevitably, there will be differences with competitors' books and even the FAA. If necessary, we will develop an UPDATE for *Fundamentals of Instructing FAA Written Exam*. Send e-mail to update@gleim.com as described at the top right of this page, and visit our Internet site for the latest updates and information on all of our products. To continue providing our customers with first-rate service, we request that questions about our books and software be sent to us via <u>mail</u>, <u>e-mail</u>, or <u>fax</u>. The appropriate staff member will give each question thorough consideration and a prompt response. Questions concerning orders, prices, shipments, or payments will be handled via telephone by our competent and courteous customer service staff.

TABLE OF CONTENTS

[Call (800) 87-GLEIM to order your FAA Test Prep software]

PREFACE

This book has three purposes:

1. To provide you with the easiest and fastest means of passing the Fundamentals of Instructing (FOI) Knowledge Test.

2. To help both experienced and inexperienced aviation instructors improve their instruction techniques.

3. To assist flight and/or ground instructors in organizing and presenting aviation ground schools which prepare individuals to pass the FAA pilot knowledge tests.

FOI Knowledge Test

Successful completion of the FOI knowledge test is required by the FAA for those seeking the flight instructor or ground instructor certificates. Chapter 1 of this book (beginning on the next page) contains a discussion of the requirements to obtain the flight instructor and ground instructor certificates, and a description of the FOI knowledge test, how to prepare for it and take it, and how to maximize your score with minimum effort. Chapters 2 through 7 contain outlines of exactly what you need to know to answer the FAA knowledge test questions, as well as all of the actual FAA test questions, each accompanied by a comprehensive explanation.

NOTE: Appendix A contains a practice test consisting of 50 questions from this book which reflects the subject matter composition of the FAA knowledge test.

Improving Instruction Methods

The FAA has published *Aviation Instructor's Handbook* (*AIH*, AC 60-14), which explains the basic principles and processes of teaching and learning. This is the subject matter of the FOI knowledge test. The first 56 pages of the *AIH* set forth these general concepts. This material is more easily presented and studied in outline format, as it appears in Chapters 2 through 7 of this book. Both experienced and inexperienced aviation instructors will find the study of these outlines very useful in improving their instruction methods.

Appendix B of this book (43 pages in length) is a reprint of "Section Two -- The Flight Instructor" of *Aviation Instructor's Handbook*. It is useful reading and periodic review for CFIs. It consists of three chapters:

1. Flight Instructor Characteristics and Responsibilities
2. Techniques of Flight Instruction
3. Planning Instructional Activity

Ground School Course Suggestions

Many aviation instructors would like to increase the general public's interest in learning to fly. These instructors also enjoy teaching. Appendix C of this book consists of suggestions on how to find (or become) a sponsor for a "ground school." It also contains suggestions on course organization, lecture outlines, and class presentation.

Enjoy Flying -- Safely!

Irvin N. Gleim

August 1997

CHAPTER ONE
THE FAA PILOT KNOWLEDGE TEST

The beginning of this chapter provides an overview of the process to obtain a flight instructor certificate. The ground instructor certificate is also addressed. The remainder of this chapter explains the content and procedure of relevant Federal Aviation Administration (FAA) tests. Becoming a Certificated Flight Instructor (CFI) and/or a Certificated Ground Instructor is fun. Begin today!

Fundamentals of Instructing FAA Written Exam is one of four related books for obtaining a flight and/or ground instructor certificate. The other three are *Flight/Ground Instructor FAA Written Exam*, which is in a format similar to this book, and *Flight Instructor Practical Test Prep and Flight Maneuvers* and *Pilot Handbook*, each in outline/illustration format.

Flight/Ground Instructor FAA Written Exam prepares you to pass the FAA's flight and/or ground instructor knowledge test. If you are planning to obtain both the flight and ground instructor certificates, you only need to pass the Fundamentals of Instructing (FOI) test once.

Flight Instructor Practical Test Prep and Flight Maneuvers is a comprehensive, carefully organized presentation of everything you need to know for your flight instructor practical (flight) test. It integrates material from over 100 FAA publications and other sources. This book will transfer knowledge to you and give you the confidence to do well on your FAA practical test.

Pilot Handbook is a complete pilot reference book that combines over 100 FAA books and documents including *AIM*, FARs, ACs, and much more. This book, more than any other, will help make you a better and more proficient pilot.

If you are planning on purchasing the FAA books on aviation weather, purchase Gleim's *Aviation Weather and Weather Services*, which combines all of the information from the FAA's *Aviation Weather* (AC 00-6A), *Aviation Weather Services* (AC 00-45D), and numerous FAA publications into one easy-to-understand book. It will help you study all aspects of aviation weather and provide you with a single reference book.

1.1 WHAT IS A FLIGHT INSTRUCTOR CERTIFICATE?

A flight instructor certificate is similar in appearance to your commercial pilot certificate and will allow you to give flight and ground instruction. The certificate is sent to you by the FAA upon satisfactory completion of your training program, two pilot knowledge tests, and a practical test. A sample flight instructor certificate is reproduced below.

Front   Back

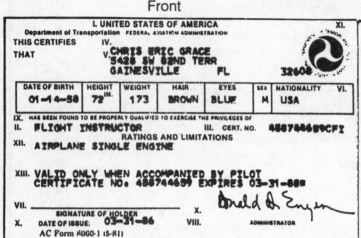

1.2 REQUIREMENTS TO OBTAIN A FLIGHT INSTRUCTOR CERTIFICATE

1. Be at least 18 years of age.

2. Be able to read, write, and converse fluently in English (certificates with operating limitations may be available for medically related deficiencies).

3. Hold a commercial or airline transport pilot (ATP) certificate with an aircraft rating appropriate to the flight instructor rating sought (e.g., airplane, glider).

    a. You must also hold an instrument rating to be a flight instructor in an airplane.

4. Receive and log ground training (such as using this book, *Flight/Ground Instructor FAA Written Exam, Flight Instructor Practical Test Prep and Flight Maneuvers*, and *Pilot Handbook*) to learn

    a. Fundamentals of instructing

    b. All subject areas in which ground training is required for recreational, private, and commercial pilot certificates and for an instrument rating

5. Pass both the FOI and the flight instructor knowledge tests with scores of 70% or better. All FAA knowledge tests are administered at FAA-designated computer testing centers. The FOI test consists of 50 multiple-choice questions selected from the 160 FOI-related questions among the 1,225 questions in the FAA's flight and ground instructor knowledge test bank; the balance of 1,065 questions are for the flight and ground instructor tests. Each of the FAA's 160 FOI questions is reproduced in this book with complete explanations to the right of each question.

    a. You are not required to take the FOI knowledge test if you

        1) Hold an FAA flight or ground instructor certificate

        2) Hold a current teacher's certificate authorizing you to teach at an educational level of the 7th grade or higher

        3) Are currently employed as a teacher at an accredited college or university

6. Demonstrate flight proficiency (FAR 61.187).

   a. You must receive and log flight and ground training and obtain a logbook endorsement from an authorized instructor in the following areas of operations for an airplane category rating with a single-engine or multiengine class rating:

      1) *Fundamentals of instructing*
      2) *Technical subject areas*
      3) *Preflight preparation*
      4) *Preflight lesson on a maneuver to be performed in flight*
      5) *Preflight procedures*
      6) *Airport and seaplane base operations*
      7) *Takeoffs, landings, and go-arounds*
      8) *Fundamentals of flight*
      9) *Performance maneuvers*
      10) *Ground reference maneuvers*
      11) *Slow flight, stalls, and spins (single-engine only)*

          a) *Slow flight and stalls (multiengine only)*

      12) *Basic instrument maneuvers*
      13) *Emergency operations*
      14) *Multiengine operations (multiengine only)*
      15) *Postflight procedures*

   b. The flight instruction must be given by a person who has held a flight instructor certificate during the 24 months immediately preceding the date the instruction is given and who has given at least 200 hr. of flight instruction as a CFI.

   c. You must also obtain a logbook endorsement by an appropriately certificated and rated flight instructor who has provided you with spin entry, spin, and spin recovery training in an airplane that is certificated for spins and has found that you are competent and possess instructional proficiency in those training areas.

7. Alternatively, enroll in an FAA-certificated pilot school that has an approved flight instructor certification course (airplane).

   a. These are known as Part 141 schools or Part 142 training centers because they are authorized by Part 141 or Part 142 of the FARs.

      1) All other regulations concerning the certification of pilots are found in Part 61 of the FARs.

   b. The Part 141 course must consist of at least 40 hr. of ground instruction and 25 hr. of flight instructor training.

8. Successfully complete a practical (flight) test which will be given by an FAA inspector or designated pilot examiner. The practical test will be conducted as specified in the FAA's Flight Instructor Practical Test Standards (FAA-S-8081-6A, dated May 1991).

   a. FAA inspectors are FAA employees and do not charge for their services.

   b. FAA-designated pilot examiners are proficient, experienced flight instructors and pilots who are authorized by the FAA to conduct flight tests. They do charge a fee.

   c. The FAA's Flight Instructor Practical Test Standards are outlined and reprinted in *Flight Instructor Practical Test Prep and Flight Maneuvers*.

1.3 REQUIREMENTS TO OBTAIN A GROUND INSTRUCTOR CERTIFICATE

1. To be eligible for a ground instructor certificate, you must

   a. Be at least 18 years of age.

   b. Be able to read, write, and converse fluently in English (certificates with operating limitations may be available for medically related deficiencies).

   c. Exhibit practical and theoretical knowledge by passing the FOI and the appropriate ground instructor pilot knowledge tests.

1)   See item 5.a. on page 2 for information on when the FOI knowledge test is not required.

2.   Ground instructor certificates cover three levels of certification:

   a.   Basic ground instructor (BGI) may provide

      1)   Ground training in the aeronautical knowledge areas required for a recreational or private pilot certificate

      2)   Ground training required for a recreational or private pilot flight review

      3)   A recommendation for the recreational or private pilot knowledge test

   b.   Advanced ground instructor (AGI) may provide

      1)   Ground training in the aeronautical knowledge areas required for any certificate or rating

      2)   Ground training required for any flight review

      3)   A recommendation for a knowledge test required for any certificate or rating

   c.   Instrument ground instructor (IGI) may provide

      1)   Ground training in the aeronautical knowledge areas required for an instrument rating to a pilot or instructor certificate

      2)   Ground training required for an instrument proficiency check

      3)   A recommendation for the instrument rating knowledge test for a pilot or instructor certificate

      4)   See Gleim's *Instrument Pilot FAA Written Exam* which covers the IGI pilot knowledge test.

1.4 FAA PILOT KNOWLEDGE TEST

   This test book is designed to help you prepare for and successfully take the FAA FOI knowledge test for the flight and/or ground instructor certificate. The remainder of this chapter explains the FAA test procedures.

1.   All of the 160 questions in the FAA's flight and ground instructor knowledge test bank that are applicable to fundamentals of instructing have been grouped into the following six categories, which are the titles of Chapters 2 through 7:

   Chapter 2 -- The Learning Process
   Chapter 3 -- Barriers to Learning
   Chapter 4 -- Human Behavior and Effective Communication
   Chapter 5 -- Teaching Methods
   Chapter 6 -- Planning Instructional Activity
   Chapter 7 -- Critique and Evaluation

   Note that, in the official FAA flight and ground instructor knowledge test bank containing all of the questions, the FAA's questions are **not** grouped together by topic. We have unscrambled them for you in this book.

2.   Within each of the chapters listed, questions relating to the same subtopic are grouped together to facilitate your study program. Each subtopic is called a module.

3.   To the right of each question are

   a.   The correct answer,
   b.   The FAA question number, and
   c.   A reference for the answer explanation.

      1)   EXAMPLE: *AIH Chap I* means *Aviation Instructor's Handbook*, Chapter I.

4.   Each chapter begins with an outline of the material tested on the FAA knowledge test. The outlines in this part of the book are somewhat brief and have only one purpose: to help you pass the FAA FOI knowledge test.

    a.   **CAUTION:** The **sole purpose** of this book is to expedite your passing the FAA FOI knowledge test for the flight and/or ground instructor certificate. Accordingly, all extraneous material (i.e., not directly tested on the FAA knowledge test) is omitted even though much more information and knowledge are necessary to be a proficient flight or ground instructor. This additional material is presented in three related books: *Flight/Ground Instructor FAA Written Exam*, *Flight Instructor Practical Test Prep and Flight Maneuvers*, and *Pilot Handbook*.

Follow the suggestions given throughout this chapter and you will have no trouble passing the test the first time you take it.

1.5 HOW TO PREPARE FOR THE FAA PILOT KNOWLEDGE TEST

1.   Begin by carefully reading the rest of this chapter. You need to have a complete understanding of the examination process prior to beginning to study for it. This knowledge will make your studying more efficient.

2.   After you have spent an hour studying this chapter, set up a study schedule, including a target date for taking your pilot knowledge test.

    a.   Do not let the study process drag on because it will be discouraging, i.e., the quicker the better.

    b.   Consider enrolling in an organized ground school course at your local FBO, community college, etc.

    c.   Determine where and when you are going to take your pilot knowledge test.

3.   Work through each of Chapters 2 through 7.

    a.   Each chapter begins with a list of its module titles. The number in parentheses after each title is the number of FAA questions that cover the information in that module. The two numbers following the parentheses are the page numbers on which the outline and the questions for that particular module begin, respectively.

    b.   Begin by studying the outlines slowly and carefully.

    c.   Cover the answer explanations on the right side of each page with your hand or a piece of paper while you answer the multiple-choice questions.

        1)   Remember, it is very important to the learning (and understanding) process that you honestly commit yourself to an answer. If you are wrong, your memory will be reinforced by having discovered your error. Therefore, it is crucial to cover up the answer and make an honest attempt to answer the question before reading the answer.

        2)   Study the answer explanation for each question that you answer incorrectly, do not understand, or have difficulty with.

4.   Note that this test book (in contrast to most other question and answer books) contains the FAA questions grouped by topic. Thus, some questions may appear repetitive, while others may be duplicates or near-duplicates. Accordingly, do not work question after question (i.e., waste time and effort) if you are already conversant with a topic and the type of questions asked.

5.   As you move from module to module and chapter to chapter, you may need further explanation or clarification of certain topics. You may wish to obtain and use *Flight Instructor Practical Test Prep and Flight Maneuvers*, which covers in detail all the information in the FAA Flight Instructor Practical Test Standards, and other information relevant to flight instructors. This book covers the fundamentals of instructing as well as the knowledge and skills required of flight instructors.

6.   Keep track of your work!!! As you complete a module in Chapters 2 through 7, grade yourself with an A, B, C, or ? (use a ? if you need help on the subject) next to the module title at the front of the respective chapter.

   a.   The A, B, C, or ? is your self-evaluation of your comprehension of the material in that module and your ability to answer the questions.

   A   means a good understanding.
   B   means a fair understanding.
   C   means a shaky understanding.
   ?   means to ask your CFI or others about the material and/or questions, and read the pertinent sections in *Flight Instructor Practical Test Prep and Flight Maneuvers*.

   b.   This procedure will provide you with the ability to see quickly (by looking at the first page of Chapters 2 through 7) how much studying you have done (and how much remains) and how well you have done.

   c.   This procedure will also facilitate review. You can spend more time on the modules with which you had difficulty.

1.6 WHEN TO TAKE THE FAA PILOT KNOWLEDGE TEST

1.   You must be at least 16 years of age to take the FOI knowledge test.

2.   You must prepare for the test by successfully completing a ground instruction course, or you may use this book as your self-developed home study course.

   a.   See Module 1.10, Authorization to Take the Pilot Knowledge Test, on page 7.

3.   Take the FOI knowledge test within the next 30 days.

   a.   Get the test behind you.

4.   You must obtain your flight or ground instructor certificate within 24 months or you will have to retake your test.

1.7 COMPUTER TESTING CENTERS

The FAA has contracted with several computer testing services to administer FAA pilot knowledge tests. Each of these computer testing services has testing centers throughout the country. You register by calling an 800 number. Call the following testing services for information regarding the location of testing centers most convenient to you and the time allowed and cost to take their fundamentals of instructing (FOI) knowledge test.

   CATS   (800) 947-4228
   LaserGrade   (800) 211-2754
   Sylvan   (800) 274-1900

Also, about twenty Part 141 schools use the AvTEST computer testing system, which is very similar to the computer testing services described above.

1.8 GLEIM'S *FAA TEST PREP* SOFTWARE

Computer testing is consistent with modern aviation's use of computers (e.g., DUATS, flight simulators, computerized cockpits, etc.). All FAA pilot knowledge tests are administered by computer.

Computer testing is natural after computer study. Computer-assisted instruction is a very efficient and effective method of study. Gleim's *FAA Test Prep* software is designed to prepare you for computer testing. *FAA Test Prep* software contains all of the questions in this book (but not the outlines and figures). You choose either STUDY MODE or TEST MODE.

In STUDY MODE, the software provides you with an explanation of each answer you choose (correct or incorrect). You design each study session:

> Topic(s) you wish to cover
> Number of questions
> Order of questions -- FAA, Gleim, or random
> Order of answers to each question -- FAA or random
> Questions missed from last session -- test, study, or both
> Questions missed from all sessions -- test, study, or both
> Questions never answered correctly

In TEST MODE, you decide the format -- CATS, LaserGrade, Sylvan, AvTEST, or Gleim. When you finish your test, you can study the questions missed and access answer explanations. The software imitates the operation of the FAA-approved computer testing companies above. Thus, you have a complete understanding of exactly how to take an FAA knowledge test before you go to a computer testing center.

To use *FAA Test Prep*, you need an IBM-compatible computer with a hard disk, 2.0 MB of disk space, 2.0 MB of RAM, and a high-density 3.5 in. diskette drive. Learn more details about how Gleim's *FAA Test Prep* software functions beginning on page 12. Call (800) 87-GLEIM or use the order form at the back of this book to obtain your copy of this useful interactive software.

1.9 PART 141 SCHOOLS WITH FAA PILOT KNOWLEDGE TEST EXAMINING AUTHORITY

The FAA permits some FAR Part 141 schools to develop, administer, and grade their own pilot knowledge tests as long as they use the FAA knowledge test bank, i.e., the same questions as in this book. The FAA does not provide the correct answers to the Part 141 schools, and the FAA only reviews the Part 141 school test question selection sheets. Thus, some of the answers used by Part 141 test examiners may not agree with the FAA or those in this book. The latter is not a problem but may explain why you may miss a question on a Part 141 pilot knowledge test using an answer presented in this book.

1.10 AUTHORIZATION TO TAKE THE FAA PILOT KNOWLEDGE TEST

Before taking the FOI knowledge test, applicants must, according to FAR 61.185(a)(1), log ground training from an authorized instructor in all of the subjects in which ground training is required for the recreational, private, and commercial pilot certificates and an instrument rating. They must also receive an endorsement from an authorized instructor on the fundamentals of instructing, including

1. The learning process
2. Elements of effective teaching
3. Student evaluation and testing
4. Course development
5. Lesson planning
6. Classroom training techniques

For your convenience, standard authorization forms for the FOI and the flight and ground instructor knowledge tests are reproduced on page 143. They can be easily completed, signed by a flight or ground instructor, torn out, and taken to the computer testing center.

1.11 FORMAT OF THE FAA PILOT KNOWLEDGE TEST

The FAA's fundamentals of instructing knowledge test consists of 50 multiple-choice questions selected from the 160 questions that appear in the next six chapters.

Note that the FAA test will be taken from exactly the same questions that are reproduced in this book. If you study the next six chapters, including all the questions and answers, **you should be assured of passing your test.**

Additionally, all of the FAA figures are contained in a book titled *Computerized Testing Supplement for Flight and Ground Instructor*, which will be given to you for your use at the time of your test. There is only one FAA figure used for the FOI knowledge test and it is reproduced on page 65 of this book.

1.12 WHAT TO TAKE TO THE FAA PILOT KNOWLEDGE TEST

1. Authorization to take the examination (see page 143)
2. Picture identification of yourself
3. Proof of age

1.13 COMPUTER TESTING PROCEDURES

To register to take the FOI knowledge test, you should call one of the testing services listed in Module 1.7, Computer Testing Centers, on page 6, or you may call one of their testing centers. These testing centers and telephone numbers are listed in Gleim's *FAA Test Prep* software under Vendors in the main menu. When you register, you will pay the fee by credit card.

When you arrive at the computer testing center, you will be required to provide positive proof of identification and documentary evidence of your age. The identification presented must include your photograph, signature, and actual residential address. This information may be presented in more than one form of identification. Next, you sign in on the testing center's daily log. On the logsheet there must be a statement that your signature certifies that, if this is a retest, you meet the applicable requirements (see Module 1.16, Failure on the Pilot Knowledge Test, on page 10) and that you have not taken and passed this test in the past 2 years. Finally, you will present your logbook endorsement or authorization form from your instructor, which authorizes you to take the test. A standard authorization form is provided on page 143 for your use.

Next, you will be taken into the testing room and seated at a computer terminal. A person from the testing center will assist you in logging on the system, and you will be asked to confirm your personal data (e.g., name, Social Security number, etc.). Then you will be prompted and given an online introduction to the computer testing system and you will take a sample test. If you have used our *FAA Test Prep* software, you will be conversant with the computer testing methodology and environment, and you will probably want to skip the sample test and begin the actual test immediately. You will be allowed 1.5 hr. to complete the actual test. This is 1.8 minutes per question. Confirm the time permitted when you call the testing center to register to take the test by computer. When you have completed your test, an Airman Computer Test Report will be printed out, validated (usually with an embossed seal), and given to you by a person from the testing center. Before you leave, you will be required to sign out on the testing center's daily log.

Each computer testing center has certain idiosyncrasies in its paperwork, scheduling, telephone procedures, as well as in its software. It is for this reason that our *FAA Test Prep* software emulates each of these FAA-approved computer testing companies.

1.14 FAA QUESTIONS WITH TYPOGRAPHICAL ERRORS

Occasionally, FAA test questions contain typographical errors such that there is no correct answer. The FAA test development process involves many steps and people, and as you would expect, glitches occur in the system that are beyond the control of any one person. We indicate "best" rather than correct answers for some questions. Use these best answers for the indicated questions.

Note that the FAA corrects (rewrites) defective questions on the computer tests, which it cannot currently do with respect to faulty figures which are printed in the FAA computer testing supplements. Thus, it is important to carefully study questions that are noted to have a best answer in this book.

1.15 YOUR FAA PILOT KNOWLEDGE TEST REPORT

1. You will receive your Airman Computer Test Report upon completion of the test. An example computer test report is reproduced below.

   a. Note that you will receive only one grade as illustrated.

   b. The expiration date is the date by which you must take your FAA practical test.

   c. The report lists the FAA subject matter knowledge codes of the questions you missed, so you can review the topics you missed prior to your practical test.

Federal Aviation Administration
Airman Computer Test Report

EXAM TITLE: Fundamentals of Instructing

NAME: Jones David John

ID NUMBER: 123456789   TAKE: 1

DATE: 08/14/97   SCORE: 82   GRADE: Pass

Knowledge area codes in which questions were answered incorrectly. See appropriate FAA knowledge test study guide. A code may represent more than one incorrect response.

H20 H21 H22 H23

EXPIRATION DATE: 08/31/99

<u>DO NOT LOSE THIS REPORT</u>

Authorized instructor's statement. (If Applicable)

I have given Mr./Ms. _____ additional instruction in each subject area shown to be deficient and consider the applicant competent to pass the test.

Last _____ Initial _____ Cert. No. _____ Type _____
(Print Clearly)

Signature _____

CTD's Embossed Seal

2.   The following FAA subject matter knowledge codes will appear on your test report to identify which topics you had difficulty with. They are the chapter titles in the FAA's *Aviation Instructor's Handbook* (AC 60-14).

> H20 The Learning Process
> H21 Human Behavior
> H22 Effective Communication
> H23 The Teaching Process
> H24 Teaching Methods
> H25 The Instructor as a Critic
> H26 Evaluation
> H27 Instructional Aids
> H30 Flight Instructor Characteristics and Responsibilities
> H31 Techniques of Flight Instruction
> H32 Planning Instructional Activity

    a.   Look them over and review them with your CFI so (s)he can certify that (s)he reviewed the deficient areas and found you competent in them when you take your practical test.

3.   Keep your Airman Computer Test Report in a safe place because you must submit it to the FAA examiner when you take your practical test.

1.16 FAILURE ON THE FAA PILOT KNOWLEDGE TEST

1.   If you fail (less than 70%) the FOI knowledge test (virtually impossible if you follow the above instructions), you may retake it after your instructor endorses the bottom of your Airman Computer Test Report certifying that you have received the necessary ground training to retake the test.

2.   Upon retaking the test, everything is the same except you must also submit your Airman Computer Test Report indicating the previous failure to the examiner.

3.   Note that the pass rate on the FOI knowledge test is about 90%, i.e., 1 out of 10 fail the test initially. Reasons for failure include

    a.   Failure to study the material tested (contained in the outlines at the beginning of Chapters 2 through 7 of this book);

    b.   Failure to practice working the FAA exam questions under test conditions (all of the FAA questions on airplanes appear in Chapters 2 through 7 of this book); and

    c.   Poor examination technique, such as misreading questions and not understanding the requirements.

1.17 REORGANIZATION OF FAA QUESTIONS

1. The questions in the FAA's flight and ground instructor knowledge test bank are numbered 6001 to 7225. Note that questions 6001 to 6160 are Fundamentals of Instructing questions and questions 6161 to 7225 are used for the flight and ground instructor test. The FAA questions appear to be presented randomly.

    a. We have reorganized and renumbered the FAA questions into chapters and modules.

    b. The FAA question number is presented in the middle of the first line of the explanation of each answer.

2. Pages 141 and 142 contain a list of the FAA questions numbers 6001 to 6160 with cross-references to the FAA's subject matter knowledge codes and the chapters and question numbers in this book.

    a. For example, the FAA's question 6001 is cross-referenced to the FAA's subject knowledge code H20, Aviation Instructor's Handbook, Chapter I, The Learning Process. The correct answer is A, and the question appears with answer explanations in this book under 2-1, which means it is reproduced in Chapter 2 as question number 1.

With this overview of exam requirements, you are ready to begin the easy-to-study outlines and rearranged questions with answers to build your knowledge and confidence and PASS THE FAA's FUNDAMENTALS OF INSTRUCTING KNOWLEDGE TEST.

The feedback we receive from users indicates that our books and software reduce anxiety, improve FAA test scores, and build knowledge. Studying for each test becomes a useful step toward advanced certificates and ratings.

1.18 SIMULATED FAA PRACTICE TEST

Appendix A, Fundamentals of Instructing Practice Test, beginning on page 81, allows you to practice taking the FAA knowledge test without the answers next to the questions. This test has 50 questions that have been randomly selected from the 160 Fundamentals of Instructing questions in the FAA's flight and ground instructor knowledge test bank. Topical coverage in this practice test is similar to that of the FAA FOI test.

It is very important that you answer all 50 questions at one sitting. You should not consult the answers, especially when being referred to charts or tables in this book where the questions are answered and explained. Analyze your performance based on the answer key which follows the practice test.

Also rely on Gleim's *FAA Test Prep* software to simulate actual computer testing conditions including the screen layouts, instructions, etc., for CATS, LaserGrade, AvTEST, and Sylvan.

1.19 INSTRUCTIONS FOR *FAA TEST PREP* SOFTWARE

To install *FAA Test Prep*, put your install disk in your floppy drive, type A:INSTALL (if the disk is in your A: drive), and press <Enter>. If this is your first time installing the software, you will be prompted for information such as your name, Social Security number, and address. When you have completed this information and verified that it is correct, the install program will decompress the executable and data files onto your hard drive. The disk is copy protected; do not attempt to fix apparent disk errors.

Once you have installed *FAA Test Prep*, you can always begin the software by typing FAATP at your C:\> prompt (and pressing <Enter>).

The first two times you run the software, a brief introduction will appear. It gives you information about the software and can be printed by pressing <F8>. If you want to read the introduction after your second use of the software, you can access the Introduction menu item located on the Help submenu within the main menu.

The *FAA Test Prep* main menu (shown below) allows you to enter each of the submenus (which are discussed and illustrated on the next five pages) by pressing <Enter> when the cursor is on the desired submenu item. You can always go to the main menu by pressing <Esc> from anywhere in the software.

```
Library  Study  Test  History  Vendors  Options        Help  Exit
```

Library

The Library submenu allows you to select which FAA pilot knowledge test you want to study. You must have the *FAA Test Prep* software installed in order to access it. Most pilots will have only one "library" of questions installed. In the following example, private, commercial, instrument, fundamentals of instructing, flight/ground instructor, and airline transport pilot questions are installed.

```
Database  Installed  Questions

  PPWE       Yes        711
  CPWE       Yes        565
  IPWE       Yes        900
  FOI        Yes        160
  FIGI       Yes        833
  ATP        Yes       1500
```

Study

The Study submenu lets you create and grade study sessions; you can also view a grade report for your last graded study session or view performance data for all of the study sessions you have ever graded. The Study submenu looks like this:

```
Create Session
Grade Session
Return to Study

Performance Analysis
View Grade Report
```

To create a study session, select Create Session from this submenu, and the following screen will appear:

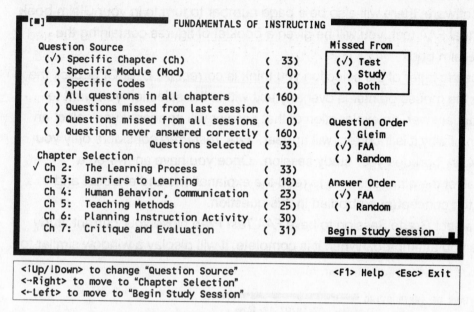

In the example screen shown above, a study session for Chapter 2 is being created. You can also specify the order of questions and the order of answers. If you select "questions missed" to study, you will need to indicate whether they should be from study sessions, test sessions, or both (see box in upper right). When you have adequately specified which questions (or which subjects) you want to practice on, depress the Begin Study Session button with your mouse (or press <Enter> when your cursor is over this control) to begin your study session, which will look somewhat like this:

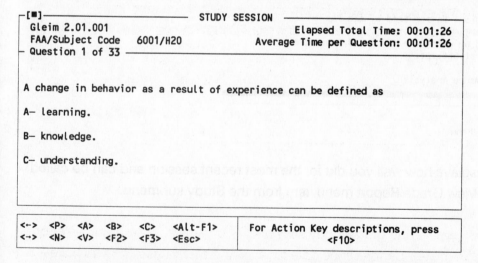

The top portion of the screen shows you generic information about your study session: the current question (Gleim and FAA number), elapsed total time, and average time per question. This allows you to gauge your ability to answer questions in a time-critical manner (without the threat of time expiring).

The middle portion of the screen is the question/answer display area; both the question text and the answer selections appear in this section. Some questions will refer you to FAA figures (as is true on the actual FAA test). In the software, there will also be a page number to turn to in your Gleim book to find the FAA figure. At the actual FAA test, you will be given a booklet of figures containing the same figures you'll find in your Gleim book.

To answer a question, press the letter of the selection you think is correct (A, B, or C) or click the left button on your mouse when the mouse pointer is over any text within the selection you want to choose. If you choose the correct answer, an explanation of that answer will appear; if you select an incorrect answer, an explanation of why it is incorrect will appear. *FAA Test Prep* considers only your first answer for each question when it grades your study session. Once you have answered a question, you can proceed to select the other answers to read the explanations and evaluate and improve your understanding of the concept(s) embodied in this question.

From the Study submenu, select Grade Session to have *FAA Test Prep* close your current study session and grade all questions you attempted. When it is complete, it will display a window similar to the one below:

```
[■]━━━━━━━━━━━━━ FUNDAMENTALS OF INSTRUCTING ━━━━━━━━━━━━━━   ▲
   Gleim Practice FAA Study Report          Tuesday, 07/18/97 12:14pm   ▨

   Number of questions in this Study Session        50
   Number of questions answered correctly           48
   Number of questions answered incorrectly          2
   Number of questions not answered                  0

   Study score based on total questions             96 %
   Study score based on questions answered          96 %

   Entire time spent in Session               1:36:40
   Average time spent per question            0:01:56

   70% score based on total questions is required by the FAA

   Your Study score is determined by using the number of questions
   answered correctly on your first attempt.

   Information updated in Performance Analysis                      ▨
━━━━━━━━━━━━━━━━━━━━━━━━━━━━━━━━━━━━━━━━━━━━━━━━━━━━━━━━━━━━━━━━━━━   ▼

┌─────────────────────────────────────────────────────────────┐
│  Press <F8> to Print this Report.                             │
│  Press <Esc> to return to the Main Menu.                      │
└─────────────────────────────────────────────────────────────┘
```

This screen is useful in that it displays how well you did for the most recent session and can be called up at any time by selecting the View Grade Report menu item from the Study submenu.

You can view performance data for your cumulative study sessions by selecting the Performance Analysis menu item from the Study submenu. It will open a window similar to the following:

```
■[■]■■■■■■■■■■ Study Performance Analysis by Chapter ■■■■■■■

 FUNDAMENTALS OF INSTRUCTING    Christopher N. Eichelberger  000-00-0000
 ─────────────Total Questions Answered and Percent Correct──────────
                                      Last      Last 3    Cumulative
                                     Session    Sessions
                              (Q's)
 All Questions                (160)  160│ 91%   479│ 89%   543│ 89% ▲
 Ch 2:  The Learning Process  ( 33)   33│ 85%    98│ 86%   131│ 85% ▓
 Ch 3:  Barriers to Learning  ( 18)   18│100%    54│ 89%    54│ 89%
 Ch 4:  Human Behavior, Communication ( 23)  23│ 91%   69│ 87%   69│ 87%
 Ch 5:  Teaching Methods      ( 25)   25│ 96%    75│ 96%    75│ 96%
 Ch 6:  Planning Instruction Activity ( 30)  30│ 87%   90│ 90%   90│ 90%
 Ch 7:  Critique and Evaluation ( 31)  31│ 87%   93│ 88%   124│ 90%
  Chapter(s) from which questions were answered in the LAST session  ▼

 ┌────────────────────────────────────────────────────────────────┐
 │ <F8> to print all Chapters              <Esc> to return         │
 │ <Enter> to view Analysis by Module                              │
 └────────────────────────────────────────────────────────────────┘
```

Test

The Test submenu contains options allowing you to create (using an AvTEST, CATS, LaserGrade, or Sylvan format), grade, and print test sessions, as well as view performance data for all cumulative test sessions taken. Selecting the Test submenu will open a menu that looks like this:

```
┌─────────────────────┐
│ Create Session      │
│ Grade Session       │
│ Return to Test      │
│ Print Session       │
├─────────────────────┤
│ Performance Analysis│
│ View Grade Report   │
└─────────────────────┘
```

To create a test session, select the Create Session option on the Test submenu, and a window will open as shown below. You may select question order, answer order, and emulation.

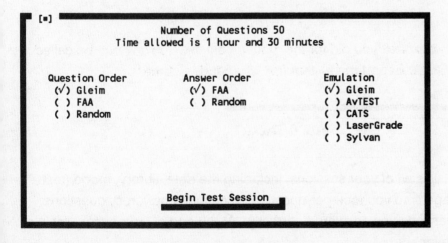

```
■[■]■■■■■■■■■■■■■■■■■■■■■■■■■■■■■■■■■■■■■■■■■■■■■■■■■■■■■■■
                       Number of Questions 50
              Time allowed is 1 hour and 30 minutes


  Question Order        Answer Order          Emulation
   (√) Gleim             (√) FAA               (√) Gleim
   ( ) FAA               ( ) Random            ( ) AvTEST
   ( ) Random                                  ( ) CATS
                                               ( ) LaserGrade
                                               ( ) Sylvan



           Begin Test Session
```

The appearance of your test session depends on which vendor emulation you selected. The Gleim emulation, for instance, looks very much like the study sessions you take with *FAA Test Prep* (except for a few missing features, such as answer explanations). The AvTEST, CATS, LaserGrade, and Sylvan emulations reproduce the screens and testing procedures that you will encounter at each of these testing centers. The objective is to make you knowledgeable and comfortable when you take your FAA test.

You can grade your current test session by selecting the Grade Session menu item on the Test submenu; the report looks very similar to the grade report for study sessions; the same applies for performance data (select the Performance Analysis menu item on the Test submenu).

History

The History submenu gives you options for viewing and purging data about your past performance. Selecting the History submenu opens the following menu:

```
History Table
History Graph
Purge History
```

The History Table submenu item lets you view summary data for each of the most recent 400 study and test sessions you have graded across all libraries (since the last time the history was purged; see below). Selecting this menu item opens a window that looks like this:

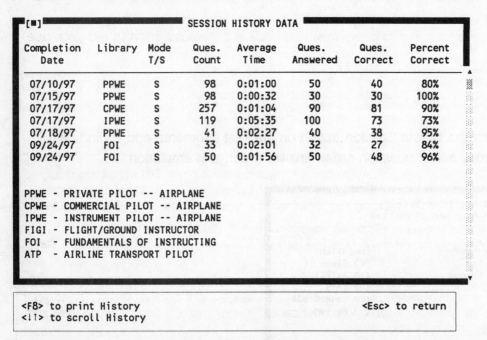

```
[■]                       SESSION HISTORY DATA

Completion   Library  Mode   Ques.    Average    Ques.     Ques.     Percent
   Date               T/S    Count     Time     Answered   Correct   Correct

  07/10/97    PPWE     S       98     0:01:00       50        40        80%
  07/15/97    PPWE     S       98     0:00:32       30        30       100%
  07/17/97    CPWE     S      257     0:01:04       90        81        90%
  07/17/97    IPWE     S      119     0:05:35      100        73        73%
  07/18/97    PPWE     S       41     0:02:27       40        38        95%
  09/24/97    FOI      S       33     0:02:01       32        27        84%
  09/24/97    FOI      S       50     0:01:56       50        48        96%


PPWE  -  PRIVATE PILOT -- AIRPLANE
CPWE  -  COMMERCIAL PILOT -- AIRPLANE
IPWE  -  INSTRUMENT PILOT -- AIRPLANE
FIGI  -  FLIGHT/GROUND INSTRUCTOR
FOI   -  FUNDAMENTALS OF INSTRUCTING
ATP   -  AIRLINE TRANSPORT PILOT


 <F8> to print History                              <Esc> to return
 <↓↑> to scroll History
```

The middle portion of the screen lists all of your sessions, including the date, library, mode (test or study), number of questions, average time you took per question, questions answered, questions correct, and the overall percent of questions you answered correctly. At the end of your history list is a legend explaining the library abbreviations.

The History Graph submenu item lets you view your percent complete for the same study sessions as the History Table option, but the History Graph display shows you the data in a bar graph format. The visual approach lets you see exactly how your studies have progressed across different libraries.

Vendors

The Vendors submenu lets you view information about the four companies who administer FAA pilot knowledge tests (AvTEST, CATS, LaserGrade, Sylvan). For each company, you can view general registration information and a list of locations (and phone numbers) for each of that vendor's test centers by state.

Options

The Options submenu lets you print an instructor sign-off form (if you have qualified), change your address, see an order form for Gleim products, change your autosave time increment, select your printer type, and select your printer port.

Help

The context-sensitive help system is a feature available everywhere throughout the software. Briefly, context-sensitive help means that, whenever you press <F1> (or <Alt-F1> if you are answering questions in a session), *FAA Test Prep* automatically brings up a window explaining what is going on, including your options on how best to proceed.

The Help submenu gives you access to some miscellaneous features designed to aid your use of *FAA Test Prep*.

Order your *FAA Test Prep* today! Call 800 87-GLEIM.

If this Gleim test book saves you time and frustration in preparing for the FAA FOI knowledge test, you should use Gleim's *Flight/Ground Instructor FAA Written Exam* to prepare for those knowledge tests, and Gleim's *Flight Instructor Practical Test Prep and Flight Maneuvers* to prepare for the FAA practical test.

Flight Instructor Practical Test Prep and Flight Maneuvers will assist you in developing the competence and confidence to pass your FAA practical test, just as this book organizes and explains the knowledge needed to pass your FAA knowledge test.

Also, flight maneuvers are quickly perfected when you understand exactly what to expect before you get into an airplane to practice the flight maneuvers. You must be ahead of (not behind) your CFI and your airplane. Gleim's practical test prep books explain and illustrate all flight maneuvers so the maneuvers and their execution are intuitively appealing to you.

END OF CHAPTER

Gleim Publications, Inc.

(800) 87-GLEIM   (352) 375-0772
FAX # (352) 375-6940
P. O. Box 12848 • University Station
Gainesville, Florida 32604

TO: Users of My Written Test Books

FROM: Irvin N. Gleim

TOPIC: My **Practical Test Prep and Flight Maneuvers** Books

Before pilots take their FAA pilot knowledge (written) test, they want to understand the answer to every FAA test question. My test books are widely used because they help pilots learn and understand exactly what they need to know to do well on their FAA pilot knowledge test.

To help you and all other pilots do well on your FAA practical test(s), I have developed a series of **Practical Test Prep and Flight Maneuvers** books (a book for each certificate and rating). An easy-to-understand, comprehensive explanation of all knowledge and skill required on your flight instructor practical test is essential to you because

1. The FAA practical tests are more demanding and require more knowledge than the FAA pilot knowledge tests.

2. The National Transportation Safety Board is pressuring the FAA to have its designated pilot examiners increase the rigor on practical tests.

3. Every flight instructor presents flight maneuvers and concept knowledge from a point of view based on training, experience, etc. The FAA, however, is intent on imposing a single, standardized set of practical test standards.

4. Just as you must learn to answer the FAA's pilot knowledge test questions, you need to know the FAA's approach to practical tests and the responses, behavior, and answers that your designated pilot examiner will expect.

5. Our clear, well-organized explanation of your practical test and all questions that can be asked of you will improve your confidence (as well as your skill level).

Flight Instructor Practical Test Prep and Flight Maneuvers will help you be prepared for the demanding flight instructor practical test. It is also an excellent reference after you earn your certificate.

If your FBO or aviation bookstore does not have *Flight Instructor Practical Test Prep and Flight Maneuvers*, call **(800) 87-GLEIM** to order your copy today. Thank you for recommending both my **FAA WRITTEN EXAM** books and **Practical Test Prep and Flight Maneuvers** books to your friends and colleagues.

CHAPTER TWO
THE LEARNING PROCESS

2.1 CHARACTERISTICS OF LEARNING (Questions 1-3)

1. Learning can be defined as a change in behavior as a result of experience.

    a. The behavior change can be physical and overt (a better glide path, for instance), or psychological and attitudinal (better motivation, more acute perceptions, insights).

2. The learning process may include any (or all) of the following elements: verbal, conceptual, perceptual, motor skills, emotional, and problem solving.

3. While learning the subject at hand, the student may be learning other useful things as well. This learning is called incidental and can have a significant impact on the student's total development.

2.2 THE LAWS OF LEARNING (Questions 4-10)

1. Educational psychology professor Edward L. Thorndike has suggested several "laws of learning" that apply to the learning process. While these laws are not absolute, they do give important insight into effective teaching.

2. The **law of readiness** states that if a student is ready to learn, and has a strong purpose, clear objective, and well-fixed reason for learning, (s)he will make more progress than if (s)he lacks motivation. Readiness implies single-mindedness.

3. The **law of exercise** states that those things most often repeated are best remembered or performed.

    a. The basis of the law is to provide opportunities for a student to practice and then direct this process towards a goal.

4. The **law of effect** relates to the emotional reaction of the learner:

    a. Learning is strengthened when accompanied by a pleasant or satisfying feeling.
    b. Learning is weakened when associated with an unpleasant feeling.

5. The **law of primacy** states that those things learned first often create a strong, almost unshakable impression.

    a. This law means that bad habits learned early are hard to break. Instructors must thus insist on correct performance from the outset of maneuvers.

6. The **law of intensity** states that a vivid, dramatic, or exciting experience teaches more than a routine or boring experience.

    a. The law of intensity thus implies that a student will learn more from the real thing than from a substitute.

7. The **law of recency** states that the things most recently learned are best remembered.

    a. Instructors recognize the law of recency when they determine the relative positions of lectures within a course syllabus.

2.3 PERCEPTION AND INSIGHT (Questions 11-20)

1. Perceiving involves more than the reception of stimuli from the five senses. Perceptions result when the person gives meaning to sensations being experienced.

    a. Thus, perceptions are the basis of all learning.

2. A person's basic need is to maintain, enhance, preserve, and perpetuate the organized self.

    a. Thus, all perceptions are affected by this basic need.

3. Self-concept, or self-image, has a great influence on the total perceptual process.

4. Fear or the element of threat narrows the student's perceptual field.

    a. The resulting anxiety may limit a person's ability to learn from perceptions.

5. Insight occurs when associated perceptions are grouped into meaningful wholes, i.e., when one "gets the whole picture."

    a. Evoking insights is the instructor's major responsibility.

    b. Instruction speeds the learning process by teaching the relationship of perceptions as they occur, thus promoting the development of insights by students.

    c. An instructor can help develop student insights by providing a safe environment in which to learn.

2.4 FORGETTING AND RETENTION (Questions 21-24)

1. The following are three theories of forgetting:

    a. The **theory of disuse** states that a person forgets those things which are not used. Students are saddened by the small amount of actual data retained several years after graduation.

    b. The **theory of interference** holds that people forget because new experiences overshadow the original learning experience. In other words, new or similar subsequent events can displace facts learned previously.

    c. The **theory of repression** states that some forgetting is due to the submerging of ideas or thoughts into the subconscious mind. Unpleasant or anxiety-producing material is forgotten by the individual, although not intentionally. This is a subconscious and protective response.

2. Responses that produce a pleasurable return are called praise.

    a. Praise stimulates remembering because responses that give a pleasurable return tend to be repeated.

2.5 TRANSFER OF LEARNING (Questions 25-27)

1. The student may be either aided or hindered by things learned previously. This process is called transfer of learning.

    a. Positive transfer occurs when the learning of one maneuver aids in learning another.

        1) EXAMPLE: Flying rectangular patterns to aid in flying traffic patterns.

    b. Negative transfer occurs when a performance of a maneuver interferes with the learning of another maneuver.

        1) EXAMPLE: Trying to steer a taxiing plane with the control yoke as one drives a car.

        2) Negative transfer thus agrees with the interference theory of forgetting.

2. By making certain the student understands that what is learned can be applied to other situations, the instructor helps facilitate a positive transfer of learning.

    a. This is the basic reason for the building-block technique of instruction, in which each simple task is performed acceptably and correctly before the next learning task is introduced.

    b. The introduction of instruction in more advanced and complex operations before the initial instruction has been mastered leads to the development of poor habit patterns in the elements of performance.

2.6 LEVELS OF LEARNING (Questions 28-31)

1. Learning may be accomplished at any of four levels.

    a. The lowest level, **rote learning**, is the ability to repeat back what one has been taught without necessarily understanding or being able to apply what has been learned.

        1) EXAMPLE: Being able to cite the maneuvering speed of an airplane.

    b. At the **understanding** level, the student not only can repeat what has been taught but also comprehends the principles and theory behind the knowledge.

        1) EXAMPLE: Being able to explain how gross weight affects maneuvering speed.

        2) Being able to explain (not demonstrate) is the understanding level.

    c. At the **application** level, the student not only understands the theory but also can apply what has been learned and perform in accordance with that knowledge.

        1) This is the level of learning at which most instructors stop teaching.

    d. At the **correlation** level, the student is able to associate various learned elements with other segments or blocks of learning or accomplishment.

        1) EXAMPLE: Know what to do if, during the flight portion of the practical test, the examiner closes the throttle and announces "simulated engine failure."

2.7 LEARNING SKILLS AND THE LEARNING CURVE (Questions 32-33)

1. The best way to prepare a student to perform a task is to provide a clear, step-by-step example. Students need a clear picture of what they are to do and how they are to do it.

2. Learning typically follows a pattern which, if shown on a graph, would be called the learning curve. The first part of the curve indicates rapid early improvement. Then the curve levels off.

    a. This normal and temporary leveling-off of an individual's learning rate is called a learning plateau.

QUESTIONS AND ANSWER EXPLANATIONS

All of the FAA questions from the Fundamentals of Instructing knowledge test relating to the learning process outlined above are reproduced on the following pages in the same modules as the outlines. To the immediate right of each question are the correct answer and answer explanation. You should cover these answers and answer explanations with your hand or a piece of paper while responding to the questions. Refer to the general discussion in Chapter 1 on how to take the FAA knowledge test.

Remember that the questions from the FAA knowledge test bank have been reordered by topic, and the topics have been organized into a meaningful sequence. Accordingly, the first line of the answer explanation gives the FAA question number and the citation of the authoritative source for the answer.

2.1 Characteristics of Learning

1.
6001. A change in behavior as a result of experience can be defined as

A— learning.
B— knowledge.
C— understanding.

Answer (A) is correct (6001). *(AIH Chap I)*
Learning can be defined as a change in behavior as a result of experience.
Answer (B) is incorrect because knowledge is awareness as a result of experience, but not necessarily a change in behavior. Answer (C) is incorrect because understanding is only one of the four levels of learning.

2.
6002. The learning process may include such elements as verbal, conceptual, and

A— habitual.
B— experiential.
C— problem solving.

Answer (C) is correct (6002). *(AIH Chap I)*
The learning process involves many elements. Verbal, conceptual, perceptual, motor skill, problem solving, and emotional elements may be used at the same time.
Answer (A) is incorrect because habits are the customary or usual way of doing things and can be changed by the learning process. Answer (B) is incorrect because all learning is by experience, but it takes place in different forms in different people.

3.
6003. While learning the material being taught, students may be learning other things as well. This additional learning is called

A— residual.
B— conceptual.
C— incidental.

Answer (C) is correct (6003). *(AIH Chap I)*
While learning the subject at hand, students may be learning other things as well. They may be developing attitudes (good or bad) about aviation depending on what they experience. This learning is called incidental, but it may have a great impact on the total development of the student.
Answer (A) is incorrect because residual is not a term used to define any type of learning. Answer (B) is incorrect because conceptual learning is an element of learning the subject at hand, not other incidental things.

2.2 The Laws of Learning

4.
6004. Individuals make more progress learning if they have a clear objective. This is one feature of the law of

A— primacy.
B— readiness.
C— willingness.

Answer (B) is correct (6004). *(AIH Chap I)*
One feature of the law of readiness is that when a student has a strong purpose, a clear objective, and a well-fixed reason to learn something, (s)he will make more progress than if (s)he lacks motivation.
Answer (A) is incorrect because the law of primacy states that first experiences create a strong, almost unshakable impression. Answer (C) is incorrect because there is no law of willingness.

5.
6007. Things most often repeated are best remembered because of which law of learning?

A— Law of effect.
B— Law of recency.
C— Law of exercise.

Answer (C) is correct (6007). *(AIH Chap I)*
The law of exercise states that those things most often repeated are best remembered. This is the basis of practice and drill.
Answer (A) is incorrect because the law of effect relates to the learner's emotional reaction to the learning experience. Answer (B) is incorrect because the law of recency states that things most recently learned are best remembered.

6.
6005. Providing opportunities for a student to practice and then directing this process towards a goal is the basis of the law of

A— exercise.
B— learning.
C— readiness.

Answer (A) is correct (6005). *(AIH Chap I)*
The law of exercise states that those things most often repeated are best remembered. You must provide opportunities for your student to practice and then direct this process towards a goal.
Answer (B) is incorrect because learning is a change in behavior as a result of experience. The law of exercise is part of the learning process. Answer (C) is incorrect because the law of readiness states that individuals learn best when they are ready to learn, not practicing a task.

7.
6006. The law that is based on the emotional reaction of the learner is the law of

A— effect.
B— primacy.
C— intensity.

Answer (A) is correct (6006). *(AIH Chap I)*
The law of effect is the one which directly relates to the learner's emotional reaction. Pleasant experiences strengthen the learning process whereas unpleasant experiences tend to weaken it.
Answer (B) is incorrect because the law of primacy states that a strong, almost unshakable impression is created by first experiences. Answer (C) is incorrect because the law of intensity states that dramatic or exciting experiences teach more than routine experiences.

8.
6010. Which law of learning often creates a strong impression?

A— Law of primacy.
B— Law of intensity.
C— Law of readiness.

Answer (A) is correct (6010). *(AIH Chap I)*
Primacy, the state of being first, often creates a strong, almost unshakable, impression. For the instructor, this means that what is taught must be right the first time. The first experience should be positive and functional, and should lay the foundation for all that is to follow.
Answer (B) is incorrect because the law of intensity means that a student will learn more from the real thing than from a substitute. Answer (C) is incorrect because the law of readiness means that a student must be willing and eager to learn.

9.
6008. Which law of learning implies that a student will learn more from the real thing than from a substitute?

A— Law of effect.
B— Law of primacy.
C— Law of intensity.

Answer (C) is correct (6008). *(AIH Chap I)*
The law of intensity states that a vivid, dramatic, or exciting learning experience teaches more than a routine or boring experience. Thus, the law of intensity implies that a student will learn more from a real thing than from a substitute.
Answer (A) is incorrect because the law of effect is based on the emotional reaction of the student. Thus, pleasant experiences strengthen the learning while unpleasant experiences weaken the learning. These may be experienced by learning from either the real thing or a substitute. Answer (B) is incorrect because the law of primacy states that a strong, almost unshakable impression is created by first experiences. These experiences may be from either a real thing or a substitute.

10.
6009. Which law of learning determines the relative positions of lectures within a course syllabus?

A— Law of primacy.
B— Law of recency.
C— Law of intensity.

Answer (B) is correct (6009). *(AIH Chap I)*
The law of recency states that the things most recently learned are best remembered. The farther a student is removed time-wise from a new fact or understanding, the more difficult it is to remember it. The law of recency often determines the relative positions of lectures within a course syllabus.
Answer (A) is incorrect because the law of primacy means to the instructor that what is taught must be right the first time. Answer (C) is incorrect because the law of intensity means that a student will learn more from the real experience than a substitute.

2.3 Perception and Insight

11.
6011. What is the basis of all learning?

A— Perception.
B— Motivation.
C— Positive self-concept.

Answer (A) is correct (6011). *(AIH Chap I)*
Initially, all learning comes from perceptions which are directed to the brain by one or more of the five senses. Perceptions result when a person gives meaning to sensations.
Answer (B) is incorrect because motivation is the dominant force which governs a student's progress and ability to learn, not the basis for all learning. Answer (C) is incorrect because positive self-concept is a factor which affects an individual's ability to learn, not the basis of all learning.

12.
6015. Perceptions result when a person

A— gives meaning to sensations being experienced.
B— is able to discern items of useful information.
C— responds to visual cues first, then aural cues, and relates these cues to ones previously learned.

Answer (A) is correct (6015). *(AIH Chap I)*
Perceptions occur when a person gives meaning to sensations being experienced. This is the difference between just seeing something and understanding what is seen.
Answer (B) is incorrect because a person who is able to discern items of useful information has learned, not just perceived. Answer (C) is incorrect because it describes the rote level of learning, i.e., memorization without concern for meaning.

13.
6012. A basic need that affects all of a person's perceptions is the need to

A— maintain and enhance the organized self.
B— accomplish a higher level of satisfaction.
C— avoid areas that pose a threat to success.

Answer (A) is correct (6012). *(AIH Chap I)*
A person's basic need is to maintain and enhance the organized self. The self is a person's past, present, and future, and is both physical and psychological. A person's most fundamental need is to preserve and perpetuate this self. Thus, all perceptions are affected by this need.
Answer (B) is incorrect because accomplishing a higher level of satisfaction is a goal, not a basic need. Answer (C) is incorrect because avoiding areas that are a threat to success is a defense mechanism, not a basic need which affects perceptions.

14.
6014. Which factor affecting perception has a great influence on the total perceptual process?

A— Self-concept.
B— Goals and values.
C— Time and opportunity.

Answer (A) is correct (6014). *(AIH Chap I)*
A student's self-concept (or self-image) has a great influence on the total perceptual process. Negative self-concepts inhibit the perceptual process by introducing psychological barriers which tend to keep a student from perceiving. Positive self-concepts allow the student to be less defensive and more ready to digest experiences by assimilating all of the instructions and demonstrations offered.
Answer (B) is incorrect because perceptions depend on one's goals and values in that every experience is colored by the individual's own beliefs and value structures, but they do not have a great influence on the total perceptual process. Answer (C) is incorrect because it takes time and opportunity to perceive, but it is not a great influence on the total perceptual process.

15.
6019. In the learning process, fear or the element of threat will

A— narrow the student's perceptual field.
B— decrease the rate of associative reactions.
C— cause a student to focus on several areas of perception.

Answer (A) is correct (6019). *(AIH Chap I)*
Fear or the element of threat will impair the student's perceptual field. This is because one tends to limit attention to the threatening object or condition, rather than to what should be learned.
Answer (B) is incorrect because the element of threat causes stress and anxiety; the mind tends to race, often irrationally, thereby increasing, not decreasing, the rate of associative reactions. Answer (C) is incorrect because fear or the element of threat will cause a student to focus only on the threatening object or condition, not on several areas of perception.

16.

6143. Which is one of the ways in which anxiety will affect a student?

A— Anxiety may limit the student's ability to learn from perceptions.

B— Anxiety will speed up the learning process for the student if properly controlled and directed by the instructor.

C— Anxiety causes dispersal of the student's attention over such a wide range of matters as to interfere with normal reactions.

Answer (A) is correct (6143). *(AIH Chap IX)*

Anxiety is a state of mental uneasiness arising from fear of anything, real or imagined, which threatens the person who experiences it. Anxiety may have a potent effect on actions and on the ability to learn from perceptions.

Answer (B) is incorrect because perceptions blocked by anxiety will tend to slow, not speed up, the learning process. Answer (C) is incorrect because anxiety narrows, not disperses, a student's attention.

17.

6017. The mental grouping of affiliated perceptions is called

A— insights.

B— association.

C— conceptualization.

Answer (A) is correct (6017). *(AIH Chap I)*

Many principles, theories, and learned tasks can be treated as pieces relating to other pieces in the overall pattern of the task to be learned. This mental relating or grouping of associated perceptions is called insight.

Answer (B) is incorrect because association is not the final, completed mental picture, although it is a necessary process to connect the affiliated perceptions. Answer (C) is incorrect because it refers only to the formation of individual ideas.

18.

6021. Insights, as applied to learning, involve a person's

A— association of learning with change.

B— grouping of associated perceptions into meaningful wholes.

C— ability to recognize the reason for learning a procedure.

Answer (B) is correct (6021). *(AIH Chap I)*

Insights, as applied to learning, involve a person's grouping of associated perceptions into meaningful wholes. As perceptions increase in number and are grouped to become insights by the student, learning becomes more meaningful and permanent.

Answer (A) is incorrect because insights involve the grouping of perceptions into meaningful wholes, not the association of learning with change. Answer (C) is incorrect because the ability to recognize the reason for learning a procedure is a feature of the law of readiness, not insight.

19.

6013. Instruction, as opposed to the trial and error method of learning, is desirable because competent instruction speeds the learning process by

A— motivating the student to a better performance.

B— emphasizing only the important points of training.

C— teaching the relationship of perceptions as they occur.

Answer (C) is correct (6013). *(AIH Chap I)*

Competent instruction speeds the learning process by teaching the relationship of perceptions as they occur, thus promoting the development of insights by the student.

Answer (A) is incorrect because motivating a student to a better performance is just one element of instruction. Answer (B) is incorrect because instructors must emphasize all points of training, not just the major, important points.

20.

6020. Name one way an instructor can help develop student insights.

A— Provide a safe environment in which to learn.

B— Point out various items to avoid during the learning process.

C— Keep learning blocks small so they are easier to understand.

Answer (A) is correct (6020). *(AIH Chap I)*

Pointing out the relationships of perceptions as they occur, providing a safe and nonthreatening environment in which to learn, and helping the student acquire and maintain a favorable self-concept are most important in fostering the development of insights.

Answer (B) is incorrect because the instructor should point out the relationships of perceptions as they occur, not point out various items to avoid during the learning process. Answer (C) is incorrect because insights develop when a student's perceptions increase in number and are assembled into larger, not smaller, blocks of learning.

2.4 Forgetting and Retention

21.
6036. When a person has difficulty recalling facts after several years, this is known as

A— disuse.
B— repression.
C— poor retention.

Answer (A) is correct (6036). *(AIH Chap I)*
The theory of disuse states that a person forgets those things that are not used or, at least, not used frequently.
Answer (B) is incorrect because repression is the practice of submerging an unpleasant experience into the subconscious. Answer (C) is incorrect because poor retention results in forgetting due to disuse, interference, or repression.

22.
6035. When the learning of similar things overshadows other learning experiences, it is called

A— suppression.
B— correlation.
C— interference.

Answer (C) is correct (6035). *(AIH Chap I)*
The theory of interference states that new or similar events can often replace previously learned facts. Most susceptible to this replacement by interference are closely similar materials and materials not well learned to begin with.
Answer (A) is incorrect because suppression is not a consideration (or theory) as to why a person forgets. Answer (B) is incorrect because correlation is the highest level of learning, which means that it is resistant to forgetting.

23.
6034. According to one theory, some forgetting is due to the practice of submerging an unpleasant experience into the subconscious. This is called

A— blanking.
B— immersion.
C— repression.

Answer (C) is correct (6034). *(AIH Chap I)*
The theory of repression states that some forgetting is due to the submersion of ideas or thoughts into the subconscious mind. For instance, information learned during an unpleasant experience may be buried out of reach of memory.
Answer (A) is incorrect because blanking refers to a temporary inability to remember, not to a theory of forgetting. Answer (B) is incorrect because immersion is not a theory of forgetting.

24.
6037. Responses that produce a pleasurable return are called

A— reward.
B— praise.
C— positive feedback.

Answer (B) is correct (6037). *(AIH Chap I)*
Responses which give a pleasurable return, called praise, tend to be repeated, thus stimulating and encouraging retention.
Answer (A) is incorrect because rewards are motivators, and are not usually responses (i.e., praise); that is, they are normally financial, self-interest, or public recognition. Answer (C) is incorrect because positive feedback (i.e., constructive criticism) is part of the learning, not retention, process. Positive feedback teaches a student how to capitalize on things done well and to use them to compensate for lesser accomplishments.

2.5 Transfer of Learning

25.
6039. The performance of rectangular patterns helps a student fly traffic patterns. What type transfer of learning is this?

A— Lateral.
B— Positive.
C— Deliberate.

Answer (B) is correct (6039). *(AIH Chap I)*
Transfers of learning can be negative or positive. Since the learning of Task A (flying rectangular patterns) helps in the learning of Task B (flying traffic patterns), it is advantageous and, therefore, a positive transfer of learning.
Answer (A) is incorrect because there is no lateral transfer of learning, only positive or negative. Answer (C) is incorrect because there is no deliberate transfer of learning, only positive or negative.

26.
6038. Which transfer of learning occurs when the performance of a maneuver interferes with the learning of another maneuver?

A— Adverse.
B— Positive.
C— Negative.

Answer (C) is correct (6038). *(AIH Chap I)*
Transfers of learning can be negative or positive. If the learning of Task A helps in the learning of Task B, the transfer of learning is deemed to be positive. If, on the other hand, Task A interferes with Task B, the transfer is a hindrance to learning and is thus negative.
Answer (A) is incorrect because there is no adverse transfer of learning, only positive or negative.
Answer (B) is incorrect because the transfer of learning is a hindrance and is thus negative.

27.
6040. To ensure proper habits and correct techniques during training, an instructor should

A— use the building block technique of instruction.
B— repeat subject matter the student has already learned.
C— introduce challenging material to continually motivate the student.

Answer (A) is correct (6040). *(AIH Chap I)*
The building-block technique of teaching insists that each simple task be performed correctly before the next is introduced. This technique fosters thorough and meaningful performance and good habits, which will be carried over into future learning.
Answer (B) is incorrect because too much repetition can lead to boredom. The instructor must mix teaching methods to sustain interest and promote learning.
Answer (C) is incorrect because complex or difficult tasks introduced before simpler ones are mastered can be frustrating, not motivating, for the student. This approach will not ensure proper habits; the student will likely develop bad habits from trying to perform tasks not completely understood.

2.6 Levels of Learning

28.
6027. What level of knowledge is being tested if asked, "What is the maneuvering speed of the aircraft listed in the owner's manual?"

A— Rote.
B— Application.
C— Understanding.

Answer (A) is correct (6027). *(AIH Chap I)*
The lowest level, rote learning, is the ability to repeat something back that one has been taught, without understanding or being able to apply what has been learned. An example of rote learning is to be able to cite the maneuvering speed of the aircraft listed in the owner's manual.
Answer (B) is incorrect because application is the ability of a student to apply what has been taught. This is the third level of learning and is achieved after the student understands, has practiced, and can consistently perform a task. Answer (C) is incorrect because the second level of learning is understanding, which has been achieved when a student can put together a block of learning and develop an insight into the performance of a task.

29.
6028. During the flight portion of a practical test, the examiner simulates complete loss of engine power by closing the throttle and announcing "simulated engine failure." What level of learning is being tested?

A— Application.
B— Correlation.
C— Understanding.

Answer (B) is correct (6028). *(AIH Chap I)*
When the examiner simulates complete loss of engine power by closing the throttle and announcing "simulated engine failure," the examiner is testing at the correlation level of learning. The applicant must be able to correlate (associate) the engine failure with the requirements to perform the elements of an emergency approach and landing; i.e., establish best-glide speed, select a field, perform restart checklist, plan a flight pattern to the selected field, complete all appropriate checklists, etc.
Answer (A) is incorrect because the application level of learning is tested when the examiner closes the throttle and tells the applicant to perform an emergency approach and landing. Answer (C) is incorrect because the understanding level of learning is tested when the examiner asks the applicant to explain the elements of an emergency approach and landing.

30.
6030. At which level of learning do most instructors stop teaching?

A— Application.
B— Correlation.
C— Understanding.

Answer (A) is correct (6030). *(AIH Chap I)*
Most instructors stop teaching at the application level of learning. Discontinuing instruction on an element at this point and directing subsequent instruction exclusively to other elements is characteristic of piecemeal instruction, which is usually inefficient. It violates the building block concept of instruction by failing to apply what has been learned to future learning tasks.
Answer (B) is incorrect because correlation is the highest level of learning and should be the goal of each instructor. Instructions all too often stop at the application level. Answer (C) is incorrect because understanding is the second level of learning, and at this point, a student understands a task but may not be able to do it. Instructors will usually continue teaching to the next level, which is application.

31.
6029. When asking a student to explain how gross weight affects maneuvering speed, what level of learning is being tested?

A— Application.
B— Correlation.
C— Understanding.

Answer (C) is correct (6029). *(AIH Chap I)*
At the understanding level of learning, a student will be able to explain how gross weight affects maneuvering speed (V_A). Understanding is the next level after rote memorization and the level before acquiring the skill to apply knowledge, which is application (correlation is the fourth and highest level of learning). Being able to explain (not demonstrate) is the understanding level of learning, not the application or correlation level.
Answer (A) is incorrect because, at the application level, a student will be able to apply the knowledge that gross weight affects maneuvering speed when determining the appropriate airspeed for entering turbulent air or maneuvers that require an airspeed at or below V_A. Answer (B) is incorrect because, at the correlation level, a student has developed the ability to correlate the elements of maneuvering speed with other concepts such as gust loads, accelerated stalls, load factors, acceleration forces in the aircraft, etc.

2.7 Learning Skills and the Learning Curve

32.
6031. The best way to prepare a student to perform a task is to

A— explain the purpose of the task.
B— provide a clear, step-by-step example.
C— give the student an outline of the task.

Answer (B) is correct (6031). *(AIH Chap I)*
The best way to prepare a student to perform a task is to provide a clear, step-by-step example. Having a model to follow permits a student to get a clear picture of each step in the sequence (i.e., what it is, how to do it).
Answer (A) is incorrect because, while a student should know the purpose of a task, (s)he must be provided with a clear, step-by-step example showing how to perform the task. Answer (C) is incorrect because an outline is not as useful as a clear, step-by-step example.

33.
6033. A learning plateau may be defined as the

A— point in the learning curve at which skill proficiency retrogresses.
B— normal and temporary leveling-off of an individual's learning rate.
C— achievement of the highest possible level of competence for a particular individual.

Answer (B) is correct (6033). *(AIH Chap I)*
A learning plateau may be defined as the normal and temporary leveling-off of an individual's learning rate. This is normal and should be expected by you and your student after an initial period of rapid improvement.
Answer (A) is incorrect because a learning plateau is a temporary leveling-off or slower rate of learning, not retrogression. Answer (C) is incorrect because a learning plateau is a temporary leveling-off of an individual's learning rate, not achievement of the highest possible level of competence.

END OF CHAPTER

CHAPTER THREE
BARRIERS TO LEARNING

3.1 SELF-CONCEPT (Questions 1-2)

1. Self-concept is how one pictures oneself.

    a. This is the most powerful determinant in learning.
    b. Self-concept has a great influence on the total perceptual process.

2. Negative self-concept contributes most to a student's failure to remain receptive to new experiences and creates a tendency to reject additional training.

3. Thus, an instructor can foster the development of insights by helping the student acquire and maintain a favorable self-concept.

3.2 DEFENSE MECHANISMS (Questions 3-10)

1. Certain behavior patterns are called defense mechanisms because they are subconscious defenses against the reality of unpleasant situations. People use these defenses to soften feelings of failure, alleviate feelings of guilt, and protect feelings of personal worth and adequacy.

2. Although defense mechanisms can serve a useful purpose, they can also be a hindrance to learning because they involve some self-deception and distortion of reality.

    a. They alleviate symptoms, not causes.

3. Common defense mechanisms:

    a. **Rationalization** -- When a person cannot accept the real reasons for his/her own behavior, this device permits the substitution of excuses for reasons. Rationalization is a subconscious technique for justifying actions that otherwise would be unacceptable.

    b. **Flight** -- Students escape from frustration by taking physical or mental flight.

        1) To flee physically, students may develop symptoms or ailments that give them excuses for removing themselves from the frustration.

        2) More frequent than physical flight is mental flight or daydreaming.

    c. **Aggression** -- A person can avoid a frustrating situation by means of aggressive behavior. Shouting and accusing others are typical defense mechanisms. Social pressure usually forces student aggressiveness into more subtle forms. Typically, students may

        1) Ask irrelevant questions,
        2) Refuse to participate in class activities, or
        3) Disrupt activities.

    d. **Resignation** -- Students become so frustrated that they lose interest and give up.

        1) They may no longer believe it profitable or even possible to work further.

        2) Resignation usually occurs when the student has completed early lessons without grasping the fundamentals and then becomes bewildered and lost in the advanced phase.

3.3 STRESS AND ANXIETY (Questions 11-14)

1. Normal individuals react to stress by responding rapidly and exactly, often automatically, within their experience and training.

   a. This underlines the need for proper training prior to emergency situations.

   b. The effective individual thinks rapidly, acts rapidly, and is extremely sensitive to his/her surroundings.

2. Some abnormal reactions to stress include:

   a. Inappropriate reactions such as extreme overcooperation, painstaking self-control, inappropriate laughter or singing, and very rapid changes in emotion.

   b. Marked changes in mood (e.g., high spirits followed by deep depression).

   c. Severe, unreasonable anger toward the flight instructor, service personnel, or others.

3. Anxiety is probably the most significant psychological barrier affecting flight instruction. It is the extreme worry brought on by stressful situations (e.g., an emergency, an exam, etc.). Anxiety can be countered by

   a. Treating fears as a normal reaction rather than ignoring them,
   b. Reinforcing the student's enjoyment of flying, and
   c. Teaching students to cope with fears.

3.4 THE OVERCONFIDENT OR IMPATIENT STUDENT (Questions 15-18)

1. Impatience is a greater deterrent to learning pilot skills than is generally recognized.

   a. The impatient student fails to understand the need for preliminary training. (S)he seeks only the final objective without considering the means necessary to reach it.

   b. Impatience can be corrected by the instructor by presenting the necessary preliminary training one step at a time, with clearly stated goals for each step.

2. Because they make few mistakes, apt students may assume that the correction of those errors is unimportant.

   a. This overconfidence soon results in faulty performance.

   b. For apt students a good instructor will constantly raise the standard of performance for each lesson, demanding greater effort.

QUESTIONS AND ANSWER EXPLANATIONS

All of the FAA questions from the Fundamentals of Instructing knowledge test relating to the barriers to learning material outlined above are reproduced on the following pages in the same modules as the outlines. To the immediate right of each question are the correct answer and answer explanation. You should cover these answers and answer explanations with your hand or a piece of paper while responding to the questions. Refer to the general discussion in Chapter 1 on how to take the FAA pilot knowledge test.

Remember that the questions from the FAA pilot knowledge test bank have been reordered by topic, and the topics have been organized into a meaningful sequence. Accordingly, the first line of the answer explanation gives the FAA question number and the citation of the authoritative source for the answer.

3.1 Self-Concept

1.
6016. The factor which contributes most to a student's failure to remain receptive to new experiences and which creates a tendency to reject additional training is

A— basic needs.
B— element of threat.
C— negative self-concept.

Answer (C) is correct (6016). *(AIH Chap I)*
A student with a negative self-concept is resistant to new experiences and may reject additional training. People tend to avoid experiences which contradict their self-concept.
Answer (A) is incorrect because a student's basic needs can be used by the instructor to promote learning. For instance, personal safety is one of the most important basic needs, and aviation training heavily emphasizes this need. Answer (B) is incorrect because an element of threat will cause a student to limit his/her attention to the threatening object or condition. Once this is removed, the student will be able to learn.

2.
6018. An instructor may foster the development of insights by

A— helping the student acquire and maintain a favorable self-concept.
B— pointing out the attractive features of the activity to be learned.
C— keeping the rate of learning consistent so that it is predictable.

Answer (A) is correct (6018). *(AIH Chap I)*
Especially in a field such as aviation training, the instructor can foster the development of insights by helping the student acquire and maintain a favorable self-concept. The student who feels sure of his/her knowledge, skills, and judgments learned in class will also feel better about actual performance and his/her own ability to fly.
Answer (B) is incorrect because the attractive features in a learning situation tend to increase motivation rather than insight. Answer (C) is incorrect because learning rates will vary, not stay constant, with each training lesson.

3.2 Defense Mechanisms

3.
6045. Although defense mechanisms can serve a useful purpose, they can also be a hindrance because they

A— provide feelings of adequacy.
B— alleviate the cause of problems.
C— involve self-deception and distortion of reality.

Answer (C) is correct (6045). *(AIH Chap II)*
Although defense mechanisms can serve a useful purpose, they can also be hindrances. Because they involve some self-deception and distortion of reality, defense mechanisms do not solve problems.
Answer (A) is incorrect because defense mechanisms mask and protect feelings of adequacy rather than provide them. Answer (B) is incorrect because defense mechanisms alleviate symptoms, not causes, of problems.

4.
6044. When a student uses excuses to justify inadequate performance, it is an indication of the defense mechanism known as

A— flight.
B— aggression.
C— rationalization.

Answer (C) is correct (6044). *(AIH Chap II)*
Rationalization is a subconscious technique for justifying unacceptable actions or performance. This allows a student to substitute excuses for reasons, and to make those excuses plausible and acceptable to themselves.
Answer (A) is incorrect because flight is the defense mechanism in which the student escapes (either physically or mentally) from a frustrating experience. Answer (B) is incorrect because aggression is the defense mechanism in which the student uses aggressive behavior to deal with feelings of frustration.

5.
6047. Taking physical or mental flight is a defense mechanism students use when they

A— want to escape from frustrating situations.
B— cannot accept the real reasons for their behavior.
C— lose interest during the advanced stages of training.

Answer (A) is correct (6047). *(AIH Chap II)*
The defense mechanism of flight allows a student to escape from a frustrating situation. This escape can be physical flight (absenteeism, illness, etc.) or mental flight (daydreaming).
Answer (B) is incorrect because, if a student cannot accept the real reasons for his/her behavior, (s)he may rationalize, not take flight. Answer (C) is incorrect because a student who loses interest during the advanced stages of training may resign, not take flight, and give up. This is common if a student has not understood the fundamentals.

6.
6048. When students subconsciously use the defense mechanism called rationalization, they

A— use excuses to justify acceptable behavior.
B— cannot accept the real reasons for their behavior.
C— develop symptoms that give them excuses for removing themselves from frustration.

Answer (B) is correct (6048). *(AIH Chap II)*
Rationalization is a subconscious technique for justifying unacceptable actions or performance. This allows a student to substitute excuses for reasons, and to make those excuses plausible and acceptable to themselves.
Answer (A) is incorrect because, in rationalization, excuses are used to justify unacceptable, not acceptable, behavior. Answer (C) is incorrect because, when students develop symptoms that give them excuses for removing themselves from frustration, they are using the defense mechanism of physical flight.

7.
6050. When a student engages in daydreaming, it is the defense mechanism of

A— flight.
B— fantasy.
C— avoidance.

Answer (A) is correct (6050). *(AIH Chap II)*
A student engaging in daydreaming is an example of flight or mental escape.
Answer (B) is incorrect because fantasy is not a defense mechanism in and of itself, yet it is involved in the defense mechanism of flight: fantasy in mental flight (daydreaming). Answer (C) is incorrect because avoidance is not a defense mechanism in and of itself, yet it is involved in the defense mechanism of flight: avoidance in physical flight.

8.
6049. When students display the defense mechanism called aggression, they

A— become visibly angry, upset, and childish.
B— may refuse to participate in class activities.
C— attempt to justify actions by asking numerous questions.

Answer (B) is correct (6049). *(AIH Chap II)*
Examples of subtle aggression include students who ask irrelevant questions, refuse to participate in class activities, or disrupt activities within the group. Aggressive behavior is used to avoid facing failure.
Answer (A) is incorrect because, although such behavior is characteristic of aggression, it is relatively uncommon in a classroom due to social strictures. Student aggressiveness is usually more subtle in nature and will thus be expressed less obviously. Answer (C) is incorrect because attempting to justify actions is an example of rationalization.

9.
6046. When a student asks irrelevant questions or refuses to participate in class activities, it usually is an indication of the defense mechanism known as

A— flight.
B— aggression.
C— resignation.

Answer (B) is correct (6046). *(AIH Chap II)*
Examples of subtle aggression include students who ask irrelevant questions, refuse to participate in class activities, or disrupt activities within the group. Aggressive behavior is used to avoid facing failure.
Answer (A) is incorrect because flight is the defense mechanism when a person removes him/herself, physically or mentally, from a frustrating situation. Answer (C) is incorrect because resignation is a process of becoming frustrated and not believing that continuing will be worthwhile, i.e., the person is resigned to failure and gives up.

10.
6051. When a student becomes bewildered and lost in the advanced phase of training after completing the early phase without grasping the fundamentals, the defense mechanism is usually in the form of

A— submission.
B— resignation.
C— rationalization.

3.3 Stress and Anxiety

11.
6130. When under stress, normal individuals usually react

A— by showing excellent morale followed by deep depression.
B— by responding rapidly and exactly, often automatically, within the limits of their experience and training.
C— inappropriately such as extreme overcooperation, painstaking self-control, and inappropriate laughing or singing.

12.
6133. Which would most likely be an indication that a student is reacting abnormally to stress?

A— Slow learning.
B— Inappropriate laughter or singing.
C— Automatic response to a given situation.

13.
6131. One possible indication of a student's abnormal reaction to stress would be

A— a hesitancy to act.
B— extreme overcooperation.
C— a noticeable lack of self-control.

14.
6132. The instructor can counteract anxiety in a student by

A— treating the student's fears as a normal reaction.
B— discontinuing instruction in tasks that cause anxiety.
C— allowing the student to decide when he/she is ready for a new maneuver to be introduced.

Answer (B) is correct (6051). *(AIH Chap II)*
When a student has become frustrated, lost interest, given up, and no longer believes it profitable or possible to work further, resignation has taken place. A student in this frame of mind accepts defeat. Typically, such a student has not grasped the fundamentals and is bewildered by later lessons.
Answer (A) is incorrect because submission is not a defense mechanism, but may be characteristic of resignation. Answer (C) is incorrect because rationalization is a process of making excuses for unacceptable behavior.

Answer (B) is correct (6130). *(AIH Chap IX)*
When under stress, normal individuals begin to respond rapidly and exactly, within the limits of their experience and training. Many responses are automatic, which indicates the need for proper training in emergency operations prior to an actual emergency.
Answer (A) is incorrect because marked changes in mood, e.g., excellent morale followed by deep depression is an abnormal, not a normal, reaction to stress. Answer (C) is incorrect because inappropriate reactions such as extreme overcooperation, painstaking self-control, and inappropriate laughter or singing are abnormal, not normal, reactions to stress.

Answer (B) is correct (6133). *(AIH Chap IX)*
Inappropriate laughter or singing is an abnormal reaction to stress. The instructor should be alert for other inappropriate (and possibly dangerous) reactions.
Answer (A) is incorrect because slow learning is a normal, not an abnormal, reaction to stress. Answer (C) is incorrect because automatic response to a given situation is a normal, not an abnormal, reaction to stress.

Answer (B) is correct (6131). *(AIH Chap IX)*
Extreme overcooperation is an indication that a student is reacting abnormally to stress. The abnormally tense or anxious student may be noticeably over-agreeable.
Answer (A) is incorrect because a hesitancy to act is an indication of anxiety, not an abnormal reaction to stress. Answer (C) is incorrect because painstaking self-control, not a lack thereof, is an indication of an abnormal reaction to stress.

Answer (A) is correct (6132). *(AIH Chap IX)*
Psychologists tell us that a student's fear is a normal reaction and should be treated as such by an instructor. Treating fear as normal will help in counteracting anxiety.
Answer (B) is incorrect because discontinuing instruction in stressful tasks will not help the student to overcome the anxiety. Perhaps a different approach to the task is necessary. Answer (C) is incorrect because it describes an example of negative motivation which would tend to contribute to the student's anxiety.

3.4 The Overconfident or Impatient Student

15.
6140. Which obstacle to learning is a greater deterrent to learning pilot skills than is generally recognized?

A— Anxiety.
B— Impatience.
C— Physical discomfort.

Answer (B) is correct (6140). *(AIH Chap X)*
Failing to understand the need for preliminary training, the impatient student can only see the ultimate objective of flying an airplane. (S)he may desire to make an early solo or cross-country flight before certain basic elements of flight have been learned. This impatience can be detrimental to the usual, careful acquisition of pilot skills.
Answer (A) is incorrect because, although anxiety may be detrimental to the learning process, it is generally recognized as such, whereas impatience has an equal effect and is not widely recognized. Answer (C) is incorrect because, although physical discomfort may be detrimental to the learning process, it is generally recognized as such, whereas impatience has an equal effect and is not widely recognized.

16.
6139. Students who grow impatient when learning the basic elements of a task are those who

A— are less easily discouraged than the unaggressive students.
B— should have the preliminary training presented one step at a time with clearly stated goals for each step.
C— should be advanced to the next higher level of learning and not held back by insisting that the immediate goal be reached before they proceed to the next level.

Answer (B) is correct (6139). *(AIH Chap X)*
Impatient students fail to see why they must learn one step thoroughly before they move to the next. Presenting the preliminary training with clearly stated goals for each step will minimize student impatience.
Answer (A) is incorrect because impatient students are often aggressive and more easily discouraged than unaggressive students. Answer (C) is incorrect because it is necessary to hold a student until (s)he masters the basics if the whole task is to be performed competently and safely. This is the basis of the building block technique of instruction.

17.
6126. What should an instructor do with a student who assumes that correction of errors is unimportant?

A— Divide complex flight maneuvers into elements.
B— Try to reduce the student's overconfidence to reduce the chance of an accident.
C— Raise the standard of performance for each lesson, demanding greater effort.

Answer (C) is correct (6126). *(AIH Chap IX)*
Because apt students make few mistakes, they may assume that the correction of errors is not important. Such overconfidence soon results in faulty performance. For such students, a good instructor will constantly raise the standard of performance for each lesson, demanding greater effort.
Answer (A) is incorrect because dividing complex tasks into simpler elements should be done with students whose slow progress is due to a lack of confidence, not apt students. Answer (B) is incorrect because reducing students' overconfidence would be inefficient for properly motivating the apt student. After realizing the impatience of such students comes only from improperly paced instruction, instructors should give them challenges fitting their abilities.

18.
6125. Faulty performance due to student overconfidence should be corrected by

A— increasing the standard of performance for each lesson.
B— praising the student only when the performance is perfect.
C— providing strong, negative evaluation at the end of each lesson.

Answer (A) is correct (6125). *(AIH Chap IX)*
Because apt students make few mistakes, they may assume that the correction of errors is not important. Such overconfidence soon results in faulty performance. For such students, a good instructor will constantly raise the standard of performance for each lesson, demanding greater effort.
Answer (B) is incorrect because students need consistent, fair critique of every performance, perfect or not. Overly high standards also frustrate students by making them work too hard without reward (and for an unrealistic goal). Answer (C) is incorrect because the law of effect states that learning is weakened when associated with an unpleasant feeling. Aside from being unfair, the continual negative evaluations will also increasingly frustrate students.

END OF CHAPTER

CHAPTER FOUR
HUMAN BEHAVIOR AND EFFECTIVE COMMUNICATION

4.1 HUMAN NEEDS (Questions 1-3)

1. Human needs can be organized into a series of levels. The "pyramid of human needs" has been suggested by Abraham Maslow. For instance, physical needs must be satisfied before so-called "higher" needs can be used as motivators. He suggests that needs must be satisfied in the following ascending order:

   a. **Physical needs** pertain to food, rest, exercise, sex, etc. Until these needs are satisfied to a reasonable degree, a student cannot concentrate on learning.

   b. **Safety needs** include shelter and protection against danger, threat, and deprivation.

   c. **Social needs** are the needs to belong and to associate with other people.

   d. **Egoistic needs** will usually have a direct influence on the student-instructor relationship. Egoistic needs are of two kinds:

      1) Relating to one's self-esteem: needs for self-confidence, independence, achievement, and knowledge.

      2) Relating to one's reputation: needs for status, appreciation, and the deserved respect of one's fellow beings.

   e. **Self-fulfillment needs** are at the top of the hierarchy of human needs. These are the needs for realizing one's own potentialities, for continued development, and for being creative.

      1) This need of a student should offer the greatest challenge to an instructor.

      2) Helping students realize self-fulfillment is perhaps the most worthwhile accomplishment an instructor can achieve.

4.2 MOTIVATION (Questions 4-10)

1. Motivation is probably the dominant force governing the student's progress and ability to learn.

   a. Slumps in learning very often go hand-in-hand with slumps in motivation.

2. Positive motivations are provided by the promise or achievement of rewards.

3. Negative motivations are those which cause a student to react with fear and anxiety.

   a. Negative motivations in the form of reproof and threats should be avoided with all but the most overconfident and impulsive students.

4. It is important for an instructor to make the student aware that a particular lesson can help him/her reach an important goal.

   a. When students are unable to see the benefits or purpose of a lesson, they will be less motivated.

5. Motivations may be
    a. Positive or negative,
    b. Tangible or intangible,
    c. Obvious or subtle and difficult to identify.

6. Students are like any worker in wanting tangible returns for his/her efforts. If such motivation is to be effective, students must believe that their efforts will be suitably rewarded. Instructors should remember always to tailor individual lessons to the objective.

7. An instructor can most effectively maintain a high level of student motivation by making each lesson a pleasurable experience.

4.3 EFFECTIVE COMMUNICATION (Questions 11-15)

1. The process of communication is composed of three dynamically interrelated elements:
    a. A source (instructor)
    b. The symbols used in composing and transmitting the message (e.g., words)
    c. The receiver (student)

2. Communication takes place when one person transmits ideas or feelings to another person or to a group of people.

    a. The effectiveness of communication is measured by the similarity between the idea transmitted and the idea received.

    b. Effective communication has taken place when, and only when, the receivers react with understanding and change their behavior accordingly.

3. The effectiveness of persons acting in the role of communicators is related to at least three basic factors.

    a. First, their ability to select symbols that are meaningful to the listener.

    b. Second, communicators consciously or unconsciously reveal attitudes toward themselves, toward the ideas they are trying to transmit, and toward their receivers.

        1) Thus, to communicate effectively, instructors must reveal a positive attitude while delivering their message.

    c. Third, successful communicators speak or write from a broad background of accurate, up-to-date, stimulating material.

4. To understand the process of communication, at least three characteristics of receivers must be understood.

    a. First, they exercise their ability to question and comprehend the ideas that have been transmitted.

    b. Second, the receiver's attitude may be one of resistance, willingness, or of passive neutrality. Communicators must gain the receiver's attention and then retain it.

        1) The communicator will be more successful in this area by using a varied communicative approach.

    c. Third, the receiver's background, experience, and education frame the target at which communicators must aim.

4.4 BARRIERS TO EFFECTIVE COMMUNICATION (Questions 16-19)

1. Probably the greatest single barrier to effective communication is the lack of a common core of experience between communicator and receiver.

    a. A communicator's words cannot communicate the desired meaning to another person unless the listener or reader has had some experience with the objects or concepts to which these words refer.

2. Overuse of abstractions should be avoided.

    a. Concrete words refer to objects that human beings can experience directly.

    b. Abstract words stand for ideas that cannot be directly experienced or things that do not call forth specific mental images.

        1) Abstractions thus serve as shorthand symbols that sum up large areas of experience.

    c. The danger with using abstract words is that they may not evoke in the listener's mind the specific items of experience the communicator intends.

    d. By using concrete words, the communicator narrows (and gains better control of) the image produced in the minds of the listeners and readers.

4.5 INSTRUCTOR PROFESSIONALISM (Questions 20-23)

1. Although the term professionalism is widely used, it is rarely defined. In fact, no single definition can encompass all of the qualifications and considerations of true professionalism. The following are some of the major considerations.

2. Professionals must be able to reason logically and accurately.

3. Professionalism requires good decision-making ability.

    a. Professionals cannot limit their actions and decisions to standard patterns and practice.

4. Professionalism demands a code of ethics.

5. The professional flight instructor should be straightforward and honest.

    a. Anything less than a sincere performance is quickly detected and immediately destroys instructor effectiveness.

    b. Student confidence tends to be destroyed if instructors bluff when in doubt about some point.

    c. The well-prepared instructor instills not only confidence but good habits, since preparing well for a flight is a basic requirement for safe flying. Students quickly become apathetic when they recognize that the flight instructor is inadequately prepared.

6. The attitude, movements, and general demeanor of the flight instructor contribute a great deal to his/her professional image.

    a. The instructor should avoid erratic movements, distracting speech habits, and capricious changes in mood. The professional image requires development of a calm, thoughtful, and disciplined, but not somber, demeanor.

7. The professional relationship between the instructor and the student should be based on a mutual acknowledgment that both the student and the instructor are important to each other and that both are working toward the same objective.

    a. Accepting lower-than-normal standards to please a student will **NOT** help the student/instructor relationship.

    b. Reasonable standards strictly enforced are not resented by an earnest student.

8. The professional flight instructor should accept students as they are with all of their faults and problems.

    a. However, (s)he should also build student self-confidence, set challenges, and generally create an atmosphere for learning.

9. A flight instructor who is not completely familiar with current pilot certification and rating requirements cannot do a competent job of flight instruction.

    a. For a professional performance as a flight instructor, it is essential that the instructor maintain current copies of:

        1) The *Federal Aviation Regulations*, especially Parts 1, 61, and 91.
        2) An *Airman's Information Manual*,
        3) *Practical Test Standards*, and
        4) Appropriate pilot training manuals.

10. Flight instructors fail to provide competent instruction when they permit students to partially learn an important item of knowledge or skill.

    a. More importantly, such deficiencies may in themselves allow hazardous inadequacies to develop in the student's ongoing piloting performance.

QUESTIONS AND ANSWER EXPLANATIONS

All of the FAA questions from the Fundamentals of Instructing knowledge test relating to human behavior and effective communication outlined above are reproduced below in the same modules as the outlines. To the immediate right of each question are the correct answer and answer explanation. You should cover these answers and answer explanations with your hand or a piece of paper while responding to the questions. Refer to the general discussion in Chapter 1 on how to take the FAA pilot knowledge test.

Remember that the questions from the FAA pilot knowledge test bank have been reordered by topic, and the topics have been organized into a meaningful sequence. Accordingly, the first line of the answer explanation gives the FAA question number and the citation of the authoritative source for the answer.

4.1 Human Needs

1.
6041. Before a student can concentrate on learning, which human needs must be satisfied?

A— Safety.
B— Physical.
C— Security.

Answer (B) is correct (6041). *(AIM Chap II)*
Physical needs are the most basic of the human needs. Thus, they must be met before any learning can take place. Until the needs of food, water, rest, etc., are satisfied, the student cannot concentrate on learning.
Answer (A) is incorrect because physical, not safety, needs must be satisfied before a student can concentrate on learning. Safety needs are protection from danger, threat, and deprivation. Answer (C) is incorrect because physical, not security, needs must be satisfied before a student can concentrate on learning. Security (or safety) needs are protection from danger, threat, and deprivation.

2.
6042. After individuals are physically comfortable and have no fear for their safety, which human needs become the prime influence on their behavior?

A— Social.
B— Physical.
C— Egoistic.

Answer (A) is correct (6042). *(AIM Chap II)*
The order of human needs according to Abraham Maslow are (1) physical, (2) safety, (3) social, (4) egoistic, and (5) self-fulfillment. In this hierarchy, social needs come after physical and safety needs are satisfied.
Answer (B) is incorrect because the question states that the individuals are physically comfortable.
Answer (C) is incorrect because egoistic needs have the fourth priority, not the third priority as the question asks.

3.
6043. Which of the student's human needs offer the greatest challenge to an instructor?

A— Social.
B— Egoistic.
C— Self-fulfillment.

Answer (C) is correct (6043). *(AIM Chap II)*
The greatest challenge for an instructor is to help the student realize his/her potentialities for continued development. This is helping the student meet the need for self-fulfillment.
Answer (A) is incorrect because social needs are not a challenge to the instructor. Social needs are those to belong and to give and receive friendship, which the student must satisfy on his/her own. Answer (B) is incorrect because, although making a student feel self-confident and deserving of respect (egoism) is important and usually has a direct influence on the instructor-student relationship, it is not the instructor's greatest challenge.

4.2 Motivation

4.
6025. Which is generally the more effective way for an instructor to properly motivate students?

A— Maintain pleasant personal relationships with students.
B— Provide positive motivations by the promise or achievement of rewards.
C— Reinforce their self-confidence by requiring no tasks beyond their ability to perform.

Answer (B) is correct (6025). *(AIM Chap I)*
Providing positive motivation is generally considered the most effective way to properly motivate people. Positive motivations are provided by the promise or achievement of rewards.
Answer (A) is incorrect because maintaining pleasant personal relationships with students (while desirable) is not the more effective way for an instructor to properly motivate students. Answer (C) is incorrect because a student who is not required to perform a task beyond present abilities will neither be motivated nor make any progress.

5.
6023. Motivations that cause a student to react with fear and anxiety are

A— tangible.
B— negative.
C— difficult to identify.

Answer (B) is correct (6023). *(AIM Chap I)*
Negative motivations may produce fears and may thus be seen by the student as threats. Negative motivation generally intimidates students and should be avoided.
Answer (A) is incorrect because motivations, whether tangible or intangible, can be either positive or negative. Answer (C) is incorrect because motivations, whether very subtle or difficult to identify, can be either positive or negative.

6.
6026. Motivations in the form of reproof and threats should be avoided with all but the student who is

A— overconfident and impulsive.
B— avidly seeking group approval.
C— experiencing a learning plateau.

Answer (A) is correct (6026). *(AIH Chap I)*
Educational experts have shown that negative motivation is useful only for a student who is overconfident and impulsive. Otherwise, negative motivation in the form of reproof and threats tends to discourage student behavior.
Answer (B) is incorrect because group approval is a strong motivating force. Use of reproofs and threats with a student seeking group approval would only alienate him/her from the group. Answer (C) is incorrect because one of the reasons a student has reached a learning plateau is due to a lack of motivation. Use of reproofs and threats would only cause a student to remain at the plateau longer.

7.
6053. When students are unable to see the benefits or purpose of a lesson, they will

A— be less motivated.
B— not learn as quickly.
C— be expected to increase their efforts.

8.
6022. Which statement is true concerning motivations?

A— Motivations must be tangible to be effective.
B— Motivations may be very subtle and difficult to identify.
C— Negative motivations often are as effective as positive motivations.

9.
6024. For a motivation to be effective, students must believe their efforts will be rewarded in a definite manner. This type of motivation is

A— subtle.
B— negative.
C— tangible.

10.
6124. An instructor can most effectively maintain a high level of student motivation by

A— making each lesson a pleasurable experience.
B— relaxing the standards of performance required during the early phase of training.
C— continually challenging the student to meet the highest objectives of training that can be established.

Answer (A) is correct (6053). *(AIH Chap I)*
Students will be less motivated if they are unable to see the benefits or purpose of a lesson. It is important for the instructor to make the student aware that a particular lesson can help him/her reach an important goal.
Answer (B) is incorrect because, while a student may not learn as quickly when (s)he is unable to see the benefits or purpose of a lesson, (s)he will become less motivated. Answer (C) is incorrect because the frustration of working without a known goal will likely decrease, not increase, their efforts.

Answer (B) is correct (6022). *(AIH Chap I)*
Motivations may be subtle, subconscious, and difficult to identify. A student may be motivated without even being aware (s)he is being influenced.
Answer (A) is incorrect because intangible motivations can be as effective (or even more effective) than tangible motivations. Rewards such as accomplishment, fame, and peer acceptance are intangible, but they are among the best positive motivators. Answer (C) is incorrect because negative motivation tends to discourage the student.

Answer (C) is correct (6024). *(AIH Chap I)*
Students, like any worker, need and want tangible returns for their efforts. These rewards must be constantly apparent to the student during instruction.
Answer (A) is incorrect because the student is often unaware of the application of subtle motivation and thus feels unrewarded for his/her effort. Answer (B) is incorrect because negative motivations are not as effective as positive motivations, as they tend to intimidate students and cause unpleasant experiences.

Answer (A) is correct (6124). *(AIH Chap I)*
An instructor can most effectively maintain a high level of motivation by making each lesson a pleasant experience. People avoid negative experiences, but they will seek out and want to repeat positive experiences.
Answer (B) is incorrect because relaxing the standards of performance required during the early phase of training may actually reduce a student's motivation. Reasonable standards strictly enforced are not resented by an earnest student. Answer (C) is incorrect because performance standards should be set to the student's potential and not his/her current ability or to unrealistically high objectives. Improvement must be fostered.

4.3 Effective Communication

11.
6056. The effectiveness of communication between instructor and student is measured by the

A— degree of dynamic, interrelated elements.
B— similarity between the idea transmitted and the idea received.
C— relationship between communicative and dynamic elements.

Answer (B) is correct (6056). *(AIH Chap III)*
Communication takes place when one person transmits ideas or feelings to another person or group of people. Its effectiveness is measured by the similarity between the idea transmitted and the idea received.
Answer (A) is incorrect because the process, not the effectiveness, of communication is composed of three dynamic, interrelated elements -- the source, the symbols, and the receiver. Answer (C) is incorrect because the relationship between the communicative elements (source, symbols, and receiver) is dynamic. There are no dynamic elements.

12.
6059. Effective communication has taken place when, and only when, the

A— information is transmitted and received.
B— receivers react with understanding and change their behavior accordingly.
C— receivers have the ability to question and comprehend ideas that have been transmitted.

Answer (B) is correct (6059). *(AIH Chap III)*
The rule of thumb among communicators is that communication succeeds only in relation to the reaction of the receiver. Effective communication has taken place only when the receivers react with understanding and change their behavior.
Answer (A) is incorrect because information may be transmitted and received without effective communication. Only when the receiver reacts to the information being transmitted and received with understanding, and changes his/her behavior accordingly, has effective communication taken place. Answer (C) is incorrect because the ability to question and comprehend ideas that have been transmitted is only one characteristic of a receiver.

13.
6058. To communicate effectively, instructors must

A— recognize the level of comprehension.
B— provide an atmosphere which encourages questioning.
C— reveal a positive attitude while delivering their message.

Answer (C) is correct (6058). *(AIH Chap III)*
Communicators consciously or unconsciously reveal attitudes toward themselves, the ideas they are trying to transmit, and their receivers. These attitudes must be positive if the communicators are to communicate effectively.
Answer (A) is incorrect because an instructor can recognize the level of a student's comprehension in the application step of the teaching process, not during the communication process. Answer (B) is incorrect because, while an instructor should provide an atmosphere which encourages questioning, the student must exercise his/her ability to ask questions to communicate effectively.

14.
6057. In order to be successful, communicators must speak or write from a background of

A— technical expertise.
B— knowing the ideas presented.
C— up-to-date, stimulating material.

Answer (C) is correct (6057). *(AIH Chap III)*
A basic factor of a communicator's effectiveness is the ability to speak or write from a broad background of accurate, up-to-date, and stimulating material.
Answer (A) is incorrect because a speaker or writer with technical expertise may depend on technical jargon. Reliance on technical language can impede effective communication, especially when the receiver lacks a similar background. Answer (B) is incorrect because just knowing the ideas presented does not ensure that effective communication will take place. A communicator must be able to make the receiver react with understanding and change his/her behavior accordingly.

15.

6060. In the communication process, the communicator will be more successful in gaining and retaining the receiver's attention by

A— being friendly and informative.
B— using a varied communicative approach.
C— using a variety of audiovisual aids in class.

Answer (B) is correct (6060). *(AIH Chap III)*

The most successful communicator will use the variety of channels that best communicates the necessary ideas and techniques, i.e., a varied communicative approach.

Answer (A) is incorrect because effective, engaging communication is more complex than merely being friendly. The source, the symbols, and the receiver are all interrelated in the communication process.

Answer (C) is incorrect because audio-visual aids can often further the learning, not the communication, process by supporting, supplementing, or reinforcing important ideas. By presenting the material in a new manner, instructional aids can even improve communication between instructor and student.

4.4 Barriers to Effective Communication

16.

6063. Probably the greatest single barrier to effective communication in the teaching process is a lack of

A— respect for the instructor.
B— personality harmony between instructor and student.
C— a common experience level between instructor and student.

Answer (C) is correct (6063). *(AIH Chap III)*

The greatest single barrier to effective communication is the lack of common experience between the communicator and the receiver. Those with the least in common usually find it difficult to communicate.

Answer (A) is incorrect because, while lack of respect for the instructor is a barrier to communication, it is not as great and as prevalent as a lack of common experience between the communicator and the receiver.

Answer (B) is incorrect because, while lack of personality harmony is a barrier to communication, it is not as great and as prevalent as a lack of common experience between the communicator and the receiver.

17.

6064. A communicator's words cannot communicate the desired meaning to another person unless the

A— words have meaningful referents.
B— words give the meaning that is in the mind of the receiver.
C— listener or reader has had some experience with the objects or concepts to which these words refer.

Answer (C) is correct (6064). *(AIH Chap III)*

Since a common core of experience is basic to effective communication, a communicator's words cannot communicate the desired meaning to another person unless the listener or the reader has had some experience with the objects or concepts to which these words refer.

Answer (A) is incorrect because the words must have not only meaningful referents, but the exact same meaningful referents in order for the communicator and the receiver to share a desired meaning. Answer (B) is incorrect because words only arouse desired meanings if the communicator generates the desired response in the mind of the receiver. The nature of this response is determined by the receiver's past experiences with the words and the concepts to which they refer.

18.

6062. The danger in using abstract words is that they

A— sum up vast areas of experience.
B— call forth different mental images in the minds of the receivers.
C— will not evoke the specific items of experience in the listener's mind that the communicator intends.

Answer (C) is correct (6062). *(AIH Chap III)*

The purpose of abstract words is not to bring forth specific ideas in the mind of the receiver but to serve as shorthand symbols that sum up vast areas of experience. The danger in using abstract words is that they will not evoke the specific items in the listener's mind that the communicator intends.

Answer (A) is incorrect because the purpose, not the danger, of using abstract words is to use them as shorthand symbols that sum up vast areas of experience. Answer (B) is incorrect because abstract words do not call forth mental images; on the contrary, they stand for ideas that cannot be directly experienced.

19.
6061. By using abstractions in the communication process, the communicator will

A— bring forth specific items of experience in the minds of the receivers.

B— be using words which refer to objects or ideas that human beings can experience directly.

C— not evoke in the listener's or reader's mind the specific items of experience the communicator intends.

Answer (C) is correct (6061). *(AIH Chap III)*
Abstract words are necessary and useful. Their purpose is not to bring forth specific items of experience in the minds of receivers but to serve as shorthand symbols that refer to thoughts or ideas. The danger is that an abstract term might not evoke in the listener's mind the specific item of experience the communicator intended.
Answer (A) is incorrect because abstract words are not used to bring forth specific items of experience in the minds of the receivers. Answer (B) is incorrect because concrete, not abstract, words refer to objects or ideas that human beings can experience directly.

4.5 Instructor Professionalism

20.
6123. Which statement is true regarding true professionalism as an instructor?

A— Anything less than sincere performance destroys the effectiveness of the professional instructor.

B— To achieve professionalism, actions and decisions must be limited to standard patterns and practices.

C— A single definition of professionalism would encompass all of the qualifications and considerations which must be present.

Answer (A) is correct (6123). *(AIH Chap IX)*
Professionalism demands a code of ethics. Professionals must be true to themselves and to those they serve. Anything less than a sincere performance will be detected by students and immediately destroy instructor effectiveness.
Answer (B) is incorrect because professionalism requires good judgment. Professionals cannot limit their actions and decisions to standard patterns and practice. Answer (C) is incorrect because professionalism is so multi-dimensional that no single definition can encompass all of the qualifications and considerations.

21.
6055. Student confidence tends to be destroyed if instructors

A— bluff whenever in doubt about some point.

B— continually identify student errors and failures.

C— direct and control the student's actions and behavior.

Answer (A) is correct (6055). *(AIH Chap II)*
No one, including students, expects an instructor to be perfect. An instructor can gain the respect of students by honestly acknowledging mistakes. If the instructor tries to cover up or bluff, students will be quick to sense it and lose their confidence in the instructor.
Answer (B) is incorrect because identifying the student's errors and failures helps the student to progress and gain confidence. Answer (C) is incorrect because directing the student's actions and behavior is a basic responsibility of the flight instructor.

22.
6142. Students quickly become apathetic when they

A— realize material is being withheld by the instructor.

B— understand the objectives toward which they are working.

C— recognize that the instructor is not adequately prepared.

Answer (C) is correct (6142). *(AIH Chap X)*
Students become apathetic when they recognize that the instructor has made inadequate preparations for the instruction being given, or when the instruction appears to be deficient, contradictory, or insincere.
Answer (A) is incorrect because students will lose respect for the instructor (not become apathetic) when they realize material is being withheld by the instructor. Answer (B) is incorrect because it is optimal that both the student and instructor understand the objectives so that they may work cooperatively toward them.

23.
6127. Which statement is true regarding the achievement of an adequate standard of performance?

A— A flight instructor should devote major effort and attention to the continuous evaluation of student performance.

B— Flight instructors can affect a genuine improvement in the student/instructor relationship by not strictly enforcing standards.

C— Flight instructors fail to provide competent instruction when they permit students to partially learn an important item of knowledge or skill.

Answer (C) is correct (6127). *(AIH Chap IX)*
Flight instructors fail to provide competent instruction when they permit their students to partially learn an important item of knowledge or skill. More importantly, such deficiencies may in themselves allow hazardous inadequacies in the student's later piloting performance.
Answer (A) is incorrect because a flight instructor should devote major effort and attention to all areas of the teaching process, not only to the evaluation of student performance. Answer (B) is incorrect because it is a fallacy to believe that a flight instructor can affect a genuine improvement in the student/instructor relationship by not strictly enforcing standards. Reasonable standards strictly enforced are not resented by an earnest student.

END OF CHAPTER

CHAPTER FIVE
TEACHING METHODS

5.1 LECTURE METHOD (Questions 1-8)

1. The lecture is used primarily for

    a. Introducing students to new subject material,
    b. Summarizing ideas,
    c. Showing relationships between theory and practice, and
    d. Reemphasizing main points.

2. There are four types of lectures:

    a. The illustrated talk in which the speaker relies heavily on visual aids to convey his ideas to the listeners;

    b. The briefing in which the speaker presents a concise array of facts to the listeners who do not expect elaboration or supporting material;

    c. The formal speech in which the speaker's purpose is to inform, persuade, or entertain; and

    d. The teaching lecture for which the instructor must plan and deliver an oral presentation in a manner that helps the students reach the desired learning outcomes.

3. One advantage of a teaching lecture is that the instructor can present many ideas in a relatively short time. Facts and ideas that have been logically organized can be concisely presented in rapid sequence.

    a. Thus, a teaching lecture is the most economical of all teaching methods in terms of the time required to present a given amount of material.

4. One disadvantage of a teaching lecture is that the instructor does not receive direct reaction (either words or actions) from the students when using the teaching lecture.

    a. Thus, the instructor must develop a keen perception for subtle response from the class and must be able to interpret the meaning of these reactions and adjust the lesson accordingly.

        1) These reactions could be in the form of facial expressions, manner of taking notes, and apparent interest or lack of interest in the lesson.

    b. The instructor must recognize that the lecture method is least useful for evaluating student performance.

5. The following four steps should be followed in preparing a lecture:

    a. Establish the objective and desired outcomes,
    b. Research the subject,
    c. Organize the material, and
    d. Plan productive classroom activities.

6. The teaching lecture is probably best delivered extemporaneously but from a written outline.

    a. Because the exact words which express an idea are chosen at the moment of delivery, the lecture can be personalized or suited to the moment more easily than one that is read or spoken from memory.

7. In the teaching lecture, use simple rather than complex words whenever possible.

    a. Picturesque slang and free-and-easy colloquialisms, if they suit the subject, can add variety and vividness to a teaching lecture.

    b. Errors in grammar and use of vulgarisms detract from an instructor's dignity and reflect upon the intelligence of the students.

8. The lecture can be formal or informal.

    a. A formal lecture provides no active student participation.

    b. The distinguishing characteristic of an informal lecture is the active student participation.

        1) The instructor can inspire active student participation during the lecture through the use of questions.

5.2 GUIDED DISCUSSION METHOD (Questions 9-14)

1. Fundamentally, the guided discussion method of teaching is the reverse of the lecture method. The instructor uses questions to guide and stimulate discussion among students. The instructor does not present new ideas.

2. In the guided discussion, learning is produced through the skillful use of questions.

    a. Questions facilitate discussion, which in turn develops an understanding of the subject.

3. Questions used in a guided discussion can be broken into several types, each with its usefulness in the guided discussion:

    a. **Overhead** -- directed to the entire group to stimulate thought.

        1) The overhead question should be used to begin a guided discussion.

    b. **Rhetorical** -- also stimulates thought, but instructor will answer it him/herself. This is normally used in a lecture, not a guided discussion.

    c. **Direct** -- question addressed to an individual for a response.

    d. **Reverse** -- The instructor answers a student's question by redirecting the question for that student to provide the answer.

    e. **Relay** -- The reverse question is addressed to the entire group, not the individual.

4. In preparing questions, the instructor should remember that the purpose is to bring about discussion, not merely to get answers.

    a. Leadoff questions should be open-ended, i.e., they should start with "how" or "why."

    b. Avoid questions that begin with "what," "when," or "does" because they only require short, categorical answers such as "yes," "no," "green," "one," etc.

5. Each question, in order to be effective, should

    a. Have a specific purpose,
    b. Be clear in meaning,
    c. Contain a single idea,
    d. Stimulate thought,
    e. Require definite answers, and
    f. Relate to previously taught information.

6. When it appears the students have adequately discussed the ideas that support a particular part of the lesson, the instructor should summarize what they have accomplished.

    a. This interim summary is one of the most effective tools available to the instructor.

        1) This summary can be made immediately after the discussion of each learning outcome.

        2) It consolidates what students learned, emphasizes how much they know already, and points out any aspects they missed.

7. Unless the students have some knowledge to exchange with each other, they cannot reach the desired learning outcomes.

    a. Students without some background in a subject should not be asked to discuss that subject.

5.3 DEMONSTRATION/PERFORMANCE METHOD (Questions 15-19)

1. The demonstration/performance method is based on the principle that we learn by doing.

    a. It is the most commonly used teaching method of flight instructors.
    b. This is the ideal method for teaching a skill such as cross-country planning.

2. The demonstration/performance method of instruction has five essential steps:

    a. Explanation -- the instructor must explain the objectives of the particular lesson to the student.

    b. Demonstration -- the instructor must show the student how to perform a skill.

    c. Student performance -- the student must act and do, i.e., practice.

    d. Instructor supervision -- this is done concurrently with student performance. The instructor coaches, as necessary, the student's practice.

    e. Evaluation -- the instructor judges the student performance.

3. The telling and doing technique of flight instruction is basically the demonstration/performance method of instruction. This consists of performing several steps in proper order.

    a. Instructor tells -- instructor does
    b. Student tells -- instructor does
    c. Student tells -- student does
    d. Student does -- instructor evaluates

5.4 INTEGRATED METHOD OF FLIGHT INSTRUCTION (Questions 20-23)

1.   Integrated flight instruction is flight instruction during which students are taught to perform flight maneuvers both by outside visual references and by reference to flight instruments, from the first time each maneuver is introduced.

   a.   In a student's first instruction on the function of flight controls you would include the instrument indication to be expected, as well as the outside references used in attitude control.

2.   The primary objective of integrated flight instruction is to form the habit patterns for the observance of and reliance on flight instruments.

   a.   Such habits have been proved to produce more capable and safer pilots.

   b.   The ability to fly in instrument meteorological conditions (IMC) is not the objective of this type of primary training.

3.   During the conduct of integrated flight instruction, you are responsible for collision avoidance while your student is flying by simulated instruments, i.e., under the hood.

   a.   You must guard against diverting your attention to the student's performance for extended periods.

4.   At the same time, you must be sure that your student develops, from the first lesson, the habit of looking for other traffic when (s)he is not operating under simulated instrument conditions.

   a.   Any observed tendency of a student to enter a maneuver without clearing the area must be corrected immediately.

5.5 THE POSITIVE APPROACH IN FLIGHT INSTRUCTION (Questions 24-25)

1.   In flight instruction, an effective positive approach will point out the pleasurable features of flying before the unpleasant possibilities are discussed.

2.   EXAMPLE: A positive first flight lesson:

   a.   A preflight inspection familiarizing the student with the airplane and its components.
   b.   A perfectly normal flight to a nearby airport and back.

      1)   The instructor calls the student's attention to how easy the trip was in comparison with other ways to travel and the fact that no critical incidents were encountered or expected.

3.   EXAMPLE: A negative first flight lesson:

   a.   An exhaustive indoctrination on preflight procedures with emphasis on the potential for disastrous mechanical failures in flight.

   b.   Instructions on the dangers of taxiing an airplane too fast.

   c.   A series of stalls with emphasis on the difficulties in recovering from them. (The side effect of this performance is likely to be airsickness.)

   d.   A series of simulated forced landings, stating that every pilot should always be prepared to cope with an engine failure.

QUESTIONS AND ANSWER EXPLANATIONS

All of the FAA questions from the Fundamentals of Instructing knowledge test relating to the teaching methods outlined above are reproduced below in the same modules as the outlines. To the immediate right of each question are the correct answer and answer explanation. You should cover these answers and answer explanations with your hand or a piece of paper while responding to the questions. Refer to the general discussion in Chapter 1 on how to take the FAA pilot knowledge test.

Remember that the questions from the FAA pilot knowledge test bank have been reordered by topic, and the topics have been organized into a meaningful sequence. Accordingly, the first line of the answer explanation gives the FAA question number and the citation of the authoritative source for the answer.

5.1 Lecture Method

1.
6068. In the teaching process, which method of presentation is suitable for presenting new material, for summarizing ideas, and for showing relationships between theory and practice?

A— Lecture method.
B— Integrated instruction method.
C— Demonstration/performance method.

Answer (A) is correct (6068). *(AIH Chap V)*
The lecture is used primarily to introduce students to new material. It is also valuable for summarizing ideas, showing relationships between theory and practice, and reemphasizing main points. The lecture is the most efficient teaching method in terms of time and student numbers, if not in other ways.
Answer (B) is incorrect because the integrated method of flight instruction means that, from the first time a maneuver is introduced, students are taught to perform it both by outside visual references and by reference to flight instruments. Answer (C) is incorrect because the demonstration/performance method is better suited to teaching a skill (i.e., flight instruction).

2.
6079. What is one advantage of a lecture?

A— Uses time economically.
B— Excellent when additional research is required.
C— Allows for maximum attainment of certain types of learning outcomes.

Answer (A) is correct (6079). *(AIH Chap V)*
In a lecture, the instructor can present many ideas in a relatively short time. Facts and ideas that have been logically organized can be concisely presented in rapid sequence. Lecturing is unquestionably the most economical of all teaching methods in terms of time required to present a given amount of material.
Answer (B) is incorrect because one advantage of the lecture is that it can be used to present information without requiring students to do additional research. Answer (C) is incorrect because a disadvantage, not an advantage, of a lecture is that the lecture does not enable the instructor to estimate the student's progress, thus learning may not be maximized.

3.
6082. Which teaching method is most economical in terms of the time required to present a given amount of material?

A— Briefing.
B— Teaching lecture.
C— Demonstration/performance.

Answer (B) is correct (6082). *(AIH Chap V)*
The teaching lecture is unquestionably the most economical of all teaching methods in terms of the time required to present a given amount of material. The instructor can concisely present many ideas that have been logically organized in rapid sequence.
Answer (A) is incorrect because, although a briefing is a type of lecture, it is used to present a concise array of facts to the listeners who do not expect elaboration or supporting material. Answer (C) is incorrect because the demonstration/performance method is the least, not the most, economical in terms of time required to present a given amount of material.

4.
6077. Which is a true statement regarding the teaching lecture?

A— Delivering the lecture in an extemporaneous manner is not recommended.
B— Instructor receives direct feedback from students which is easy to interpret.
C— Instructor must develop a keen perception for subtle responses and be able to interpret the meaning of these reactions.

Answer (C) is correct (6077). *(AIH Chap V)*
    In the teaching lecture, the instructor must develop a keen perception for subtle responses from the class (e.g., facial expressions, manner of taking notes, and apparent interest or lack of interest in the lesson), and must be able to interpret the meaning of these reactions and adjust the lesson accordingly.
    Answer (A) is incorrect because the lecture is best delivered extemporaneously, but from a written outline. The lecture can thus be personalized to suit different audience moods. Answer (B) is incorrect because, in the teaching lecture, the instructor's feedback is not as direct as other teaching methods and therefore is harder, not easier, to interpret.

5.
6076. The first step in preparing a lecture is to

A— research the subject.
B— develop the main ideas or key points.
C— establish the objective and desired outcome.

Answer (C) is correct (6076). *(AIH Chap V)*
    The following four steps, in order, should be used in preparing a lecture.

1. Establish the objectives and desired outcomes
2. Research the subject
3. Organize the material
4. Plan productive classroom activities

    Answer (A) is incorrect because researching the subject is the second, not the first, step in preparing a lecture. Answer (B) is incorrect because developing the main ideas or key points is the third, not the first, step in preparing a lecture.

6.
6078. During a teaching lecture, what would detract from an instructor's dignity and reflect upon the student's intelligence?

A— Use of figurative language.
B— Errors in grammar and use of vulgarisms.
C— Using picturesque slang and colloquialisms.

Answer (B) is correct (6078). *(AIH Chap V)*
    During a teaching lecture, errors in grammar and the use of vulgarisms detract from an instructor's dignity and reflect upon the student's intelligence.
    Answer (A) is incorrect because figurative language, when used properly, can add interest and color to a lecture. Answer (C) is incorrect because picturesque slang and colloquialisms, if they suit the subject, can add variety and vividness to a lecture.

7.
6081. The distinguishing characteristic of an informal lecture is the

A— use of visual aids.
B— student's participation.
C— requirement for informal notes.

Answer (B) is correct (6081). *(AIH Chap V)*
    The distinguishing characteristic of an informal lecture is the active student participation. A formal lecture does not include student participation.
    Answer (A) is incorrect because visual aids can be used in either the formal or informal lecture. Answer (C) is incorrect because the requirement for informal notes is not the distinguishing characteristic of an informal lecture. Notes may or may not be used in the formal or informal lecture.

8.
6080. An instructor can best inspire active student participation during lectures through the use of

A— questions.
B— visual aids.
C— encouragement.

Answer (A) is correct (6080). *(AIH Chap V)*
    An instructor can best inspire student participation during lectures (i.e., an informal lecture) through the use of questions. In this way, the students are encouraged to make contributions that supplement the lecture.
    Answer (B) is incorrect because visual aids emphasize and enhance the lecture but do not help get the students actively involved. Answer (C) is incorrect because encouragement aids learning in all situations, not just participation during lectures.

5.2 Guided Discussion Method

9.
6085. In a guided discussion, learning is produced through the

A— skillful use of questions.
B— use of questions, each of which contains several ideas.
C— use of reverse questions directed to the class as a whole.

10.
6083. Which type question should an instructor use to begin a guided discussion with a group of students?

A— Relay.
B— Overhead.
C— Rhetorical.

11.
6087. In a guided discussion, leadoff questions should usually begin with

A— why.
B— what.
C— when.

12.
6086. Which question would be best as a leadoff question for a guided discussion on the subject of torque?

A— Does torque affect an airplane?
B— How does torque affect an airplane?
C— What effect does torque have on an airplane in a turn?

Answer (A) is correct (6085). *(AIM Chap V)*
The guided discussion method relies on the students to provide ideas, experiences, opinions, and information. The instructor guides the discussion by use of questions which are aimed to draw out what the students know. Thus, learning is produced through the skillful use of questions.
Answer (B) is incorrect because, in a guided discussion, each question used should contain only one, not several, ideas. Answer (C) is incorrect because a relay, not reverse, question is redirected to the class as a whole.

Answer (B) is correct (6083). *(AIH Chap V)*
In the guided discussion, learning is produced through skillful use of questions. To begin a guided discussion, the instructor should use an overhead question. This type of question is directed to the entire group to stimulate thought and response from each student.
Answer (A) is incorrect because a relay question responds to a student's question by redirecting it back to the rest of the group. Answer (C) is incorrect because a rhetorical question is similar in nature to an overhead question, but the instructor answers the question. This is more commonly used in lecturing than in guided discussion.

Answer (A) is correct (6087). *(AIH Chap V)*
In preparing questions, the instructor should remember that the purpose is to bring about discussion, not merely to get only short categorical answers (i.e., yes, no, one, etc.). Thus, lead-off questions should usually begin with "how" or "why."
Answer (B) is incorrect because a question beginning with "what" usually requires only a short categorical answer and will not encourage a discussion. Answer (C) is incorrect because a question beginning with "when" usually requires a short answer and will not encourage a discussion.

Answer (B) is correct (6086). *(AIH Chap V)*
In preparing questions to lead off a guided discussion, the instructor should remember that the purpose is to bring about discussion, not merely answers. Avoid questions that require only short, categorical (i.e., yes or no) answers. Lead-off questions should usually begin with "how" or "why."
Answer (A) is incorrect because a question beginning with "does" only requires a yes or no answer and will not encourage a discussion. Answer (C) is incorrect because a question beginning with "what" only requires a short, categorical answer and will not encourage a discussion.

13.
6088. When it appears students have adequately discussed the ideas presented during a guided discussion, one of the most valuable tools an instructor can use is

A— a session of verbal testing.
B— a written test on the subject discussed.
C— an interim summary of what the students accomplished.

Answer (C) is correct (6088). *(AIH Chap V)*
When it appears the students have discussed the ideas that support a particular part of the lesson, the instructor should summarize what the students have accomplished. This interim summary is one of the most effective tools available to the instructor in a guided discussion. To bring ideas together and help in transition, an interim summary should be made after the discussion of each desired learning outcome.
Answer (A) is incorrect because a session of verbal testing goes against the intention of the guided discussion, where the instructor aims to "draw out" what the students know in a structured but personable manner. Answer (B) is incorrect because a written test on the subject without an instructor summary would be testing student opinions and experiences rather than facts.

14.
6084. Which statement about the guided discussion method of teaching is true?

A— The lesson objective becomes apparent at the application level of learning.
B— Students without a background in the subject can also be included in the discussion.
C— Unless the students have some knowledge to exchange with each other, they cannot reach the desired learning outcomes.

Answer (C) is correct (6084). *(AIH Chap V)*
Throughout the time the instructor prepares the students for their discussion (e.g., early lectures, homework assignments), the students should be made aware of the lesson objectives. This gives them the background for a fruitful guided discussion. Students without some background in a subject should not be asked to discuss that subject.
Answer (A) is incorrect because the lesson objective should be known while the students are preparing for the guided discussion, or at least during the introduction, not afterward at the application level of learning. Answer (B) is incorrect because students with no background in the subject will not be able to contribute to an effective discussion.

5.3 Demonstration/Performance Method

15.
6066. Which method of presentation is desirable for teaching a skill such as cross-country planning?

A— Lecture/application.
B— Presentation/practice.
C— Demonstration/performance.

Answer (C) is correct (6066). *(AIH Chap V)*
The demonstration/performance method of teaching is based on the principle that you learn by doing. Students learn physical or mental skills best by actually performing them under supervision. Learning to do cross-country planning is an ideal application of this teaching method.
Answer (A) is incorrect because the lecture method is not suitable to teach cross-country planning because the lecture does not provide for student participation and, as a consequence, lets the instructor do all the work.
Answer (B) is incorrect because presentation/practice is not a method of presentation.

16.
6089. What are the essential steps in the demonstration/ performance method of teaching?

A— Demonstration, practice, and evaluation.
B— Demonstration, student performance, and evaluation.
C— Explanation, demonstration, student performance, instructor supervision, and evaluation.

17.
6091. What is the last step in the demonstration/ performance method?

A— Summary.
B— Evaluation.
C— Student performance.

18.
6090. In the demonstration/performance method of instruction, which two separate actions are performed concurrently?

A— Instructor explanation and demonstration.
B— Student performance and instructor supervision.
C— Instructor explanation and student demonstration.

Answer (C) is correct (6089). *(AIH Chap V)*
The demonstration/performance method of teaching is based on the principle that we learn by doing. Thus, it is used by flight instructors in teaching procedures and maneuvers. The five essential steps are:

1. Explanation
2. Demonstration
3. Student performance
4. Instructor supervision
5. Evaluation

Answer (A) is incorrect because the five, not three, essential steps in the demonstration/performance method of teaching are explanation, demonstration, student performance, not practice, instructor supervision, and evaluation. Answer (B) is incorrect because the five, not three, essential steps in the demonstration/performance method of teaching are explanation, demonstration, student performance, instructor supervision, and evaluation.

Answer (B) is correct (6091). *(AIH Chap V)*
The demonstration/performance method of teaching is based on the principle that we learn by doing. Thus, it is used by flight instructors in teaching procedures and maneuvers. The five essential steps are:

1. Explanation
2. Demonstration
3. Student performance
4. Instructor supervision
5. Evaluation

Answer (A) is incorrect because summary is not a step in the demonstration/performance method.
Answer (C) is incorrect because student performance is the third, not last, step in the demonstration/performance method.

Answer (B) is correct (6090). *(AIH Chap V)*
In the demonstration/performance method of instruction, student performance and instructor supervision are performed concurrently. As the student practices to learn, the instructor supervises and coaches as necessary.
Answer (A) is incorrect because, during the explanation phase, the instructor explains to the student the actions they are to perform. This is accomplished during the preflight discussion. The demonstration is done in the airplane as the instructor shows the student how to perform a maneuver. Answer (C) is incorrect because instructor supervision, not explanation, and student performance, not demonstration, are performed concurrently.

19.
6134. The basic demonstration/performance method of instruction consists of several steps in proper order. They are

A— instructor tells--student does; student tells--student does; student does--instructor evaluates.

B— instructor tells--instructor does; student tells--instructor does; student does--instructor evaluates.

C— instructor tells--instructor does; student tells--instructor does; student tells--student does; student does--instructor evaluates.

5.4 Integrated Method of Flight Instruction

20.
6136. The primary objective of integrated flight instruction is the

A— formation of firm habit patterns for observing and relying on flight instruments.

B— difference in the pilot's operation of the flight controls during both VMC and IMC.

C— developing of the habit of occasionally monitoring their own and the aircraft's performance.

21.
6135. Integrated flight instruction has many benefits, but the main objective is to

A— develop the student's ability to fly the aircraft during inadvertent IMC.

B— ensure the student is not overly dependent on instruments during VFR flight.

C— help the student develop habit patterns for observance of and reliance on flight instruments.

22.
6137. Which is an acceptable procedure when using the integrated method of flight instruction?

A— Use alternate and distinct periods devoted entirely to instrument flight or to visual flight.

B— Prior to the first flight, clearly explain the differences in the manipulation of flight controls for maintaining aircraft control when under simulated instrument conditions and when using references outside the aircraft.

C— Include in the student's first instruction on the function of flight controls the instrument indication to be expected, as well as the outside references used in attitude control.

Answer (C) is correct (6134). *(AIH Chap X)*
The telling and doing technique of flight instruction (basically the demonstration/performance method) is very effective and valuable in teaching procedures and maneuvers. First, the instructor explains, then demonstrates. Then the student performs, first by explaining as the instructor does, then by explaining and doing it him/herself while the instructor supervises. Finally, the instructor evaluates how the student performs.
Answer (A) is incorrect because it omits the first step, which is instructor tells--instructor does. The second step is student tells--instructor does, not vice versa. Answer (B) is incorrect because it omits the third step of student tells--student does.

Answer (A) is correct (6136). *(AIH Chap X)*
The primary objective of the integrated flight training method is the formation of firm habit patterns for observing and relying on flight instruments from the student's first piloting experience. The goal is to teach proper use of flight instruments in VFR flight.
Answer (B) is incorrect because there should be no difference in the pilot's operation of the flight controls in either VMC or IMC. The manipulation of the flight controls is identical, regardless of which references are used to determine the attitude of the airplane. Answer (C) is incorrect because the pilot's habit of occasionally monitoring his/her own performance along with the aircraft's is an objective of basic flight instruction, not integrated flight instruction.

Answer (C) is correct (6135). *(AIH Chap X)*
The primary objective of the integrated method of flight training is to develop firm habit patterns for observance of and reliance on flight instruments as well as outside references from the student's first piloting experience. The goal is to teach proper use of flight instruments in VFR flight.
Answer (A) is incorrect because the ability to fly the aircraft in IMC is not an objective of integrated flight instruction. Answer (B) is incorrect because the objective of integrated flight instruction is to ensure that the student is not overly dependent on outside visual references, not flight instruments.

Answer (C) is correct (6137). *(AIH Chap X)*
When using the integrated method of flight instruction, you should include in the student's first instruction on the function of flight controls the instrument indications to be expected, as well as the outside references used in attitude control.
Answer (A) is incorrect because integrated flight instruction means simultaneous, not alternate, instruction in instrument and visual references. Answer (B) is incorrect because there is no distinction in the student's operation of the flight controls, regardless of whether outside references or instrument indications are used for the performance of a maneuver.

23.
6138. During integrated flight instruction, the instructor must be sure the student

A— develops the habit of looking for other traffic.
B— is able to control the aircraft for extended periods under IMC.
C— can depend on the flight instruments when maneuvering by outside references.

5.5 The Positive Approach in Flight Instruction

24.
6129. Which is an example of a positive approach in the first flight lesson of a student with no previous aviation experience?

A— Conducting a thorough preflight.
B— A normal flight to a nearby airport and return.
C— Instruction in the care which must be taken when taxiing an airplane.

25.
6128. Which statement is true regarding positive or negative approaches in aviation instructional techniques?

A— A student with normal abilities should not be affected by an instructor who emphasizes emergency procedures early in training.
B— A positive approach, to be effective, will point out the pleasurable features of aviation before the unpleasant possibilities are discussed.
C— The introduction of emergency procedures before the student is acquainted with normal operations is likely to be neither discouraging nor affect learning.

Answer (A) is correct (6138). *(AIH Chap X)*
If students are allowed to believe that the instructor assumes all responsibility for avoiding other traffic, they cannot develop the habit of keeping a constant watch, which is essential to safety. Any observed tendency of a student to enter flight maneuvers without first making a careful check for other possible air traffic must be corrected immediately.
Answer (B) is incorrect because the ability to control the aircraft for extended periods under IMC is not the objective of integrated flight instruction. Answer (C) is incorrect because the instructor must be sure not to let the student focus his attention on the instruments at the expense of looking for other traffic.

Answer (B) is correct (6129). *(AIH Chap IX)*
A normal flight to a nearby airport and back shows the student some of the pleasant aspects of aviation. Such an introductory lesson leaves a positive impression in the new student's mind. Positive teaching results in positive learning.
Answer (A) is incorrect because, in the first flight lesson of a student with no aviation experience, conducting a thorough, exhausting preflight is an example of a negative, not a positive, approach. The student may question whether learning to fly is a good idea or not. Answer (C) is incorrect because, in the first flight lesson of a student with no aviation experience, instruction in the care which must be taken when taxiing an airplane is an example of a negative, not a positive, approach. The student may question whether learning to fly is a good idea or not.

Answer (B) is correct (6128). *(AIH Chap IX)*
Flight instructor success depends, in large measure, on the ability to frame instructions so that students develop a positive image of flying. A positive approach, to be effective, will point out the pleasurable features of aviation before the unpleasant possibilities are discussed. A negative approach generally results in negative learning because the student's perceptual process would be adversely affected by fear.
Answer (A) is incorrect because an instructor who emphasizes emergency procedures early in training will most likely have a negative effect on the learning process regardless of a student's abilities. The student new to aviation is still quite impressionable. Answer (C) is incorrect because the introduction of emergency procedures before the student is acquainted with normal operations most likely will be discouraging, threatening, and will adversely affect learning.

END OF CHAPTER

CHAPTER SIX
PLANNING INSTRUCTIONAL ACTIVITY

6.1 COURSE DEVELOPMENT (Questions 1-5)

1. Any instructional activity must be competently planned and organized if it is to achieve the desired learning outcomes.

    a. First, you must determine the overall objectives and standards of the course.

    b. Then, you must identify the blocks of learning which constitute the necessary parts of the total objective.

        1) You must ensure that each block of learning identified is truly an integral part of the overall objective.

            a) Extraneous blocks of instruction are expensive frills, especially in flight instruction, and detract from the completion of the final objective.

        2) The blocks of learning must be developed and arranged in their proper sequence.

            a) In this way, a student can master the segments of the overall pilot performance requirements individually and can progressively combine these with other related segments until their sum meets the final objective.

2. A training syllabus is an abstract or digest of the course of training. It consists of the blocks of learning to be completed in the most efficient order.

    a. The order of training can and should be altered, when necessary, to suit the progress of the student and the demands of special circumstances.

        1) However, it is often preferable to skip to a completely different part of the syllabus when the conduct of a scheduled lesson is impossible, rather than proceeding to the next lesson, which may be predicated completely on skills to be developed during the lesson which is being postponed.

6.2 ORGANIZATION OF MATERIAL (Questions 6-11)

1. The teaching process can be broken down into four basic steps: preparation, presentation, application, and review/evaluation.

2. Regardless of the teaching method used (lecture, guided discussion or demonstration-performance), an instructor must properly organize the material. One effective way to organize a lesson is -- introduction, development, and conclusion.

    a. The **introduction** contains a clear statement of objective, with key ideas, relating this lesson's coverage to the entire course. The introduction can be divided into three subparts.

        1) **Attention** -- The instructor must gain the students' attention and focus it on the subject.

2) **Motivation** -- The instructor should offer specific reasons why they need to learn the material. This motivation should appeal to each student personally and accentuate the desire to learn.

3) **Overview** -- Each lesson introduction should contain an overview that tells the group what is to be covered during the period.

b. The **development** is the main part of the lesson during which the instructor organizes the explanations and demonstrations in a manner that helps the students achieve the desired learning outcomes.

1) The instructor must logically organize the material to show the relationships of the main points to each other. This is done by developing the main points in one of the following ways:

a) From past to present

b) From simple to complex

c) From known to unknown (i.e., using a student's previous experiences and knowledge to acquire new concepts)

d) From most frequently used (most familiar) to least frequently used

c. The **conclusion** retraces the important elements of the lesson and relates them to the objective.

1) This reinforces the student's learning and improves retention of what has been learned.

2) New ideas should not be introduced in the conclusion because doing so at this point in the lesson will only confuse the student.

6.3 LESSON PLAN (Questions 12-26)

1. Each lesson of the training syllabus includes an objective, content, and completion standards.

2. A lesson plan is an organized outline that is developed for a single instructional period.

a. A properly constructed lesson plan will provide an outline that tells the instructor what to do, in what order to do it, and what teaching procedure to use.

b. The lesson plan must be appropriate for the particular student.

1) Standard lesson plans may not be effective for students requiring a different approach.

3. A lesson plan should be prepared in writing for each instructional period, regardless of the instructor's experience.

a. A so-called mental outline is not a lesson plan.

b. Another instructor should be able to take the lesson plan and know what to do in conducting the same period of instruction.

4. Lesson plans help instructors keep a constant check on their own activity, as well as that of their students.

5. A characteristic of a well-planned lesson is that it should contain new material that is related to the lesson previously presented.

a. In flight training, a short review of earlier lessons is usually necessary.

6. Each lesson plan should contain the following items: lesson objective, elements, schedule, equipment, instructor's actions, student's actions, and completion standards. See the illustration on the next page.

LESSON GROUND REFERENCE MANEUVERS **STUDENT** _____ **DATE** ____

OBJECTIVE
- TO DEVELOP THE STUDENT'S SKILL IN PLANNING AND FOLLOWING A PATTERN OVER THE GROUND COMPENSATING FOR WIND DRIFT AT VARYING ANGLES

ELEMENTS
- USE OF GROUND REFERENCES TO CONTROL PATH
- OBSERVATION AND CONTROL OF WIND EFFECT
- CONTROL OF AIRPLANE ATTITUDE, ALTITUDE, AND HEADING

SCHEDULE
- PREFLIGHT DISCUSSION : 10
- INSTRUCTOR DEMONSTRATIONS : 25
- STUDENT PRACTICE : 45
- POSTFLIGHT CRITIQUE : 10

EQUIPMENT
- CHALKBOARD FOR PREFLIGHT DISCUSSION
- IFR VISOR FOR MANEUVERS REVIEWED

INSTRUCTOR'S ACTIONS
- PREFLIGHT-DISCUSS LESSON OBJECTIVE. DIAGRAM "S" TURNS, EIGHTS ALONG A ROAD, AND RECTANGULAR COURSE ON CHALKBOARD
- INFLIGHT-DEMONSTRATE ELEMENTS. DEMONSTRATE FOLLOWING A ROAD, "S" TURNS, EIGHTS ALONG A ROAD, AND RECTANGULAR COURSE. COACH STUDENT PRACTICE
- POSTFLIGHT-CRITIQUE STUDENT PERFORMANCE AND MAKE STUDY ASSIGNMENT

STUDENT'S ACTIONS
- PREFLIGHT-DISCUSS LESSON OBJECTIVE AND RESOLVE QUESTIONS
- INFLIGHT-REVIEW PREVIOUS MANEUVERS INCLUDING POWER-OFF STALLS AND FLIGHT AT MINIMUM CONTROLLABLE AIRSPEED. PERFORM EACH NEW MANEUVER AS DIRECTED.
- POSTFLIGHT-ASK PERTINENT QUESTIONS

COMPLETION STANDARDS
- STUDENT SHOULD DEMONSTRATE COMPETENCY IN MAINTAINING ORIENTATION, AIRSPEED WITHIN 10 KNOTS, ALTITUDE WITHIN 100 FEET, AND HEADINGS WITHIN 10 DEGREES, AND IN MAKING PROPER CORRECTION FOR WIND DRIFT.

7. The objectives of each lesson should be clearly stated.

   a. The objective is the reason for the lesson--what the student is expected to know or be able to do at the end of the lesson.

   b. Keeping the student informed of lesson objectives and completion standards minimizes the student's insecurity.

8. Fatigue is the primary consideration in determining the length and frequency of flight instruction periods.

   a. Fatigue, resulting from excessive or lengthy instruction, reduces a student's learning ability.

9. When planning time for student performance, a primary consideration is the length of the practice session.

   a. A beginning student reaches a point where additional practice is not only unproductive but may be harmful.

   b. As a student gains experience, longer periods of practice are profitable.

10. A blank lesson plan is provided on page 146 so you may make copies for your use.

6.4 INSTRUCTIONAL AIDS (Questions 27-30)

1. Instructional (or visual) aids are useful tools to emphasize, support, and supplement the key points in a lesson.

   a. Instructional aids include models, chalkboards, charts, and projected material (i.e., videotapes, movies, slides, etc.).

2. The following four-step procedure should be used to determine if and when instructional aids are necessary.

   a. Clearly establish the lesson objective, being certain what must be communicated.

   b. Gather the necessary data by researching for support material.

   c. Organize the material into an outline or lesson plan. The outline should include all key points to be presented.

   d. Finally, determine what ideas should be supported with instructional aids.

      1) They should be compatible with the learning outcomes to be achieved.
      2) They can be used to emphasize the key points in a lesson.

3. Instructional aids used in the teaching/learning process should not be used as a crutch by the instructor.

QUESTIONS AND ANSWER EXPLANATIONS

All of the FAA questions from the Fundamentals of Instructing knowledge test relating to planning instructional activity outlined above are reproduced on the following pages in the same modules as the outlines. To the immediate right of each question are the correct answer and answer explanation. You should cover these answers and answer explanations with your hand or a piece of paper while responding to the questions. Refer to the general discussion in Chapter 1 on how to take the FAA knowledge test.

Remember that the questions from the FAA knowledge test bank have been reordered by topic, and the topics have been organized into a meaningful sequence. Accordingly, the first line of the answer explanation gives the FAA question number and the citation of the authoritative source for the answer.

6.1 Course Development

1.

6144. In planning any instructional activity, the first consideration should be to

A— determine the overall objectives and standards.
B— establish common ground between the instructor and student.
C— identify the blocks of learning which make up the overall objective.

Answer (A) is correct (6144). *(AIH Chap XI)*
The first step in planning any instructional activity is to determine the overall objectives and standards. If the instructor does not have a logical view of what is to be achieved, then the students will not.
Answer (B) is incorrect because establishing a common ground between the instructor and student is the purpose of a lesson introduction, not the first step in planning instructional activity. Answer (C) is incorrect because the second, not the first, consideration in planning for any instructional activity is to identify the blocks of learning which make up the overall objective.

2.

6147. In planning instructional activity, the second step is to

A— develop lesson plans for each period or unit of instruction.
B— identify blocks of learning which constitute the necessary parts of the total objective.
C— develop a training syllabus that will serve as a guide for conducting training at each level of learning.

Answer (B) is correct (6147). *(AIH Chap XI)*
In planning instructional activity, the second step (after the overall training objectives have been established) is the identification of the blocks of learning which constitute the necessary parts of the total objective.
Answer (A) is incorrect because, to develop lesson plans for each period or unit of instruction, an instructor must first determine the overall objectives, then identify the blocks of learning necessary to meet those objectives. Answer (C) is incorrect because a training syllabus is an abstract of the course of training. It consists of the blocks of learning to be completed in the most efficient order, and thus, must be developed after the blocks have been identified.

3.

6146. Development and assembly of blocks of learning in their proper relationship will provide a means for

A— both the instructor and student to easily correct faulty habit patterns.
B— challenging the student by progressively increasing the units of learning.
C— allowing the student to master the segments of the overall pilot performance requirements individually and combining these with other related segments.

Answer (C) is correct (6146). *(AIH Chap XI)*
Training for a skill as complicated and involved as piloting an aircraft requires the development and assembly, in their appropriate sequence, of many segments or blocks of learning. In this way, a student can master the segments of the overall pilot performance requirements individually and can progressively combine these with other related segments until (s)he learns to fly, which is the final objective.
Answer (A) is incorrect because organizing the appropriate blocks of learning in their proper relationship should prevent the formation of bad habits. This is the basic reason for the building block technique of instruction. Answer (B) is incorrect because the challenge presented to the student is one way to test for a useful size of a minimum block of learning, but progressively increasing the blocks of learning may deter the student's progress.

4.

6145. Which statement is true concerning extraneous blocks of instruction during a course of training?

A— They are usually necessary parts of the total objective.
B— They detract from the completion of the final objective.
C— They assist in the attainment of the lesson's objective.

Answer (B) is correct (6145). *(AIH Chap XI)*
While identifying the blocks of learning to be used in the course, the instructor must examine each carefully to see that it is truly an integral part of the structure. Extraneous blocks of instruction can detract from, rather than assist, in the completion of the final objective.
Answer (A) is incorrect because extraneous blocks of instruction are unnecessary, not necessary, parts of the total objective. Answer (C) is incorrect because extraneous blocks of instruction detract, not assist, in the attainment of the lesson's objective.

5.

6149. When it is impossible to conduct a scheduled lesson, it is preferable for the instructor to

A— review and possibly revise the training syllabus.
B— proceed to the next scheduled lesson, or if this is not practical, cancel the lesson.
C— conduct a lesson that is not predicated completely on skills to be developed during the lesson which was postponed.

Answer (C) is correct (6149). *(AIH Chap XI)*
It is preferable for the instructor to skip to a completely different part of the syllabus when it is impossible to conduct a scheduled lesson, rather than proceeding to the next lesson, which may be predicated completely on skills to be developed during the lesson which was postponed.
Answer (A) is incorrect because an instructor should review and possibly revise the training syllabus when there is an applicable change to the FARs or PTSs, not because a lesson had to be postponed. Answer (B) is incorrect because the next lesson may need skills that were to be learned in the postponed lesson.

6.2 Organization of Material

6.

6065. What is the proper sequence in which an instructor should employ the four basic steps in the teaching process?

A— Preparation, presentation, application, and review and evaluation.
B— Preparation, demonstration, practice, and review.
C— Explanation, demonstration, practice, and evaluation.

Answer (A) is correct (6065). *(AIH Chap IV)*
The proper sequence in which an instructor should employ the four basic steps in the teaching process is preparation, presentation, application, and review and evaluation.
Answer (B) is incorrect because evaluation is an important part of the final step in the teaching process. Answer (C) is incorrect because preparation is an important first step in the teaching process.

7.

6073. The method of arranging lesson material from the simple to complex, past to present, and known to unknown, is one that

A— creates student thought pattern departures.
B— shows the relationships of the main points of the lesson.
C— requires students to actively participate in the lesson.

Answer (B) is correct (6073). *(AIH Chap V)*
An instructor must logically organize the lesson material to show the relationships of the main points. This can be done by arranging the material from the simple to the complex, past to present, known to unknown, and from the most frequently used to the least frequently used.
Answer (A) is incorrect because, by arranging lesson material from the simple to complex, past to present, and known to unknown, the instructor will make meaningful transitions from one point to another and thus keep the students oriented, not creating thought pattern departures. Answer (C) is incorrect because the objective of each lesson, not the method of arranging material, should require students to actively participate (either directly or indirectly) in the lesson in order to achieve the desired learning outcomes.

8.

6072. In organizing lesson material, which step should relate the coverage of material to the entire course?

A— Overview.
B— Conclusion.
C— Introduction.

Answer (C) is correct (6072). *(AIH Chap V)*
The introduction to a lesson should set the stage for learning, including: (1) establishing common ground between the instructor and the student, (2) capturing the student's attention, (3) indicating what is going to be covered during the presentation, (4) relating this coverage to the entire course, (5) pointing out benefits that can be expected, and (6) establishing a receptive attitude.
Answer (A) is incorrect because the overview is included in the introduction and tells the group what is to be covered during the period of instruction, not how it relates to the entire course. Answer (B) is incorrect because the conclusion retraces the important elements of the lesson and relates them to the lesson objective, not the entire course.

9.
6071. The proper sequence for the subparts of an introduction is

A— attention, motivation, and overview.
B— attention, development, and overview.
C— overview, motivation, and conclusion.

Answer (A) is correct (6071). *(AIH Chap V)*
The proper sequence for the subparts of an introduction is attention, motivation, and overview. First, the instructor must gain the student's attention and focus it on the subject at hand. Second, the introduction should offer the students specific reasons for needing to be familiar with, to know, to understand, to apply, or to be able to perform whatever they are about to learn. This motivation should appeal to each student personally and accentuate the desire to learn. Third, every lesson introduction should contain an overview that tells the group what is to be covered during the period.
Answer (B) is incorrect because development is the main part of the lesson, not a subpart of the introduction. Answer (C) is incorrect because conclusion is the review portion of the lesson, not a subpart of the introduction.

10.
6075. In developing a lesson, the instructor should organize explanations and demonstrations to help the student

A— achieve the desired learning outcome.
B— acquire a thorough understanding of the material presented.
C— acquire new concepts, generally progressing from the known to the unknown.

Answer (A) is correct (6075). *(AIH Chap V)*
In developing a lesson, the instructor should organize the subject matter (explanations and demonstrations) in a manner that helps the student achieve the desired learning outcome.
Answer (B) is incorrect because the student's ability to acquire a thorough understanding of the material is dependent on more than an instructor's organized presentation, e.g., motivation, needs, etc. Answer (C) is incorrect because progressing from the known to the unknown is a way of logically organizing the lesson material to show the relationships of the main points, not the intent of developing a lesson, which is to help the student achieve the desired learning outcome.

11.
6074. When teaching from the known to the unknown, an instructor is using the student's

A— current knowledge of the subject.
B— previous experiences and knowledge.
C— previously held opinions, both valid and invalid.

Answer (B) is correct (6074). *(AIH Chap V)*
Teaching from the known to the unknown allows the instructor to use the student's previous experience and knowledge as the point of departure from which to lead into new ideas and concepts.
Answer (A) is incorrect because, when teaching from the known to the unknown, an instructor is using a student's knowledge of related subjects, not the subject at hand. Answer (C) is incorrect because organizing lessons using the known to the unknown pattern requires students' previous knowledge, not their previously held opinions.

6.3 **Lesson Plan**

12.
6153. A lesson plan, if constructed properly, will provide an outline for

A— proceeding from the unknown to the known.
B— the teaching procedure to be used in a single instructional period.
C— establishing blocks of learning that become progressively larger in scope.

Answer (B) is correct (6153). *(AIH Chap XI)*
A properly constructed lesson plan is an organized outline or blueprint for a single instructional period. It is a necessary guide for the instructor in that it tells what to do, in what order to do it, and what procedure to use in teaching the material of the lesson.
Answer (A) is incorrect because the lesson plan will usually proceed from the known to the unknown, not unknown to known. Answer (C) is incorrect because a syllabus, not a lesson plan, will provide an outline for establishing blocks of learning that become progressively larger in scope.

13.
6148. Each lesson of a training syllabus includes

A— attention, motivation, and overview.
B— introduction, development, and conclusion.
C— objective, content, and completion standards.

Answer (C) is correct (6148). *(AIH Chap XI)*
Each lesson of a written training syllabus includes an objective, content, and completion standards.
Answer (A) is incorrect because attention, motivation, and overview are the parts of an introduction to a lesson. Answer (B) is incorrect because the structure of every lesson as it is being presented to a student, not as found in a written syllabus, should be based on an introduction, a development, and a conclusion.

14.
6154. (Refer to figure 1 on page 65.) Section A is titled:

A— Overview.
B— Objective.
C— Introduction.

Answer (B) is correct (6154). *(AIH Chap XI)*
Section A of Fig. 1 is titled: Objective. The objective of the lesson is the reason for the lesson and should clearly state what the instructor expects the student to know or do at the completion of the lesson.
Answer (A) is incorrect because overview is a subpart of an introduction to a lesson, not a titled section of a lesson plan. Answer (C) is incorrect because an introduction is part of an effective way to organize a lesson, not a titled section of a lesson plan.

15.
6155. (Refer to figure 1 on page 65.) Section B is titled:

A— Elements.
B— Blocks of Learning.
C— Course of Training.

Answer (A) is correct (6155). *(AIH Chap XI)*
Section B of Fig. 1 is titled: Elements. This is a statement of the elements of knowledge and skill necessary for the fulfillment of the lesson objective. This may include both elements previously learned and those to be introduced during this lesson.
Answer (B) is incorrect because blocks of learning are identified and used in preparing lesson plans, not a titled section of a lesson plan. Answer (C) is incorrect because the course of training is the overall objective of the instruction and is comprised of many different lesson plans, not a titled section of a lesson plan.

16.
6158. (Refer to figure 1 on page 65.) Section C is titled:

A— Schedule.
B— Overview.
C— Training Schedule.

Answer (A) is correct (6158). *(AIH Chap XI)*
Section C of Fig. 1 is titled: Schedule. The instructor should estimate the amount of time to be devoted to the presentation of the elements of that lesson.
Answer (B) is incorrect because overview is a subpart of an introduction to a lesson, not a titled section of a lesson plan. Answer (C) is incorrect because the correct title is schedule, not training schedule.

17.
6159. (Refer to figure 1 on page 65.) Section D is titled:

A— Apparatus.
B— Equipment.
C— Preparation.

Answer (B) is correct (6159). *(AIH Chap XI)*
Section D of Fig. 1 is titled: Equipment. This includes all instructional materials and training aids required to teach the lesson.
Answer (A) is incorrect because the correct title is equipment, not apparatus. Answer (C) is incorrect because preparation is something both the student and instructor should do before a lesson, not a titled section of a lesson plan.

18.
6157. (Refer to figure 1 on page 65.) Section E is titled:

A— Content.
B— Discussion.
C— Instructor's Actions.

Answer (C) is correct (6157). *(AIH Chap XI)*
Section E of Fig. 1 is titled: Instructor's Actions. This is a statement of the instructor's proposed procedures for presenting the elements of knowledge and performance involved in the lesson.
Answer (A) is incorrect because content is not a titled section of a lesson plan. Answer (B) is incorrect because, while this section states that a discussion will take place, it is specifically those actions taken by the instructor and not the student.

LESSON GROUND REFERENCE MANEUVERS **STUDENT** _____ **DATE** _____

A _____
- TO DEVELOP THE STUDENT'S SKILL IN PLANNING AND FOLLOWING A PATTERN OVER THE GROUND COMPENSATING FOR WIND DRIFT AT VARYING ANGLES.

B _____
- USE OF GROUND REFERENCES TO CONTROL PATH.
- OBSERVATION AND CONTROL OF WIND EFFECT.
- CONTROL OF AIRPLANE ATTITUDE, ALTITUDE, AND HEADING.

C _____
- PREFLIGHT DISCUSSION. : 10
- INSTRUCTOR DEMONSTRATIONS. : 25
- STUDENT PRACTICE. : 45
- POSTFLIGHT CRITIQUE. : 10

D _____
- CHALKBOARD FOR PREFLIGHT DISCUSSION.
- IFR VISOR FOR MANEUVERS REVIEWED.

E _____
- PREFLIGHT – DISCUSS LESSON OBJECTIVE. DIAGRAM RECTANGULAR COURSE, S-TURNS ACROSS A ROAD, AND TURNS AROUND A POINT ON CHALKBOARD.

- INFLIGHT – DEMONSTRATE ELEMENTS. DEMONSTRATE RECTANGULAR COURSE, S-TURNS ACROSS A ROAD, AND TURNS AROUND A POINT. COACH STUDENT PRACTICE.

- POSTFLIGHT – CRITIQUE STUDENT PERFORMANCE AND MAKE STUDY ASSIGNMENT.

F _____
- PREFLIGHT – DISCUSS LESSON OBJECTIVE AND RESOLVE QUESTIONS.

- INFLIGHT – REVIEW PREVIOUS MANEUVERS INCLUDING POWER-OFF STALLS AND SLOW FLIGHT. PERFORM EACH NEW MANEUVER AS DIRECTED.

- POSTFLIGHT – ASK PERTINENT QUESTIONS.

G _____
- STUDENT SHOULD DEMONSTRATE COMPETENCY IN MAINTAINING ORIENTATION, AIRSPEED WITHIN 10 KNOTS, ALTITUDE WITHIN 100 FEET, AND HEADINGS WITHIN 10 DEGREES, AND IN MAKING PROPER CORRECTION FOR WIND DRIFT.

FIGURE 1.–Lesson Plan

19.
6160. (Refer to figure 1 on page 65.) Section F is titled:

A— Application.
B— Understanding.
C— Student's Actions.

Answer (C) is correct (6160). *(AIH Chap XI)*
Section F of Fig. 1 is titled: Student's Actions. This is a statement of desired student responses to instruction.
Answer (A) is incorrect because, while this involves application of what the instructor has presented to the student, this section is the instructor's desired student's action during the lesson. Answer (B) is incorrect because understanding is a level of learning, not a titled section of a lesson plan.

20.
6156. (Refer to figure 1 on page 65.) Section G is titled:

A— Summary.
B— Evaluation.
C— Completion Standards.

Answer (C) is correct (6156). *(AIH Chap XI)*
Section G of Fig. 1 is titled: Completion Standards. This is the evaluation basis for determining how well the student has met the objective of the lesson in terms of knowledge and skill.
Answer (A) is incorrect because a summary of a lesson would take place during the postflight discussion. Answer (B) is incorrect because evaluation is part of the teaching process and would be used by the instructor to compare the student's performance to the completion standards.

21.
6150. Which statement is true regarding lesson plans?

A— Lesson plans should not be directed toward the course objective; only to the lesson objective.
B— A well-thought-out mental outline of a lesson may be used any time as long as the instructor is well prepared.
C— Lesson plans help instructors keep a constant check on their own activity as well as that of their students.

Answer (C) is correct (6150). *(AIH Chap XI)*
Lesson plans help instructors keep a constant check on their own activity, as well as that of their students. The development of lesson plans by instructors signifies, in effect, that they have taught the lesson to themselves prior to attempting to teach the lesson to students.
Answer (A) is incorrect because a lesson plan should serve as a means of relating the lesson to the objectives of the course, as well as the lesson. Answer (B) is incorrect because a mental outline of a lesson is not a lesson plan. A lesson plan should be in written form regardless of an instructor's preparation.

22.
6054. When the instructor keeps the student informed of lesson objectives and completion standards, it minimizes the student's feelings of

A— insecurity.
B— resignation.
C— aggressiveness.

Answer (A) is correct (6054). *(AIH Chap II)*
Students feel insecure when they do not know the lesson objectives and the completion standards to which they will be held. Instructors can minimize such feelings of insecurity by telling students what is expected of them and what to anticipate.
Answer (B) is incorrect because resignation occurs when a student completes the early phase of training without understanding the fundamentals, not the objectives or completion standards, and becomes lost in the advanced phase. Answer (C) is incorrect because aggression occurs when a student becomes angry at something or someone. Aggression (or any other defense mechanism) may be used to defend a feeling of insecurity when a student is not kept informed.

23.

6152. Which statement is true about lesson plans?

A— Lesson plans should follow a prescribed format.
B— Standard prepared lesson plans are effective for teaching all students.
C— The use of standard lesson plans may not be effective for students requiring a different approach.

Answer (C) is correct (6152). *(AIH Chap XI)*
A lesson plan for an instructional period should be appropriate to the background, experience, and ability of the particular student(s). If the procedures outlined in the lesson plan are not leading to the desired results, the instructor should change the approach. Thus, the use of standard lesson plans may not be effective for students requiring a different approach.
Answer (A) is incorrect because, although lesson plans should all contain certain items, the format to be followed should be tailored to the particular student(s). Answer (B) is incorrect because lesson plans are only an outline of the lesson. An instructor may have to adapt the procedures in a standard prepared lesson plan so it will be effective with different students.

24.

6151. With regard to the characteristics of a well-planned lesson, each lesson should contain

A— new material that is related to the lesson previously presented.
B— one basic element of the principle, procedure, or skill appropriate to that lesson.
C— every bit of information needed to reach the objective of the training syllabus.

Answer (A) is correct (6151). *(AIH Chap XI)*
One characteristic of a well-planned lesson is content, which means each lesson should contain new material. However, the new facts, principles, or skills should be related to the lesson previously presented. A short review of earlier lessons is usually necessary, especially in flight training.
Answer (B) is incorrect because all of the elements, not only one, necessary to learn a simple procedure, principle, or skill should be presented. Answer (C) is incorrect because each lesson should include all of the information needed to reach the objective of a particular lesson, but not everything needed for the entire syllabus.

25.

6141. What is the primary consideration in determining the length and frequency of flight instruction periods?

A— Fatigue.
B— Mental acuity.
C— Instructor preparation.

Answer (A) is correct (6141). *(AIH Chap X)*
Fatigue is the primary consideration in determining the length and frequency of flight instruction periods. Flight instruction should be continued only so long as the student is alert, receptive to instruction, and is performing at a level consistent with experience.
Answer (B) is incorrect because fatigue, not mental acuity, is the primary consideration in determining the length and frequency of flight instruction periods. Fatigue may be either physical or mental, or both. Answer (C) is incorrect because fatigue, not instructor preparation, is the primary consideration in determining the length and frequency of flight instruction periods. Poor instructor preparation will make students become apathetic, not fatigued.

26.

6032. A primary consideration in planning for student performance is the

A— student's motivational level.
B— student's intellectual level.
C— length of the practice session.

Answer (C) is correct (6032). *(AIH Chap I)*
In planning for student performance, a primary consideration is the length of time devoted to practice. A beginning student reaches a point where additional practice is not only unproductive but may even be harmful. When that point is reached, errors increase and motivation declines. As a student gains experience, longer periods of practice are profitable.
Answer (A) is incorrect because a student's motivational level is important to an instructor since it directly relates to the student's progress and ability to learn, not as a primary consideration in planning for student performance. Answer (B) is incorrect because a primary consideration in student performance is the length of time devoted to practice, not the student's intellectual level.

6.4 Instructional Aids

27.
6119. Which is a true statement concerning the use of visual aids?

A— Visual aids ensure getting and holding the student's attention.
B— Visual aids can be used to emphasize the key points in a lesson.
C— Visual aids should not be used simply to cover a subject in less time.

28.
6122. The use of instructional aids should be based on their ability to support a specific point in the lesson. What is the first step in determining if and where instructional aids are necessary?

A— Organize subject material into an outline or a lesson plan.
B— Determine what ideas should be supported with instructional aids.
C— Clearly establish the lesson objective, being certain what must be communicated.

29.
6120. Instructional aids used in the teaching/learning process should be

A— self-supporting and require no explanation.
B— compatible with the learning outcomes to be achieved.
C— selected prior to developing and organizing the lesson plan.

30.
6121. Instructional aids used in the teaching/learning process should not be used

A— as a crutch by the instructor.
B— for teaching more in less time.
C— to visualize relationships between abstracts.

Answer (B) is correct (6119). (AIH Chap VIII)
Visual and other instructional aids are a good way to improve communication between the instructor and the students. Instructional aids are useful tools to support, supplement, and reinforce (emphasize) the key points in a lesson.
Answer (A) is incorrect because appropriate visual aids will help to get the student's attention, but they cannot ensure that it will hold the student's attention. Answer (C) is incorrect because visual aids can help get a point across quickly and clearly, thus reducing the time spent on some subjects.

Answer (C) is correct (6122). (AIH Chap VIII)
The first step in developing a lesson plan using instructional aids is, as in any lesson plan, to establish the lesson objective. Visual or other aids must help achieve the overall lesson objective. They should be strategically placed to recapture interest, shift to a new topic, or provide emphasis.
Answer (A) is incorrect because organizing the outline or lesson plan is the third, not first, step in the process. Answer (B) is incorrect because the final, not first, step in determining if and where instructional aids are necessary is to determine what ideas in the lesson should be supported with instructional aids.

Answer (B) is correct (6120). (AIH Chap VIII)
After establishing lesson objectives, researching the subject, and organizing the material into a lesson plan, the instructor should determine what needs to be supported by visual or other instructional aids. The aids should be compatible with the learning outcomes to be achieved.
Answer (A) is incorrect because instructional aids are not self-supporting and will require explanation.
Answer (C) is incorrect because instructional aids should be compatible with the desired learning outcomes, which can best be done after, not prior to, developing and organizing the lesson plan.

Answer (A) is correct (6121). (AIH Chap V)
Aids used in conjunction with oral presentation should emphasize, not distract from, the oral message. Also, the instructor should realize that such aids do not take the place of a sound lesson plan or instructor's input.
Answer (B) is incorrect because aids do help teach more in less time because they clarify and emphasize the lecture. The class can move to new material sooner.
Answer (C) is incorrect because instructional aids should be used to help students to visualize relationships between abstracts.

END OF CHAPTER

CHAPTER SEVEN
CRITIQUE AND EVALUATION

7.1 THE INSTRUCTOR'S CRITIQUE (Questions 1-8)

1. No instructor skill is more important than the ability to analyze, appraise, and judge student performance.

    a. A student looks to the instructor for guidance, suggestions for improvement, and encouragement.

    b. To enhance a student's acceptance of further instruction, the instructor should keep the student informed of the progress made.

        1) This will help to minimize student frustrations, which will keep the student motivated to learn.

2. A critique should always be conducted immediately after the student's performance, while the details are easy to recall.

    a. The instructor may critique any activity which a student performs or practices to improve skill, proficiency, and learning.

3. A critique is a step in the learning process, not the grading process.

4. A critique is not necessarily negative in content. It considers the good along with the bad, the whole in terms of its parts, and the parts in relation to each other.

5. The purpose of a critique is to improve the student's performance and to provide him/her with something constructive with which to work and on which to build.

    a. The critique should provide direction and guidance to improve performance.

6. A critique should be **objective**.

    a. The effective critique is focused on student performance, and should not reflect the personal opinions, likes, dislikes, and biases of the instructor.

    b. The critique must be based on the performance as it was, not as it could have been.

7. A critique should be **flexible**.

    a. The instructor must fit the tone, technique, and content of the critique to the occasion and the student.

    b. An effective critique is flexible enough to satisfy the requirements of the moment.

8. A critique should be **acceptable**.

    a. Before students willingly accept their instructor's criticism they must first accept the instructor.

    b. The students must have confidence in the instructor's qualifications, teaching ability, sincerity, competence, and authority.

    c. Instructors cannot rely solely on their position to make a critique acceptable to their students.

9.   A critique should be **comprehensive**.

a.   A comprehensive critique is not necessarily long, nor must it treat every aspect of the performance in detail.

b.   The instructor must decide whether the greater benefit will come from a discussion of a few major points or a number of minor points.

c.   An effective critique covers strengths as well as weaknesses.

10.   A critique should be **constructive**.

a.   A critique is pointless unless a student profits from it.

b.   Praise for praise's sake is of no value if a student is not taught how to capitalize on things which are done well and to use them to compensate for lesser accomplishments.

c.   Also, it is not enough to identify a fault or weakness.

1)   To tell students that their work is unsatisfactory with no explanation will most likely result in the students becoming frustrated.

2)   The students must be briefed on the errors made and told how to correct them so progress and accomplishment can be made.

11.   A critique should be **thoughtful**.

a.   An effective critique reflects an instructor's thoughtfulness toward the student's need for self-esteem, recognition, and approval from others.

1)   The critique should never minimize the inherent dignity and importance of the individual.

b.   Ridicule, anger, or fun at the expense of the student has no place in the critique.

12.   A critique should be **specific**.

a.   The instructor's comments and recommendations should be specific, not so general that the student can find nothing to hold onto.

b.   Express ideas with firmness and authority in terms that cannot be misunderstood.

1)   Students should have no doubt what they did well and what they did poorly, and specifically how they can improve.

7.2 ORAL QUIZZING (Questions 9-15)

1.   The most practical means of evaluation is oral quizzing of students by the instructor. Questions may be loosely classified as fact and thought questions.

a.   The answer to a fact question is based on memory or recall.

b.   Thought questions require the student to combine a knowledge of facts with an ability to analyze situations, solve problems, and arrive at conclusions.

2.   Proper quizzing by the instructor can have a number of desirable results. It can

a.   Reveal the effectiveness of training procedures,
b.   Check student retention and comprehension of what has been learned,
c.   Review material already covered,
d.   Help retain student interest and stimulate thinking,
e.   Emphasize the important points of training,
f.   Identify points that need more emphasis, and
g.   Promote active student participation.

3. Characteristics of effective questions:

   a. Each question must have only one correct answer.

      1) This is a characteristic of good objective-type (fact) questions and generally true of all good questions.

      2) Each question should call for a specific answer which can be readily evaluated by the instructor.

   b. Each question must apply to the subject being taught.

   c. Each question should be brief and concise, but must be clear and definite.

   d. Each question should center on only one idea which is limited to who, what, where, when, how, or why, not a combination.

   e. Each question should present a challenge.

      1) A question must be difficult for the students at that particular stage of training.

4. When answering student questions, the instructor needs to clearly understand the question before attempting an answer.

   a. The instructor should display interest in the student's questions and give as direct and accurate an answer as possible.

   b. If a student's question is too advanced for the particular lesson and confusion may result from a complete answer, the instructor may

      1) Carefully explain that the question was good and pertinent;

      2) Explain that to answer would unnecessarily complicate the learning task at hand; and

      3) Advise the student to reintroduce the question later at the appropriate point in training, or meet outside class for a more complete discussion.

5. Occasionally, a student will ask a question the instructor cannot answer. The best course is to freely admit not knowing the answer.

   a. The instructor should then promise to find out or offer to help the student look it up in appropriate references.

7.3 TYPES OF WRITTEN TEST QUESTIONS (Questions 16-23)

1. Written test questions fall into two general categories:

   a. Supply-type and
   b. Selection-type.

2. Supply-type questions require the student to furnish a response in the form of a word, sentence, or paragraph.

   a. Supply-type test items

      1) Require students to organize their thoughts and ideas,

      2) Demand the ability to express ideas, and

      3) Are subjective.

         a) Thus, their main disadvantage is that they cannot be graded uniformly.

         b) The same test graded by different instructors probably would be assigned different scores.

      4) Take longer for students to answer and for instructors to grade, which is another disadvantage.

3. Selection-type questions include items for which two or more alternative responses are provided.

    a. Selection-type test items

        1) Are highly objective.

            a) Thus, they are graded uniformly regardless of the student or grader.

        2) Allow direct comparison of students' accomplishments. For example, it is possible to compare student performance

            a) Within the same class,
            b) Between classes, and
            c) Under different instructors.

    b. True-false, multiple-choice, and matching type questions are prime examples of selection-type questions.

4. The true-false test item is well adapted to the testing of knowledge of facts and detail, especially when there are only two possible answers.

    a. The chief disadvantage of the true-false test item is that it creates the greatest probability of guessing since the student always has a 50% chance of guessing correctly.

5. Multiple-choice test items may be used to determine student achievement, ranging from acquisition of facts to understanding, reasoning, and ability to apply what has been learned.

    a. One of the major difficulties encountered in the construction of multiple test items is inventing plausible sounding incorrect choices (distractors) which will be attractive to students lacking knowledge or understanding.

    b. When multiple-choice items are intended to measure achievement at a higher level of learning, some or all of the alternatives should be acceptable, but one should be clearly better than the others.

    c. Multiple-choice test items should have all alternatives of approximately equal length.

        1) The common error made by instructors is to make the correct alternative longer than the incorrect ones.

6. Matching test items are particularly good for measuring the student's ability to recognize relationships and to make associations between terms, parts, words, phrases, or symbols listed in one column with related items in another column.

    a. Matching reduces the probability of guessing correct responses compared to a series of multiple-choice items covering the same material.

7.4 CHARACTERISTICS OF A GOOD TEST (Questions 24-28)

1. Reliability

    a. A written test that has reliability yields consistent results.

2. Validity

    a. A written test has validity when it actually measures what it is supposed to measure and nothing else.

3. Usability

    a. A written test is usable when it is easy to give, easy to read, the wording is clear and concise, figures are appropriate to the test items and clearly drawn, and the test is easily graded.

4. Comprehensiveness

    a. A written test is said to be comprehensive when it samples liberally whatever is being measured.

5. Discrimination

    a. A written test shows discrimination when it will measure small differences in achievement between students.

    b. A written test that distinguishes between students both low and high in achievement is said to show positive discrimination.

7.5 REVIEW AND EVALUATION (Questions 29-31)

1. Review and evaluation of the student's learning should be an integral part of each lesson.

    a. Evaluation of student performance and accomplishment should be based on the objectives and goals established in the lesson plan.

2. Performance testing is desirable for evaluating training that involves an operation, procedure, or process.

    a. This method of evaluation is particularly suited to the measurement of a student's ability in performing a task, either mental or physical.

QUESTIONS AND ANSWER EXPLANATIONS

All of the FAA questions from the Fundamentals of Instructing knowledge test relating to the learning process and the material outlined above are reproduced below in the same modules as the outlines. To the immediate right of each question are the correct answer and answer explanation. You should cover these answers and answer explanations with your hand or a piece of paper while responding to the questions. Refer to the general discussion in Chapter 1 on how to take the FAA pilot knowledge test.

Remember that the questions from the FAA pilot knowledge test bank have been reordered by topic, and the topics have been organized into a meaningful sequence. Accordingly, the first line of the answer explanation gives the FAA question number and the citation of the authoritative source for the answer.

7.1 The Instructor's Critique

1.
6070. To enhance a student's acceptance of further instruction, the instructor should

A— keep the student informed of the progress made.
B— continually prod the student to maintain motivational levels.
C— establish performance standards a little above the student's actual ability.

Answer (A) is correct (6070). *(AIH Chap II)*
    Keeping the student informed of progress will tend to enhance a student's acceptance of further instruction. A student who is unaware of progress may lose interest, which decreases motivation and hinders learning.
    Answer (B) is incorrect because, if an instructor continually prods a student, the student's motivational level will decrease, not remain the same, due to his/her becoming frustrated. This will then lead to a decrease, not increase, in the student's desire to learn. Answer (C) is incorrect because the student will become frustrated by his/her inability to reach standards above his/her actual level of skill. This will lead to a decrease, not increase, in the desire to learn.

2.
6094. When an instructor critiques a student, it should always be

A— done in private.
B— subjective rather than objective.
C— conducted immediately after the student's performance.

Answer (C) is correct (6094). *(AIH Chap VI)*
The critique should always be conducted immediately after the student's performance, while the performance is still fresh in the student's mind. Specific comments on "your third turn," for instance, would have little value a week after the maneuver was performed.
Answer (A) is incorrect because a critique may be conducted in private or before the entire class. A critique presented before the entire class can be beneficial to every student in the classroom as well as to the student who performed the exercise. Answer (B) is incorrect because the critique should be objective rather than subjective.

3.
6092. Which statement is true about an instructor's critique of a student's performance?

A— The critique should always be conducted in private.
B— It is a step in the learning process, not in the grading process.
C— Instructor comments and recommendations should be based on the performance the way it should have been.

Answer (B) is correct (6092). *(AIH Chap VI)*
A critique is a step in the learning process, not the grading process. A critique should be used to guide students to better performance.
Answer (A) is incorrect because a critique may be conducted in private or before the entire class. A critique presented before the entire class can be beneficial to every student in the classroom as well as to the student who performed the exercise. Answer (C) is incorrect because a critique must be based on the performance as it was, not as it should have been.

4.
6095. An instructor's critique of a student's performance should

A— treat every aspect of the performance in detail.
B— be private so that the student is not embarrassed.
C— provide direction and guidance to improve performance.

Answer (C) is correct (6095). *(AIH Chap VI)*
A critique should improve a student's performance and provide something constructive with which (s)he can work on and build. It should provide direction and guidance to improve performance.
Answer (A) is incorrect because a comprehensive critique is not necessarily a long one, nor must it treat every aspect of the performance in detail. The instructor must decide whether the greater benefit will come from discussing a few major points or a number of minor points. Answer (B) is incorrect because a critique may be conducted in private or before the entire class. A critique presented before the entire class can be beneficial to every student in the classroom as well as to the student who performed the exercise.

5.
6096. Which is true about an instructor's critique of a student's performance?

A— Praise for praise's sake is of value.
B— It should be constructive and objective.
C— It should treat every aspect of the performance in detail.

Answer (B) is correct (6096). *(AIH Chap VI)*
A critique must be constructive by explaining to the student how to capitalize on things which are done well and to use them to compensate for lesser accomplishments. A critique must also be objective by basing it on the performance as it was, not as it could have been.
Answer (A) is incorrect because praise for praise's sake is of no value if a student is not taught how to capitalize on things that are done well and to use them to compensate for lesser accomplishments. Answer (C) is incorrect because a comprehensive critique is not necessarily a long one, nor must it treat every aspect of the performance in detail. The instructor must decide whether the greater benefit will come from discussing a few major points or a number of minor points.

6.

6097. To be effective, a critique should

A— not contain negative remarks.

B— treat every aspect of the performance in detail.

C— be flexible enough to satisfy the requirements of the moment.

Answer (C) is correct (6097). *(AIH Chap VI)*

An effective critique is one that is flexible enough to satisfy the requirements of the moment. The instructor must fit the tone, technique, and content of the critique to the occasion and the student. Thus, the instructor is faced with the problem of what to say, what to omit, and what to minimize. The challenge of the critique is that the instructor must determine what to say at the proper moment.

Answer (A) is incorrect because a critique may contain negative remarks as long as they point toward improvement or a higher level of performance. Answer (B) is incorrect because a comprehensive critique is not necessarily a long one, nor must it treat every aspect of the performance in detail. The instructor must decide whether the greater benefit will come from discussing a few major points or a number of minor points.

7.

6093. Which statement is true about instructors' critiques?

A— Instructors should rely on their personality to make a critique more acceptable.

B— A comprehensive critique should emphasize positive aspects of student performance.

C— Before students willingly accept their instructor's critique, they must first accept the instructor.

Answer (C) is correct (6093). *(AIH Chap VI)*

Students must have confidence in the instructor's qualifications, teaching ability, sincerity, competence, and authority before they will willingly accept their instructor's criticism. A critique holds little weight if the student has no respect for the instructor.

Answer (A) is incorrect because the effective critique is focused on student performance and should not reflect the personal opinions, likes, dislikes, and biases (i.e., personality) of the instructor. Answer (B) is incorrect because a comprehensive critique means that good and bad points are covered adequately, but not necessarily in exhaustive detail.

8.

6052. Which would more likely result in students becoming frustrated?

A— Giving the students meaningless praise.

B— Telling students their work is unsatisfactory with no explanation.

C— Covering up instructor mistakes or bluffing when the instructor is in doubt.

Answer (B) is correct (6052). *(AIH Chap II)*

If a student has made an earnest effort but is told that the work is not satisfactory, with no other explanation, frustration occurs. On the other hand, if the student is briefed on the errors made and is told how to correct them, progress and accomplishment can be made.

Answer (A) is incorrect because giving meaningless praise is valueless, not frustrating, to a student. Answer (C) is incorrect because covering up instructor mistakes or bluffing when the instructor is in doubt results in destroying student confidence, not creating frustration.

7.2 Oral Quizzing

9.

6100. One desirable result of proper oral quizzing by the instructor is to

A— reveal the effectiveness of the instructor's training procedures.

B— fulfill the requirements set forth in the overall objectives of the course.

C— reveal the essential information from which the student can determine progress.

Answer (A) is correct (6100). *(AIH Chap VII)*

One desirable result of proper oral quizzing by the instructor is that it reveals the effectiveness of the instructor's training procedures.

Answer (B) is incorrect because quizzing can only measure achievement, not fulfill the requirements, of the overall objectives of the course. Answer (C) is incorrect because an instructor should use the critique, not a quiz, to reveal the essential information from which the student can determine progress.

10.
6098. Which is a valid reason for the use of proper oral quizzing during a lesson?

A— Promotes active student participation.
B— Identifies points that need less emphasis.
C— Helps the instructor determine the general intelligence level of the students.

Answer (A) is correct (6098). *(AIH Chap VII)*
A valid reason for the use of proper oral quizzing during a lesson is to promote active student participation, which is important to effective teaching.
Answer (B) is incorrect because a valid reason for the use of proper oral quizzing during a lesson is that it identifies points which need more, not less, emphasis. Answer (C) is incorrect because a valid reason for the use of proper oral quizzing during a lesson is to check the students' comprehension of what has been learned, not their general intelligence level.

11.
6099. Proper oral quizzing by the instructor during a lesson can have which result?

A— Promotes effective use of available time.
B— Identifies points which need more emphasis.
C— Permits the introduction of new material not covered previously.

Answer (B) is correct (6099). *(AIH Chap VII)*
One desirable result of oral quizzing is that it helps the instructor identify points that need more emphasis. By noting students' answers, the instructor can quickly spot weak points in understanding and give these extra attention.
Answer (A) is incorrect because the use of a lesson plan, not oral quizzing, by the instructor will promote effective use of available time. Answer (C) is incorrect because the introduction of new material is accomplished during the presentation, not evaluation, step of the teaching process.

12.
6103. To be effective in oral quizzing during the conduct of a lesson, a question should

A— be difficult for that stage of training.
B— include a combination of where, how, and why.
C— divert the student's thoughts to subjects covered in other lessons.

Answer (A) is correct (6103). *(AIH Chap VII)*
During oral quizzing, an effective question must present a challenge to the student. A question must be difficult for the student at that particular stage of training. These types of questions stimulate learning.
Answer (B) is incorrect because an effective question should be limited to who, what, when, where, how, or why, not a combination. Answer (C) is incorrect because an effective question must apply to the subject of instruction, not divert the student's thoughts to subjects covered in other lessons.

13.
6101. During oral quizzing in a given lesson, effective questions should

A— be brief and concise.
B— provide answers that can be expressed in a variety of ways.
C— divert the student's thoughts to subjects covered in previous lessons.

Answer (A) is correct (6101). *(AIH Chap VII)*
During oral quizzing, an effective question should be brief and concise, but must also be clear and definite. Enough words must be used to establish the conditions or situations exactly, so that instructor and students will have the same mental picture.
Answer (B) is incorrect because all effective questions will have only one correct answer. A thought question will only have one correct answer, although it may be expressed in a variety of ways. Answer (C) is incorrect because an effective question must apply to the subject of instruction, not divert the student's thoughts to subjects covered in previous lessons.

14.
6102. In all quizzing as a portion of the instruction process, the questions should

A— include catch questions to develop the student's perceptive power.
B— call for specific answers and be readily evaluated by the instructor.
C— include questions with more than one central idea to evaluate how completely a student understands the subject.

Answer (B) is correct (6102). *(AIH Chap VII)*
In any kind of testing, questions should have one specific answer so that the instructor can readily evaluate the student's response. General questions tend to confuse rather than help, and unanswered questions serve no useful purpose at all.
Answer (A) is incorrect because catch questions should be avoided at all times. The students will feel they are engaged in a battle of wits with the instructor, and the whole significance of the subject of instruction will be lost. Answer (C) is incorrect because effective questions used in quizzing should center on only one central idea.

15.
6104. To answer a student's question, it is most important that the instructor

A— clearly understand the question.
B— have complete knowledge of the subject.
C— introduce more complicated information to partially answer the question, if necessary.

Answer (A) is correct (6104). *(AIH Chap VII)*
The answering of students' questions can be an effective teaching method. To answer a student's question, it is most important that the instructor clearly understands the question.
Answer (B) is incorrect because, while an instructor may have knowledge of a subject, occasionally a student will ask a question which the instructor cannot answer. The instructor should admit not knowing the answer, and should promise to get the answer or help the student to find it. Answer (C) is incorrect because introducing more complicated information to partially answer the question is normally unwise. Doing so would confuse the student and complicate the learning tasks at hand.

7.3 Types of Written Test Questions

16.
6112. What is a characteristic of supply-type test items?

A— They are easily adapted to testing knowledge of facts and details.
B— Test results would be graded the same regardless of the student or the grader.
C— The same test graded by different instructors would probably be given different scores.

Answer (C) is correct (6112). *(AIH Chap VII)*
A characteristic of supply-type test items is that they cannot be graded with uniformity. The same test graded by different instructors would probably be assigned different scores. The same test graded by the same instructor on consecutive days might be assigned two different scores. There is no assurance that the grade assigned is the grade deserved.
Answer (A) is incorrect because true-false, not supply-type, test items are easily adapted to testing knowledge of facts and details. Answer (B) is incorrect because selection-type, not supply-type, test items would be graded the same regardless of the student or the grader.

17.
6111. Which is the main disadvantage of supply-type test items?

A— They cannot be graded with uniformity.
B— They are readily answered by guessing.
C— They are easily adapted to statistical analysis.

Answer (A) is correct (6111). *(AIH Chap VII)*
The main disadvantage of supply-type test items is that they cannot be graded with uniformity. The same test graded by different instructors would probably be assigned different scores. The same test graded by the same instructor on consecutive days might be assigned two different scores. There is no assurance that the grade assigned is the grade deserved.
Answer (B) is incorrect because the main disadvantage of true-false, not supply-type, test items is they are readily answered by guessing. Answer (C) is incorrect because an advantage, not disadvantage, of selection-type, not supply-type, test items is that they are easily adapted to statistical analysis.

18.
6113. One of the main advantages of selection-type test items over supply-type test items is that the selection-type

A— decreases discrimination between responses.
B— would be graded objectively regardless of the student or the grader.
C— precludes comparison of students under one instructor with those under another instructor.

Answer (B) is correct (6113). *(AIH Chap VII)*
One of the main advantages of selection-type test items over supply-type test items is that the selection-type are graded objectively regardless of the student or grader.
Answer (A) is incorrect because an advantage of the selection-type test item over the supply-type test item is that more areas of knowledge can be tested in a given time, thus increasing, not decreasing, comprehensiveness, validity, and discrimination. Answer (C) is incorrect because an advantage of the selection-type test item over supply-type test item is the ability to compare, not to preclude comparison of, student performance under one instructor with those of another instructor.

19.
6115. Which statement is true about multiple-choice test items that are intended to measure achievement at a higher level of learning?

A— It is unethical to mislead students into selecting an incorrect alternative.
B— Some or all of the alternatives should be acceptable, but only one should be clearly better than the others.
C— The use of common errors as distracting alternatives to divert the student from the correct response is ineffective and invalid.

Answer (B) is correct (6115). *(AIH Chap VII)*
When multiple-choice test items are intended to measure achievement at a higher level of learning, some or all of the alternatives should be acceptable, but only one should be clearly better than the others. The instructions given should direct the student to select the best alternative.
Answer (A) is incorrect because when using multiple-choice test items the students are not supposed to guess the correct answer; they should select it only if they know it is correct. Thus, it is ethical, not unethical, to mislead students into selecting an incorrect alternative.
Answer (C) is incorrect because when using multiple-choice test items, the use of common errors as distracting alternatives to divert the student from the correct response is effective, not ineffective, and valid, not invalid.

20.
6116. Which statement is true relative to effective multiple-choice test items?

A— Negative words or phrases need not be emphasized.
B— Items should call for abstract background knowledge.
C— Keep all alternatives of approximately equal length.

Answer (C) is correct (6116). *(AIH Chap VII)*
In preparing and reviewing the alternatives to a multiple-choice item, it is advisable to keep all alternatives approximately the same length. Research of instructor-made tests reveals that, in general, correct alternatives are longer than incorrect ones.
Answer (A) is incorrect because, when negative words or phrases are used, they should be emphasized in order to be effective. Answer (B) is incorrect because items should call for essential knowledge rather than for abstract background knowledge or unimportant facts.

21.
6110. Which type of test item creates the greatest probability of guessing?

A— True-false.
B— Supply-type.
C— Multiple-choice.

Answer (A) is correct (6110). *(AIH Chap VII)*
The true-false test item creates the greatest probability of guessing since the student always has a 50% chance of guessing correctly.
Answer (B) is incorrect because the true-false, not the supply-type, test item creates the greatest probability of guessing. Answer (C) is incorrect because the true-false, not the multiple-choice, test item creates the greatest probability of guessing.

22.
6114. Which is one of the major difficulties encountered in the construction of multiple-choice test items?

A— Adapting the items to statistical item analysis.
B— Keeping all responses approximately equal in length.
C— Inventing distractors which will be attractive to students lacking knowledge or understanding.

Answer (C) is correct (6114). *(AIH Chap VII)*
Three major difficulties are encountered in the construction of multiple-choice test items:

1. Development of a question or an item stem which can be expressed clearly without ambiguity.
2. Statement of an answer which cannot be refuted.
3. The invention of lures or distractors which will be attractive to those students who do not possess the knowledge or understanding necessary to recognize the correct answer.

Answer (A) is incorrect because it is a major advantage, not difficulty, for a multiple-choice test item to be well adapted to statistical item analysis. Answer (B) is incorrect because a principle, not difficulty, of constructing a multiple-choice test item is to keep all responses approximately equal in length.

23.
6117. In a written test, which type of selection-type test items reduces the probability of guessing correct responses?

A— Essay.
B— Matching.
C— Multiple-choice.

Answer (B) is correct (6117). *(AIH Chap VII)*
In a written test, matching test items reduces the probability of guessing correct responses compared to a series of multiple-choice items covering the same material, especially if alternatives are used more than once.
Answer (A) is incorrect because an essay question is a supply-type, not selection-type, test item. Answer (C) is incorrect because matching, not multiple-choice, test items reduce the probability of guessing correct responses.

7.4 Characteristics of a Good Test

24.
6106. A written test that has reliability

A— yields consistent results.
B— measures small differences in the achievement of students.
C— actually measures what it is supposed to measure and nothing else.

Answer (A) is correct (6106). *(AIH Chap VII)*
A written test that has reliability is one which yields consistent results.
Answer (B) is incorrect because a written test which shows discrimination, not reliability, measures small differences in the achievement of students. Answer (C) is incorrect because a written test which has validity, not reliability, actually measures what it is supposed to measure and nothing else.

25.
6105. A written test has validity when it

A— yields consistent results.
B— samples liberally whatever is being measured.
C— actually measures what it is supposed to measure and nothing else.

Answer (C) is correct (6105). *(AIH Chap VII)*
A written test has validity when it actually measures what it is supposed to measure and nothing else.
Answer (A) is incorrect because a written test has reliability, not validity, when it yields consistent results. Answer (B) is incorrect because a written test has comprehensiveness, not validity, when it samples liberally whatever is being measured.

26.
6109. A written test is said to be comprehensive when it

A— includes all levels of difficulty.
B— samples liberally whatever is being measured.
C— measures knowledge of the same topic in many different ways.

Answer (B) is correct (6109). *(AIH Chap VII)*
A written test is said to be comprehensive when it samples liberally whatever is being measured.
Answer (A) is incorrect because a written test shows discrimination, not comprehensiveness, when it includes all levels of difficulty. Answer (C) is incorrect because a written test shows discrimination, not comprehensiveness, when it measures knowledge of the same topic in many different ways.

27.
6107. The characteristic of a written test, which measures small differences in achievement between students, is its

A— validity.
B— reliability.
C— discrimination.

Answer (C) is correct (6107). *(AIH Chap VII)*
The characteristic of a written test which measures small differences in achievement between students is its discrimination.
Answer (A) is incorrect because a written test has validity when it measures what it is supposed to and nothing else, not when it measures small differences in achievement between students. Answer (B) is incorrect because a written test that has reliability is one which yields consistent results, not which measures small differences in achievement between students.

28.
6108. When a written test shows positive discrimination, it will

A— cover several levels of difficulty.
B— distinguish between students both low and high in achievement.
C— include a representative and comprehensive sampling of the course objectives.

7.5 Review and Evaluation

29.
6069. Evaluation of student performance and accomplishment during a lesson should be based on

A— objectives and goals established in the lesson plan.
B— performance of each student compared to an objective standard.
C— each student's ability to make an objective evaluation of their own progress.

30.
6067. Which statement is true regarding student evaluation?

A— The student's own evaluations can only be objective.
B— Evaluation of the student's learning should be an integral part of each lesson.
C— If deficiencies or faults not associated with the present lesson are revealed, they should be corrected immediately.

31.
6118. Which type test is desirable for evaluating training that involves an operation, procedure, or process?

A— Oral.
B— Performance.
C— Proficiency.

Answer (B) is correct (6108). *(AIH Chap VII)*
When a written test shows positive discrimination, it will distinguish between students both low and high in achievement of the course objectives.
Answer (A) is incorrect because, when a written test shows positive discrimination, it will cover all, not several, levels of difficulty. Answer (C) is incorrect because a written test shows comprehensiveness, not discrimination, when it includes a representative and comprehensive sampling of the course objectives.

Answer (A) is correct (6069). *(AIH Chap IV)*
The evaluation of student performance and accomplishment during a lesson should be based on the objectives and goals that were established in the instructor's lesson plan.
Answer (B) is incorrect because a critique, not an evaluation, is based on comparing a student's performance to an objective standard. Answer (C) is incorrect because a student's own evaluation can only be subjective, not objective. Only the instructor can provide a realistic evaluation of performance and progress.

Answer (B) is correct (6067). *(AIH Chap IV)*
Review and evaluation should be an integral part of each classroom or flight lesson. At the end of each class period, the instructor should review what has been covered during the lesson and require the students to demonstrate the extent to which the lesson objectives have been met. Evaluation can be formal (performance, written tests) or informal (oral quiz or guided discussion).
Answer (A) is incorrect because the student's own evaluations can only be subjective, not objective. Answer (C) is incorrect because, if deficiencies or faults not associated with the present lesson are revealed, they should be noted and pointed out. Corrective measures that are practicable at the time should be taken immediately, but more thorough remedial actions must be included in future lesson plans.

Answer (B) is correct (6118). *(AIH Chap VII)*
Performance testing is desirable for evaluating training that involves an operation, procedure, or process. This method of evaluation is particularly suited to the measurement of a student's ability in performing a task, either mental or physical.
Answer (A) is incorrect because performance, not oral, testing is desirable for evaluating training that involves an operation, procedure, or process. Answer (C) is incorrect because there is no proficiency-type test in evaluation, only oral, written, or performance.

END OF CHAPTER

APPENDIX A
FUNDAMENTALS OF INSTRUCTING
PRACTICE TEST

The following 50 questions have been randomly selected from the 160 fundamental of instructing questions in the FAA's flight and ground instructor test bank. Topical coverage in this practice test is similar to that of the FAA knowledge test. Use the correct answer listing on page 88 to grade your practice test.

1.
6001. A change in behavior as a result of experience can be defined as

A— learning.
B— knowledge.
C— understanding.

2.
6004. Individuals make more progress learning if they have a clear objective. This is one feature of the law of

A— primacy.
B— readiness.
C— willingness.

3.
6007. Things most often repeated are best remembered because of which law of learning?

A— Law of effect.
B— Law of recency.
C— Law of exercise.

4.
6010. Which law of learning often creates a strong impression?

A— Law of primacy.
B— Law of intensity.
C— Law of readiness.

5.
6013. Instruction, as opposed to the trial and error method of learning, is desirable because competent instruction speeds the learning process by

A— motivating the student to a better performance.
B— emphasizing only the important points of training.
C— teaching the relationship of perceptions as they occur.

6.
6016. The factor which contributes most to a student's failure to remain receptive to new experiences and which creates a tendency to reject additional training is

A— basic needs.
B— element of threat.
C— negative self-concept.

7.
6019. In the learning process, fear or the element of threat will

A— narrow the student's perceptual field.
B— decrease the rate of associative reactions.
C— cause a student to focus on several areas of perception.

8.
6022. Which statement is true concerning motivations?

A— Motivations must be tangible to be effective.
B— Motivations may be very subtle and difficult to identify.
C— Negative motivations often are as effective as positive motivations.

9.
6025. Which is generally the more effective way for an instructor to properly motivate students?

A— Maintain pleasant personal relationships with students.
B— Provide positive motivations by the promise or achievement of rewards.
C— Reinforce their self-confidence by requiring no tasks beyond their ability to perform.

10.
6028. During the flight portion of a practical test, the examiner simulates complete loss of engine power by closing the throttle and announcing "simulated engine failure." What level of learning is being tested?

A— Application.
B— Correlation.
C— Understanding.

11.
6031. The best way to prepare a student to perform a task is to

A— explain the purpose of the task.
B— provide a clear, step-by-step example.
C— give the student an outline of the task.

12.
6034. According to one theory, some forgetting is due to the practice of submerging an unpleasant experience into the subconscious. This is called

A— blanking.
B— immersion.
C— repression.

13.
6037. Responses that produce a pleasurable return are called

A— reward.
B— praise.
C— positive feedback.

14.
6040. To ensure proper habits and correct techniques during training, an instructor should

A— use the building block technique of instruction.
B— repeat subject matter the student has already learned.
C— introduce challenging material to continually motivate the student.

15.
6043. Which of the student's human needs offer the greatest challenge to an instructor?

A— Social.
B— Egoistic.
C— Self-fulfillment.

16.
6046. When a student asks irrelevant questions or refuses to participate in class activities, it usually is an indication of the defense mechanism known as

A— flight.
B— aggression.
C— resignation.

17.
6049. When students display the defense mechanism called aggression, they

A— become visibly angry, upset, and childish.
B— may refuse to participate in class activities.
C— attempt to justify actions by asking numerous questions.

18.
6052. Which would more likely result in students becoming frustrated?

A— Giving the students meaningless praise.
B— Telling students their work is unsatisfactory with no explanation.
C— Covering up instructor mistakes or bluffing when the instructor is in doubt.

19.
6055. Student confidence tends to be destroyed if instructors

A— bluff whenever in doubt about some point.
B— continually identify student errors and failures.
C— direct and control the student's actions and behavior.

20.
6058. To communicate effectively, instructors must

A— recognize the level of comprehension.
B— provide an atmosphere which encourages questioning.
C— reveal a positive attitude while delivering their message.

21.
6061. By using abstractions in the communication process, the communicator will

A— bring forth specific items of experience in the minds of the receivers.
B— be using words which refer to objects or ideas that human beings can experience directly.
C— not evoke in the listener's or reader's mind the specific items of experience the communicator intends.

22.
6064. A communicator's words cannot communicate the desired meaning to another person unless the

A— words have meaningful referents.
B— words give the meaning that is in the mind of the receiver.
C— listener or reader has had some experience with the objects or concepts to which these words refer.

23.
6067. Which statement is true regarding student evaluation?

A— The student's own evaluations can only be objective.
B— Evaluation of the student's learning should be an integral part of each lesson.
C— If deficiencies or faults not associated with the present lesson are revealed, they should be corrected immediately.

24.
6070. To enhance a student's acceptance of further instruction, the instructor should

A— keep the student informed of the progress made.
B— continually prod the student to maintain motivational levels.
C— establish performance standards a little above the student's actual ability.

25.
6073. The method of arranging lesson material from the simple to complex, past to present, and known to unknown, is one that

A— creates student thought pattern departures.
B— shows the relationships of the main points of the lesson.
C— requires students to actively participate in the lesson.

26.
6076. The first step in preparing a lecture is to

A— research the subject.
B— develop the main ideas or key points.
C— establish the objective and desired outcome.

27.
6079. What is one advantage of a lecture?

A— Uses time economically.
B— Excellent when additional research is required.
C— Allows for maximum attainment of certain types of learning outcomes.

28.
6082. Which teaching method is most economical in terms of the time required to present a given amount of material?

A— Briefing.
B— Teaching lecture.
C— Demonstration/performance.

29.
6085. In a guided discussion, learning is produced through the

A— skillful use of questions.
B— use of questions, each of which contains several ideas.
C— use of reverse questions directed to the class as a whole.

30.
6088. When it appears students have adequately dis-cussed the ideas presented during a guided discussion, one of the most valuable tools an instructor can use is

A— a session of verbal testing.
B— a written test on the subject discussed.
C— an interim summary of what the students accomplished.

31.
6091. What is the last step in the demonstration/performance method?

A— Summary.
B— Evaluation.
C— Student performance.

32.
6094. When an instructor critiques a student, it should always be

A— done in private.
B— subjective rather than objective.
C— conducted immediately after the student's performance.

33.
6097. To be effective, a critique should

A— not contain negative remarks.
B— treat every aspect of the performance in detail.
C— be flexible enough to satisfy the requirements of the moment.

34.
6100. One desirable result of proper oral quizzing by the instructor is to

A— reveal the effectiveness of the instructor's training procedures.
B— fulfill the requirements set forth in the overall objectives of the course.
C— reveal the essential information from which the student can determine progress.

35.
6103. To be effective in oral quizzing during the conduct of a lesson, a question should

A— be difficult for that stage of training.
B— include a combination of where, how, and why.
C— divert the student's thoughts to subjects covered in other lessons.

36.
6106. A written test that has reliability

A— yields consistent results.
B— measures small differences in the achievement of students.
C— actually measures what it is supposed to measure and nothing else.

37.
6109. A written test is said to be comprehensive when it

A— includes all levels of difficulty.
B— samples liberally whatever is being measured.
C— measures knowledge of the same topic in many different ways.

38.
6113. One of the main advantages of selection-type test items over supply-type test items is that the selection-type

A— decreases discrimination between responses.
B— would be graded objectively regardless of the student or the grader.
C— precludes comparison of students under one instructor with those under another instructor.

39.
6117. In a written test, which type of selection-type test items reduces the probability of guessing correct responses?

A— Essay.
B— Matching.
C— Multiple-choice.

40.
6121. Instructional aids used in the teaching/learning process should not be used

A— as a crutch by the instructor.
B— for teaching more in less time.
C— to visualize relationships between abstracts.

41.
6123. Which statement is true regarding true professionalism as an instructor?

A— Anything less than sincere performance destroys the effectiveness of the professional instructor.
B— To achieve professionalism, actions and decisions must be limited to standard patterns and practices.
C— A single definition of professionalism would encompass all of the qualifications and considerations which must be present.

42.
6126. What should an instructor do with a student who assumes that correction of errors is unimportant?

A— Divide complex flight maneuvers into elements.
B— Try to reduce the student's overconfidence to reduce the chance of an accident.
C— Raise the standard of performance for each lesson, demanding greater effort.

43.
6130. When under stress, normal individuals usually react

A— by showing excellent morale followed by deep depression.
B— by responding rapidly and exactly, often automatically, within the limits of their experience and training.
C— inappropriately such as extreme overcooperation, painstaking self-control, and inappropriate laughing or singing.

44.
6134. The basic demonstration/performance method of instruction consists of several steps in proper order. They are

A— instructor tells--student does; student tells--student does; student does--instructor evaluates.
B— instructor tells--instructor does; student tells-- instructor does; student does--instructor evaluates.
C— instructor tells--instructor does; student tells-- instructor does; student tells--student does; student does--instructor evaluates.

45.
6138. During integrated flight instruction, the instructor must be sure the student

A— develops the habit of looking for other traffic.
B— is able to control the aircraft for extended periods under IMC.
C— can depend on the flight instruments when maneuvering by outside references.

46.
6142. Students quickly become apathetic when they

A— realize material is being withheld by the instructor.
B— understand the objectives toward which they are working.
C— recognize that the instructor is not adequately prepared.

47.
6146. Development and assembly of blocks of learning in their proper relationship will provide a means for

A— both the instructor and student to easily correct faulty habit patterns.
B— challenging the student by progressively increasing the units of learning.
C— allowing the student to master the segments of the overall pilot performance requirements individually and combining these with other related segments.

48.
6150. Which statement is true regarding lesson plans?

A— Lesson plans should not be directed toward the course objective; only to the lesson objective.
B— A well-thought-out mental outline of a lesson may be used any time as long as the instructor is well prepared.
C— Lesson plans help instructors keep a constant check on their own activity as well as that of their students.

49.
6154. (Refer to figure 1 below.) Section A is titled:

A— Overview.
B— Objective.
C— Introduction.

50.
6158. (Refer to figure 1 below.) Section C is titled:

A— Schedule.
B— Overview.
C— Training Schedule.

	GROUND		
LESSON	REFERENCE MANEUVERS	STUDENT _____	DATE _____

A _____ • TO DEVELOP THE STUDENT'S SKILL IN PLANNING AND FOLLOWING A PATTERN OVER THE GROUND COMPENSATING FOR WIND DRIFT AT VARYING ANGLES.

B _____ • USE OF GROUND REFERENCES TO CONTROL PATH.
• OBSERVATION AND CONTROL OF WIND EFFECT.
• CONTROL OF AIRPLANE ATTITUDE, ALTITUDE, AND HEADING.

C _____ • PREFLIGHT DISCUSSION.   :10
• INSTRUCTOR DEMONSTRATIONS.   :25
• STUDENT PRACTICE.   :45
• POSTFLIGHT CRITIQUE.   :10

D _____ • CHALKBOARD FOR PREFLIGHT DISCUSSION.
• IFR VISOR FOR MANEUVERS REVIEWED.

E _____ • PREFLIGHT – DISCUSS LESSON OBJECTIVE. DIAGRAM RECTANGULAR COURSE, S-TURNS ACROSS A ROAD, AND TURNS AROUND A POINT ON CHALKBOARD.

• INFLIGHT – DEMONSTRATE ELEMENTS. DEMONSTRATE RECTANGULAR COURSE, S-TURNS ACROSS A ROAD, AND TURNS AROUND A POINT. COACH STUDENT PRACTICE.

• POSTFLIGHT – CRITIQUE STUDENT PERFORMANCE AND MAKE STUDY ASSIGNMENT.

F _____ • PREFLIGHT – DISCUSS LESSON OBJECTIVE AND RESOLVE QUESTIONS.

• INFLIGHT – REVIEW PREVIOUS MANEUVERS INCLUDING POWER-OFF STALLS AND SLOW FLIGHT. PERFORM EACH NEW MANEUVER AS DIRECTED.

• POSTFLIGHT – ASK PERTINENT QUESTIONS.

G _____ • STUDENT SHOULD DEMONSTRATE COMPETENCY IN MAINTAINING ORIENTATION, AIRSPEED WITHIN 10 KNOTS, ALTITUDE WITHIN 100 FEET, AND HEADINGS WITHIN 10 DEGREES, AND IN MAKING PROPER CORRECTION FOR WIND DRIFT.

FIGURE 1.–Lesson Plan

CORRECT ANSWER LISTING -- PRACTICE TEST

Ques.	Ans.	Page	Ques.	Ans.	Page	Ques.	Ans.	Page	Ques.	Ans.	Page	Ques.	Ans.	Page
1.	A	22	11.	B	28	21.	C	43	31.	B	53	41.	A	43
2.	B	22	12.	C	26	22.	C	42	32.	C	74	42.	C	34
3.	C	22	13.	B	26	23.	B	80	33.	C	75	43.	B	33
4.	A	23	14.	A	27	24.	A	73	34.	A	75	44.	C	54
5.	C	25	15.	C	39	25.	B	62	35.	A	76	45.	A	55
6.	C	31	16.	B	32	26.	C	50	36.	A	79	46.	C	43
7.	A	24	17.	B	32	27.	A	49	37.	B	79	47.	C	61
8.	B	40	18.	B	75	28.	B	49	38.	B	77	48.	C	66
9.	B	39	19.	A	43	29.	A	51	39.	B	79	49.	B	64
10.	B	27	20.	C	41	30.	C	52	40.	A	68	50.	A	64

For additional practice tests, use *FAA Test Prep* software. Call (800) 87-GLEIM to order. Its cost is $30. The advantage of this software is that you cannot cheat (yourself) when taking practice tests. You can make up as many tests as you desire and you can also have the software rearrange the question sequence and answer order. The questions on each test are randomly selected from the FAA's actual test questions so that the coverage of topics (laws of learning, lesson plan, etc.) is the same as on actual FAA tests. It also emulates AvTEST, CATS, LaserGrade, and Sylvan to help you understand exactly what will occur at your FOI knowledge test.

APPENDIX B
THE FLIGHT INSTRUCTOR SECTION OF
THE FAA'S AVIATION INSTRUCTOR'S HANDBOOK
REPRINTED

The FAA's *Aviation Instructor's Handbook* (AC 60-14) consists of three sections comprising 14 chapters. The first eight chapters are the General Education Theory Section, which is outlined in Chapters 2 through 7 of this book. The Flight Instructor Section consists of three chapters:

Chapter IX: Flight Instructor Characteristics and Responsibilities
Chapter X: Techniques of Flight Instruction
Chapter XI: Planning Instructional Activity

They are reprinted beginning below and continue through page 131. The final three chapters concern aircraft maintenance instruction and are not relevant to this book.

CHAPTER IX. FLIGHT INSTRUCTOR CHARACTERISTICS AND RESPONSIBILITES

PROFESSIONALISM

As stated in the preamble of FAR Part 61, the flight instructor is the keystone of the new total operational concept and is responsible for all phases of required training. In light of this statement, it is clear that the flight instructor must be a true "professional."

The flight instructor must be fully qualified as a pilot; however, the instructor's ability must go far beyond this if the requirements of professionalism are to be met. Although the term "professionalism" is widely used, it is rarely defined. In fact, no single definition can encompass all of the qualifications and considerations which must be present before true professionalism can exist.

One noted educator has listed the major considerations and qualifications which must be included:

1. Professionalism exists only when a service is performed for someone, or for the common good.
2. Professionalism is achieved only after extended training and preparation.

3. True performance as a professional is based on study and research.
4. Professionalism presupposes an intellectual requirement. Professionals must be able to reason logically and accurately.
5. Professionalism requires the ability to make good judgmental decisions. Professionals cannot limit their actions and decisions to standard patterns and practice.
6. Professionalism demands a code of ethics. Professionals must be true to themselves, and to those they serve. Anything less than a sincere performance is quickly detected, and immediately destroys their effectiveness.

The flight instructor and prospective flight instructor certificate applicant should carefully consider this list. Attempts to operate as a flight instructor without any one of the qualities listed can only result in poor performance and deficient students. Preparation and performance as a flight instructor with these qualities constantly in mind will command recognition as a professional in the field of flight instruction.

Professionalism also includes a flight instructor's public image. In the past, flight instructors have all too often been willing to accept a less-than-professional status in the public view by relaxing their demeanor, appearance, and approach to their profession. A flight instructor who gives the impression that interest in flight instruction is secondary to interest in other activities cannot retain the reputation of a professional. This does not mean that the part-time instructor cannot be a professional. During the time devoted to flight instruction, however, this individual should present a professional image to the public.

If the role of the flight instructor in the aviation industry is to be upgraded, it must be done through the efforts of flight instructors themselves. The professional flight instructor commands the respect of associates; asks for and deserves higher pay; and, most importantly, delivers more effective flight instruction. The following is a discussion of several basic performance factors which should be considered by a flight instructor who seeks to be a professional.

Sincerity

The professional flight instructor should be straightforward and honest. Attempting to hide some inadequacy behind a smokescreen of unrelated instruction will make it impossible for the instructor to command the interested attention of a student.

Teaching a student pilot is predicated upon acceptance of the flight instructor as a competent, qualified teacher and an expert pilot. Any facade of instructor pretentiousness, whether it be real or mistakenly assumed by the student, will immediately cause a loss of confidence by the student in the instructor, and little learning will be accomplished.

The effectiveness of instructor emphasis on the precepts of safety will be lost if the instructor appears to disregard them; the same applies to the instructor's insistence on precision and accuracy in handling an airplane. The professional flight instructor should be honest in every way.

Acceptance of the Student

The professional flight instructor must accept students as they are, with all their faults and all their problems. The student is a person who wants to learn to fly, and the instructor is a person who is available to help in the learning process. Beginning with this understanding, the professional relationship of the instructor with the student should be based on a mutual acknowledgment that both the student and the instructor are important to each other, and that both are working toward the same objective.

Under no circumstances should the professional instructor do anything which implies degrading the student. Acceptance, rather than ridicule, and support, rather than reproof, will encourage learning, regardless of whether the student is quick to learn or is slow and apprehensive. Criticizing a student pilot who does not learn rapidly is not unlike a doctor reprimanding a patient who does not get well as rapidly as was hoped.

Personal Appearance and Habits

Personal appearance has an important effect on the professional image of the instructor. Today's aviation customers are people who expect their associates to be neat, clean, and appropriately dressed. It is not intended that the flight instructor should assume an attire foreign to the flight environment; however, since the instructor is engaged in a learning situation with professional people, the attire worn should be appropriate to a professional status.

Personal habits have a significant effect on the professional image. The exercise of common courtesy is perhaps the most important of these. A flight instructor who is rude, thoughtless, and inattentive cannot hold the respect of the students, regardless of piloting ability.

Cleanliness of body and breath is important to flight instruction. The airplane cabin is a close, tightly-sealed area, where an instructor and a student work in close proximity, and where even little annoyances provide serious distractions from the learning tasks at hand. Smoking by the instructor may, for example, be most unpleasant and distracting for a non-smoking student.

The use of alcohol in public, especially around an airport, has a serious impact on the flight instructor's image. The smell of alcohol on an instructor's breath during a period of flight instruction is inexcusable.

Demeanor

The attitude and movements of the flight instructor can contribute much to a professional image. The instructor should avoid erratic movements, distracting speech habits, and capricious changes in mood. The professional image requires development of a calm, thoughtful, and disciplined, but not somber, demeanor.

The instructor should avoid any tendency toward frequently countermanding directions, reacting differently to similar or identical errors at different times, demanding unreasonable performances or progress, or criticizing a student unfairly.

A forbidding or imperious demeanor is as much to be avoided as is an air of flippancy. Effective instruction is best fostered by a calm, pleasant, thoughtful demeanor which puts the student at ease, and maintains the instructor's personal image of competence and genuine interest in the student's learning tasks.

Safety Practices and Accident Prevention

The flying habits of the flight instructor, both during flight instruction and as observed by students when conducting other pilot operations, have a vital effect on safety. Students consider their flight instructor to be a paragon of flying proficiency whose flying habits they, consciously or unconsciously, attempt to imitate. The instructor's advocacy and description of safety practices mean little to a student if the instructor is observed to violate them.

For this reason, a flight instructor must meticulously observe the safety practices taught the students. A good example is the use of a checklist before takeoff. If a student sees the instructor start an airplane and take off without referring to a checklist, no amount of instruction in the use of a checklist will assure that the student will use one conscientiously when solo flight operations begin.

A flight instructor must carefully observe all regulations and recognized safety practices during all flight operations if a professional image is to be maintained. An instructor who is observed to fly with apparent disregard for loading limitations or weather minimums creates an image of irresponsibility which many hours of conscientious flight instruction cannot correct.

Habitual observance of regulations, safety precautions, and the precepts of courtesy will enhance the instructor's image of professionalism. Further and more important, such habits make the instructor more effective by developing the same habits in the students.

Perhaps the most productive action a flight instructor can take to enhance flying safety is to actively participate in the Federal Aviation Administration Accident Prevention Program. Although all segments of the FAA are vitally concerned with the program, the flight instructor will be involved chiefly through the General Aviation District Office Accident Prevention Specialist (APS). The program's objective is to improve safety in general aviation by: (1) improving attitudes, (2) increasing knowledge and proficiency through education, and (3) reducing environmental hazards. The GADO Accident Prevention Specialist utilizes the following programs to reduce hazards in these three areas:

1. *Safety meetings.* These meetings are very effective in updating knowledge and proficiency. In planning a safety meeting, the flight instructor should coordinate with the FAA Accident Prevention Specialist regarding time, place, and subject matter. The District Office has the necessary equipment and numerous audio-visual presentations available on various safety subjects, which are appropriate for such meetings.

2. *Accident Prevention Counselors.* These individuals are selected by the District Office Chief and are well-known and highly respected members of the community. They generally are pilots, flight instructors, or aviation maintenance technicians; however, this is not a prerequisite for selection. Counselors are volunteers who are willing to devote time, energy, and thought toward the objective of solving aviation safety problems in their community. To accomplish this

objective, these individuals: (1) counsel airmen who commit unsafe acts; (2) offer assistance and provide information to pilots and aviation organizations in the community in establishing safety programs; (3) make recommendations on matters designed to reduce aviation accidents; (4) publicize accident prevention program activities and accomplishments; (5) encourage the scheduling and assist in the conduct of local aviation safety education meetings, clinics, and seminars; (6) advise the GADO Accident Prevention Specialist when unable to remedy a hazardous situation; and (7) promote and conduct proficiency flights.

3. *Flight Assists.* The Accident Prevention Specialist uses information contained in ATC Flight Assist Reports to help pilots fly safely. No actual or implied punitive action is involved in the utilization of these reports.

The flight instructor must go beyond the requirements of developing technically proficient students who are knowledgeable in the areas of their equipment, flight procedures, and maneuvers. The flight instructor must not only teach students to know their own and their equipment's limitations, but must also teach them to be guided by those limitations. In brief, the flight instructor must make a strenuous effort to *develop good judgment* on the part of the students.

Proper Language

In flight instruction, as in other professional activities, the use of profanity and obscene language leads to distrust or, at best, to a lack of complete confidence. To many people, such language is actually objectionable to the point of being painful. The professional flight instructor must speak normally and without inhibitions, but must not develop the inability to speak positively and descriptively without excesses of language.

The beginning student pilot is entering a realm of new concepts and experiences and is also encountering new terms and phrases which are often confusing. Words such as "traffic," "stall," "elevator," and "lift" are familiar but are given entirely new meanings. Coined words, such as "vortac," "unicom," and

"pireps" cause further difficulty. Phrases such as "clear the area," "monitor ATIS," or "lower the pitch attitude" are completely incomprehensible.

The flight instructor does, and properly should, use these terms and phrases during instruction. Although the language of aviation is new and strange, it is part of the new world of flying which the beginning student is eager to learn about and adopt. Difficulty arises, however, when the instructor introduces these new expressions for the first time during an inflight situation, which may be difficult for the student under the best of circumstances.

At the beginning of the student's flight training, and before each flight lesson during early dual instruction, the flight instructor should carefully define the terms and phrases which will be used during the forthcoming lesson. The instructor should then be careful to limit instruction to those terms and phrases, unless the exact meaning and intent of any new expression are explained immediately.

Serious student errors and confusion involving unfamiliar terms and phrases result from the use of the colloquial expressions of aviation, which are rarely specific, and have endless variations. Instructing the student to "give it the needle," "throw the cobs to it," or "firewall it" when it is intended that the throttle should be opened for takeoff may be picturesque and brighten the instruction given; however, the use of such an expression can have serious consequences if one is used for the first time in a critical flight situation. There is the apocryphal story of the pilot of a large airplane faced with an emergency pullup who shouted "takeoff power" to the flight engineer who immediately closed all four throttles.

Self-Improvement

Professional flight instructors must never become complacent or satisfied with their own qualifications and ability. They should be constantly active and alert for ways to improve their qualifications, effectiveness, and the services they provide to students. Flight instructors are considered authorities on aeronautical matters and are the experts to whom many pilots refer questions concerning regulations, requirements, and new operating techniques. They have the opportunity and responsibility of introducing new procedures and techniques through their students and through certificated pilots with whom they come in contact.

There are many means of self-improvement available to flight instructors. Properly organized pilot safety symposiums and flight training clinics are valuable sources of refresher training and of opportunities to exchange information with instructors from other areas. Aviation periodicals, government publications, and technical issuances from the aviation industry are sources of valuable information for flight instructors.

For a professional performance as a flight instructor, it is essential that the instructor maintain current copies of the *Federal Aviation Regulations* that are pertinent to pilot qualification and certification, an *Airman's Information Manual*, current FAA *Flight Test Guides*, and pilot training manuals. A flight instructor who is not completely familiar with current pilot certification and rating requirements cannot do a competent job of flight instruction. The FAA Advisory Circular Checklist and Status of Federal Aviation Regulations, AC 00–2, includes a number of government publications which the instructor should consider for inclusion in a library. The Appendix gives instructions for ordering the checklist and also for obtaining other government reference and training materials. In addition to government publications, a number of excellent handbooks and other reference materials are available from commercial publishers. Also, many public and institutional libraries have excellent resource material on educational psychology, teaching methods, testing, and aviation-related subjects.

HELPING STUDENT PILOTS LEARN

Learning to fly should be an enjoyable experience. By making each lesson a pleasurable experience for the student, the flight instructor can maintain a high level of student motivation. This does not mean the instructor must make things easy for the student or sacrifice standards of performance to please the student. The student will experience pleasure

from a learning task well done or from successfully meeting the challenge of a difficult operation.

The idea that people must be led to learning by making it easy has no basis in fact. People are not always attracted to something which is pleasant and easy. Actually, they devote more effort to things which bring rewards, such as self-enhancement and personal satisfaction. People want to feel capable; they are proud of difficult achievements.

Learning to fly should be interesting. Knowing the objective of each period of instruction gives meaning and interest to the instructor's and student's efforts. Not knowing the objective involved leads to confusion, disinterest, and uneasiness on the part of the student.

Learning to fly should provide an opportunity for exploration and experimentation for students. Students should be allowed time to explore and evaluate the various elements of each maneuver or operation presented and thereby discover their own capabilities and acquire self-confidence. This can also be fostered by using alternative presentations for different students.

Learning to fly should be a habit-building period during which students devote their attention, memory, and judgment to the development of correct habit patterns. Any goal other than a desire to learn the right way makes students impatient of the instruction and practice they need and should be trying to obtain. The instructor should keep this goal before the students by example and by a logical presentation of learning tasks.

As was stated at the beginning of this chapter, flight instructors have full responsibility for all phases of required training. To meet this responsibility, flight instructors must be clear regarding their objectives. After the objectives have been established, teaching methods and activities must be organized to best achieve them.

Instructors must take specific steps if student learning is to be effectively fostered. They must (1) devise a plan of action, (2) create a positive student-instructor relationship, (3) present information and guidance effectively, (4) transfer responsibility to the student as learning occurs, and (5) evaluate student learning and thereby their own teaching effectiveness. While these distinct factors involved in instruction are not apparent to the student during learning, the disregard of any one of them results in a difficult and inefficient learning experience.

Helping the student learn does not mean that the instructor has the responsibility for performing learning tasks which students can do for themselves. This is not effective instruction. The best instructors provide only the information, guidance, and opportunity for student learning, and support their motivation while they are in a learning situation.

Providing Adequate Instruction

The flight instructor must attempt to analyze carefully and correctly the personality, thinking, and ability of each student. No two students are alike, and the same methods of instruction cannot be equally effective for all students. The instructor must talk with a student at some length to learn about the student's background, interests, way of thinking, and temperament. The instructor's methods may change as the student advances through successive stages of training; a gentle introduction must sometimes be followed by strict instruction if progress is to continue in advanced stages.

An instructor who has not correctly analyzed a student may soon find that the instruction is not producing the desired results. This could mean, for example, that the instructor has analyzed as a slow thinker a student who is actually a quick thinker but is hesitant to act. Such a student may fail to act at the proper time due to lack of self-confidence, even though the situation is correctly understood. In this case, the correction would obviously be instruction directed toward developing student self-confidence, rather than drill on flight fundamentals.

The slow student requires instructional methods which combine tact, keen perception, and delicate handling. If such a student receives too much help and encouragement, a feeling of incompetence may develop. Too much criticism may completely subdue a timid person, whereas brisk instruction may force a more diligent application to the learning task.

A student whose slow progress is due to discouragement and a lack of confidence should be assigned "subgoals" which can be attained more easily than the normal learning goals. For this purpose, complex flight maneuvers can be separated into their elements, and each element practiced until an acceptable performance is achieved before the whole maneuver or operation is attempted. As an example, instruction in turns across a road may begin with consideration at first for headings only, and the problems of altitude control, drift correction, and coordination can be introduced separately, one at a time. As the student gains confidence and ability, goals should be increased in difficulty until progress is normal.

Apt students can also create problems. Because they make few mistakes, they may assume that the correction of errors is unimportant. Such overconfidence soon results in faulty performance. For such students, a good instructor will constantly raise the standard of performance for each lesson, demanding greater effort. Individuals learn when they are aware of their errors. Students who are permitted to complete every flight lesson without corrections and guidance will not retain what they have practiced as well as those students who have their attention constantly directed to the analysis of their performance. This does not mean that deficiencies must be invented for their benefit, because unfair criticism immediately destroys a student's confidence in the instructor.

The demands on an instructor to serve as a practical psychologist are much greater than is generally realized. An instructor can meet this responsibility only through a careful analysis of the students and through a continuing deep interest in them.

Demanding Adequate Standard of Performance

Flight instructors must continuously evaluate their own effectiveness and the standard of learning and performance achieved by the students. The desire to maintain pleasant personal relationships with the students must not cause the acceptance of a slow rate of learning or a low level of flight performance. It is a fallacy to believe that accepting lower standards to please a student will affect a genuine improvement in the student-instructor relationship. Reasonable standards strictly enforced are not resented by an earnest student.

Flight instructors fail to provide competent instruction when they permit their students to get by with a substandard performance, or without learning thoroughly some item of knowledge pertinent to safe piloting. More importantly such deficiencies may in themselves allow hazardous inadequacies in the students' later piloting performance.

Emphasizing the "Positive"

Flight instructors have a tremendous influence on their students' "image" of aviation in general and piloting in particular. The way flight instructors conduct themselves, the attitudes they display, and the manner in which they develop their instruction all contribute to the formation of either *positive* or *negative* impressions by their students. Flight instructor success depends, in large measure, on the ability to frame instructions so that students develop a positive image of flying.

In Chapter I, it was emphasized that negative self-concepts inhibit the perceptual process, that fear adversely affects the students' perceptions, that threat limits their ability to perceive, and that negative motivations are not as effective as positive motivations. A knowledge of these factors, which have such a profound effect on the students' ability to absorb instruction is not enough. Instructors must be constantly aware of these and other "negativisms" and not allow them to creep into their instruction.

Consider how the following not-too-exaggerated first flight lesson might impress a new student pilot without previous experience in aviation:

1. An exhaustive indoctrination in preflight procedures, with emphasis on the extreme precautions which must be taken before every flight, because mechanical failures in flight are often disastrous.

2. Instruction in the extreme care which must be taken in taxiing an airplane, because "if you go too fast, it's likely to get away from you."

3. A series of stalls, because "this is how so many people lose their lives in airplanes."

(The side effect of this performance on the first lesson is likely to be airsickness.)

4. A series of simulated forced landings, because one should always be prepared to cope with an engine failure.

These are a series of new experiences which might make the new student wonder whether learning to fly is a good idea or not.

For contrast, one might consider a first flight lesson in which the preflight inspection is presented to familiarize the student with the airplane and its components, and the flight consists of a perfectly normal flight to a nearby airport and return. Following the flight, the instructor can call the student's attention to the ease with which the trip was made in comparison with other modes of transportation, and the fact that no critical incidents were encountered or expected.

This by no means proposes that preflight inspections, stalls, and emergency procedures should be omitted from training. It only illustrates the "positive" approach, in which the student is not overwhelmed with the critical possibilities of aviation before having an opportunity to see its potential and pleasurable features. The introduction of emergency procedures after the student has developed an acquaintance with normal operations is not so likely to be discouraging and frightening, or to retard learning by the imposition of fear.

There is no creed in aviation which demands that students must suffer as part of their flight instruction. This has often been the case because of the unthinking use of "negative" explanations and motivations for all flight operations. Every effort should be made to assure that flight instruction is given under the most favorable conditions.

There is the unfamiliar vibration, the strange noises, the eerie sensations due to "g" loads, or the "woozy" feeling in the stomach. Instructors, to be effective, cannot ignore the existence of these negative factors, nor should they ridicule students who are adversely affected by them. Rather, these negativisms must be overcome by positive instruction.

An instructor may explain to a student that a flight maneuver or procedure must be accomplished in a certain manner. To perform it otherwise, the instructor points out, is to flirt with disaster or to suffer serious consequences. Justifications such as these may be very convenient, and the instructor may consider such negative justifications sufficiently dramatic to assure that the point is committed to memory. The final test, however, must be whether the stated reasons contribute to the learning situation. With very few exceptions, the results which can be expected should be very apparent. *Negative teaching generally results in negative learning.*

Most new flight instructors tend to adopt those teaching methods used when they were students. These methods may or may not have been good. The fact that one has learned to fly under one system of instruction does not mean that this is necessarily the best way it can be done, regardless of the respect one retains for the ability of an old instructor. Some students learn to fly in spite of their instruction, rather than because of it.

EVALUATION OF STUDENT PILOTING ABILITY

This is one of the basic elements of flight instruction. In flight instruction, the instructor determines by oral quizzing that the student understands the procedure or maneuver to be learned, demonstrates its performance, allows the student to try it out and practice it under direction, and then evaluates student accomplishment by observing performance.

Evaluation of demonstrated ability during flight instruction must be based upon established standards of performance, suitably modified to apply to the student's experience and stage of development as a pilot. The evaluation, to be meaningful to the instructor, must consider the student's mastery of the elements involved in the maneuver, rather than merely the overall performance.

In flight instruction, demonstrations of piloting ability are important for exactly the same purposes as are quizzes. They have additional special significance, however, in being directly applied to the qualification of student pilots for solo and solo cross-country privileges. Also associated with pilot skill evaluations during flight instruction are the stage completion checks conducted in approved flying courses and flight checks for pilot certification flight-test recommendations.

In evaluating student demonstrations of piloting ability, as in quizzing and other instructional processes, it is important for the flight instructor to keep the student informed of progress. This may be done as each procedure or maneuver is completed or during postflight critiques.

Corrections or the explanations of errors in performance should point out the elements in which the deficiencies are believed to have originated and, if possible, appropriate corrective measures should be suggested. Correction of student errors should not include the practice of taking the controls away from the student every time a mistake is made. A student may perform a procedure or maneuver correctly and not fully understand the principles and objectives involved. When this is suspected by the instructor, the student should be required to vary the performance of the maneuver slightly, combine it with other operations, or apply the same elements to the performance of other maneuvers. A student who does not understand the principles involved will probably not be able to do this successfully.

THE FLIGHT INSTRUCTOR AS A PRACTICAL PSYCHOLOGIST

Flight instructors must be able to evaluate student personality if they are to use appropriate techniques in the presentation of instruction. While it is obviously impossible for every flight instructor to be an accomplished psychologist, there are a number of considerations which will assist in learning to analyze students before and during each lesson.

Anxiety

Anxiety is probably the most significant psychological factor affecting flight instruction. This is true because flying is a potentially threatening experience for persons who are not accustomed to being off the ground. The fear of falling is universal in human beings.

Anxiety is described by Webster as "a state of mental uneasiness arising from fear. . . ." It results from the fear of anything, real or imagined, which threatens the person who experiences it, and may have a potent effect on actions and on ability to learn from perceptions.

The responses to anxiety vary greatly. They range from a hesitancy to act to the impulse to "do something even if it's wrong!" Some persons affected by anxiety will react appropriately, adequately, and more rapidly than they would in the absence of threat. Many persons, on the other hand, may be frozen in place and incapable of doing anything to correct the situation which has caused their anxiety. Others may do things without rational thought or reason.

Both normal and abnormal reactions to anxiety are of concern to the flight instructor; the normal, because they indicate a need for special instruction to relieve the anxiety which causes them, and the abnormal, because they may be evidence of deep-seated trouble.

Anxiety can be countered by reinforcing students' enjoyment of flying, and by teaching them to cope with their fears. An effective technique is to treat fears as a normal reaction, rather than ignoring them.

Anxiety, for student pilots, is usually associated with the performance of certain flight maneuvers and operations. Instructors should introduce such maneuvers with care, so that students know what to expect, and what their reactions should be. When introducing stalls, for example, instructors should first explain the aerodynamic effects involved, and then carefully describe the sensations to be expected and the responses demanded of the pilot.

Student anxieties can be minimized throughout training by emphasizing the benefits and pleasurable experiences which can be derived from flying, rather than by continuously citing the unhappy consequences of faulty performances. Safe flying practices should be presented as conducive to satisfying, efficient, uninterrupted operations, rather than as necessary only to prevent catastrophe.

Normal Reactions to Stress

When a threat is recognized or imagined, the brain alerts the body. The adrenal gland then pours out hormones which prepare the body to meet the threat, or to retreat from it. The heart rate quickens, certain blood vessels constrict to divert blood to the organs which will need it, and other changes take place.

Normal individuals begin to respond rapidly and exactly, within the limits of their experience and training. Many responses are automatic, which points up the need for proper training in emergency operations prior to an actual emergency. The affected individual thinks rapidly, acts rapidly, and is extremely sensitive to all aspects of the surroundings.

Abnormal Reactions to Stress

With certain persons the same bodily reaction to stress does not produce actions which we regard as normal. With them, response to anxiety or stress may be completely absent or at least inadequate. Their responses may be random or illogical, or they may be more than is called for by the situation.

Flight instructors are the only persons, during flight instruction, who observe students when the "pressure is on." They are, therefore, the only individuals in a position to differentiate between potentially "safe" and "unsafe" pilots psychologically.

Flight instructors may accept the following student reactions as indicative of abnormal reactions to stress. None of them provides an absolute indication, but the presence of any of them under conditions of stress is reason for careful instructor evaluation.

1. Autonomic responses such as sweating (especially in the palms), rapid heart rate, paleness, etc.

2. Inappropriate reactions, such as extreme overcooperation, painstaking self-control, inappropriate laughter or singing, very rapid changes in emotions, and motion sickness under conditions of stress.

3. Marked changes in mood on different lessons, such as excellent morale followed by deep depression.

4. Severe anger at the flight instructor, service personnel, or others.

Flight instructors who find themselves involved with psychologically abnormal students may feel that they are not meeting the students' needs. They may believe that student actions are intended to be insulting, or more often, find student actions simply confusing. In difficult situations of this sort, flight instructors must carefully examine student responses and their own responses to the students. These responses may be the normal products of a complex learning situation, but they can also be indicative of psychological abnormalities which will inhibit learning, or be potentially very hazardous to future piloting operations.

Flight Instructor Actions Regarding Seriously Abnormal Students

A flight instructor who believes, after a careful consideration of all available evidence, that a student may be suffering from a serious psychological abnormality has a legal and moral responsibility to refrain from certifying that student to be a competent pilot.

The flight instructor's primary legal responsibility concerns the decision whether to certify the student to be competent for solo flight operations, or to execute a flight-test recommendation leading to certification as a pilot. If, after consultation, the instructor believes that the student suffers a serious psychological deficiency, such authorizations and recommendations must not be signed.

Flight instructors have the personal responsibility of assuring that such a person does not continue flight training or become certificated as a pilot. To accomplish this, the following steps are available:

1. If an instructor believes that a student may have a disqualifying psychological defect, arrangements should be made for another instructor, who is not acquainted with the student, to conduct an evaluation flight. After the flight, the two instructors should confer to determine whether they agree that further investigation or action is justified.

2. An informal discussion should be initiated with the local General Aviation or Flight Standards District Office, suggesting that the student may be able to meet the skill standards, but may be unsafe psychologically. This action should be taken as soon as a question arises regarding the student's fitness. It should not be delayed until the student feels competent to solo.

3. A discussion should be held with a local Aviation Medical Examiner, preferably the one who issued the student's medical certificate, to obtain advice and to decide on the possibility of further examination of the student.

STUDENT PILOT SUPERVISION AND SURVEILLANCE

Flight instructors have the moral obligation to provide guidance and restraint with respect to the solo operations of their students. This applies to instructors' observations of unsafe or inept operations by pilots who are not aware they are being observed, as well as pilots who have requested an instructor's evaluation or guidance. In the case of an observed unsatisfactory performance, it is the instructor's responsibility to try to correct it by the most reasonable and effective means. If unable to correct the situation by personal contacts and good advice, the instructor should report the situation which has caused the observed deficiencies to an Accident Prevention Counselor or a GADO Accident Prevention Specialist.

FLIGHT INSTRUCTOR ENDORSEMENTS

The authority and responsibility for endorsing student pilot certificates and logbooks for solo and solo cross-country flight privileges are a very important flight instructor prerogative. The rules covering these endorsements are contained in Part 61 of the Federal Aviation Regulations and are further explained in Advisory Circular 61-65, Part 61 Certification: Pilot and Flight Instructors. Failure to ascertain that a student pilot meets the requirements of regulations prior to making endorsements is a serious deficiency in performance, for which a flight instructor is held accountable. Providing a solo endorsement for a student pilot who is not fully prepared to accept the responsibility for solo flight operations is also a breach of faith with the student concerned.

Caution should be exercised regarding student pilots who seek to "learn to fly" from pilots who are not certificated flight instructors. This may not be illegal, but the accumulation of flying experience in this manner does not relieve the flight instructor of responsibility for determining that the student has met all the requirements of the regulations.

FLIGHT TEST RECOMMENDATIONS

Provision is made on all private and commercial pilot certificate application forms for the written recommendation of the flight instructor who has prepared the applicant for the flight test involved. The signing of this recommendation imposes a serious responsibility on the flight instructor.

A flight instructor who is asked to execute a flight test recommendation for a pilot certificate applicant should require the applicant to thoroughly demonstrate qualifications for the flight test sought. This demonstration should in no instance be less than the complete test procedure prescribed in the pertinent *FAA Flight Test Guide*.

A flight test recommendation based on anything less risks the presentation of an applicant who may be totally unprepared for some part of the official flight test. In such an event, the flight instructor is logically held accountable for a deficient instructional performance. This risk is especially great in signing recommendations for applicants who have not been trained by the instructor involved. Federal Aviation Regulations require a minimum of 3 hours of dual flight test preparation for a private pilot certificate and 10 hours of such instruction for a commercial certificate.

FAA inspectors and designated pilot examiners rely on flight instructor recommendations as evidence of qualification for certification, proof that a review of the subject areas found to be deficient on the airman written test has been given, and assurance that the applicant has had a thorough briefing on the flight test standards and procedures.

It is very unusual for a competently prepared applicant to fail a flight test. Failure by an incompletely prepared applicant usually results in the need for a greater amount of dual instruction than would have been required for adequate preparation for the original test.

AIRPLANE CHECKOUTS

Flight instructors are often called upon to check out certificated pilots in unfamiliar airplanes. In the case of student pilots, such checkouts and certificate endorsements are required for each make and model airplane the student is allowed to operate solo.

With the increase in popularity of high-performance personal airplanes with distinct flight characteristics, complex systems and equipment, competent checkouts are essential for their safe, efficient operation. Checkouts which consist of a demonstration of the ability to take off and land the airplane concerned are no longer adequate.

FAA Advisory Circular 61–9A, *Pilot Transition Courses for Complex Single-Engine and Light Twin-Engine Airplanes*, provides useful guidance for an instructor. All checkouts should, of course, be conducted to the performance standards required by the appropriate FAA *Flight Test Guide* for the grade of certificate held by the pilot involved.

For the conduct of a pilot checkout, it is essential that the flight instructor be fully qualified in the airplane to be used and be thoroughly familiar with its operating procedures, approved flight manual, and operating limitations. An instructor who does not meet the recent flight experience prescribed by regulations for the airplane concerned should not attempt to check out another pilot.

The flight instructor who checks out a pilot in an aircraft for which a type rating is not required by regulations is accepting a major responsibility for the safety of future passengers when certifying the competency of the pilot. Many of these newer small airplanes are comparable in performance and complexity to transport airplanes. For these, the flight instructor's checkout should be at least as thorough as an official type rating flight test.

For the benefit of the pilot concerned, and for the instructor's protection in the case of later question, the flight instructor should record in the pilot's logbook the exact extent of any checkout conducted. This can be done most easily by reference to the appropriate FAA *Flight Test Guide*.

In the event the instructor finds a pilot's performance in the airplane used sufficiently deficient to constitute a hazard, an attempt should be made to influence the pilot to obtain further instruction before continuing operation of the airplane concerned. If this is unsuccessful, and a real hazard is considered to exist, it is the instructor's responsibility to bring the situation to the attention of the appropriate FAA District Office.

REFRESHER TRAINING

The conduct of refresher training for certificated pilots is not only a responsibility of the flight instructor, but it can also be a profitable opportunity. As stated in FAR Part 61, no person may act as pilot in command unless a flight review has been accomplished within the preceding 24 months.

Effective pilot refresher training must be based on specific objectives and standards if it is to be effective. The objectives should include a thorough checkout appropriate to the grade of certificate and aircraft ratings held, and the standards should be at least those required for the issuance of that grade of certificate. Before beginning any training, the pilot and the instructor should agree fully on these objectives and standards, and, as training progresses, the pilot should be made constantly aware of progress toward their achievement.

FAA Advisory Circular 61–10A, *Refresher Courses for Private and Commercial Pilots*, contains recommended procedures and standards for general pilot refresher courses.

CHAPTER X.   TECHNIQUES OF FLIGHT INSTRUCTION

In Chapter V, three teaching methods, the lecture, the guided discussion, and the demonstration-performance, were described in general terms. In this chapter, two teaching techniques useful to the flight instructor are discussed. Both are based on the demonstration-performance teaching method. This chapter also includes a discussion of several obstacles to learning during flight instruction.

THE "TELLING AND DOING" TECHNIQUE IN FLIGHT INSTRUCTION

This technique has been in use for a long time and is very effective in teaching skills. Flight instructors find it valuable in teaching procedures and maneuvers. It is basically the demonstration-performance method and follows the four steps of the teaching process discussed in Chapter IV, except for the first step, PREPARATION. The first step is particularly important in flight instruction because of the new concepts and complexities involved. The flight instructor needs to be well prepared and highly organized if complex ideas and skills are to be taught effectively. The student must be intellectually and psychologically ready for the learning activity. The PREPARATION step is accomplished prior to the flight lesson, by a careful consideration and discussion of objectives, and by a thorough preflight discussion. Steps two, three, and four of the teaching process can be accomplished by "Telling" and "Doing."

Instructor Tells—Instructor Does

This is the second step in the teaching process—PRESENTATION. It is a continuation of preparing the student, which began in the detailed preflight discussion, and now continues by a carefully planned demonstration and accompanying verbal explanation of the procedure or maneuver. It is important that the demonstration conform to the explanation as closely as possible. If a deviation does occur, the instructor should point it out and account for it.

Student Tells—Instructor Does

This is a transition between the second and third steps in the teaching process. It assures the student and the instructor that the explanation and demonstration have been adequate and are thoroughly understood.

Student Tells—Student Does

This is the third step in the teaching process—APPLICATION. This is where learning takes place and where performance habits are formed. If the student has been adequately prepared (first step) and the procedure or maneuver fully explained and demonstrated (second step), meaningful learning will occur. The instructor should be alert during the student's practice to detect any errors in technique and to prevent the formation of erroneous ideas or faulty habits.

Student Does—Instructor Evaluates

This is the fourth step of the teaching process—REVIEW and EVALUATION, in which the instructor reviews what has been covered during the instructional flight and determines to what extent the student has met the objectives outlined during the preflight discussion.

THE INTEGRATED TECHNIQUE OF FLIGHT INSTRUCTION

"Integrated flight instruction" is flight instruction during which students are taught to perform flight maneuvers both by outside visual references and by reference to flight instruments, FROM THE FIRST TIME EACH MANEUVER IS INTRODUCED. No distinction in the pilot's operation of the flight controls is permitted, regardless of whether outside references or instrument indications are used for the performance of the maneuver.

When this training technique is used, instruction in the control of an airplane by outside visual references is "integrated" with instruction in the use of flight instrument indications for the same operations.

Objectives

Integrated flight instruction was introduced on a national scale in 1959, when an amendment to the Civil Air Regulations established certain instruction and competency in the use of flight instruments as prerequisites for the issuance of private pilot certificates. The objective of this training was, and still is, the formation of firm habit patterns for the observance of and reliance on flight instruments from the student's first piloting experience. Such habits have been proved to produce more capable and safer pilots for the efficient operation of today's airplanes. The ability to fly in instrument weather is not the objective of this type of primary training, although it does greatly facilitate later instrument flight training.

Development of Habit Patterns

The continuing observance of and reliance upon flight instruments is essential to the efficient, safe operation of modern high-performance airplanes. The habit of monitoring instruments constantly is difficult to develop after one has become accustomed to relying exclusively on outside references for heading, altitude, airspeed, and attitude information, a procedure which was adequate in most older airplanes.

General aviation accident reports provide ample support for the belief that habitual reference to flight instruments is important to safety. The safety record of pilots who hold instrument ratings is significantly better than that of pilots with comparable flight time who have never received formal instrument flight training.

Student pilots who have been required to perform all normal flight maneuvers by reference to instruments, as well as by outside references, will develop from the start the habit of continuously monitoring their own and the airplane's performance. This habit would be much more difficult for a student to develop after intensive piloting experience without it, as veteran pilots who begin formal training for an instrument rating can readily testify.

The early establishment of proper habits of instrument coverage, instrument interpretation, and aircraft control will be of great assistance to the student pilot in gaining competence in the pilot operation "Maneuvering By Reference To Instruments" which is included in the *Private Pilot Airplane Flight*

Test Guide, AC 61–54A. The habits formed at this time will also give the student a firm foundation for later training for an instrument rating.

Accuracy of Flight Control

During early experiments with the integrated technique of primary flight instruction, it was soon recognized that students trained in this manner are much more precise in their flight maneuvers and operations. This applied to all flight operations, not just when flight by reference to instruments is required.

Notable among students' achievements are better monitoring of power settings and more accurate maintenance of desired headings, altitudes, and airspeeds. As the habit of monitoring their own performance by reference to instruments is developed, students will begin to make corrections without prompting.

The habitual attention to instrument indications leads to improved landings because of more accurate airspeed control, superior cross-country navigation, better coordination, and a generally better overall pilot competency.

Operating Efficiency

As student pilots become more proficient in monitoring and correcting their own flight technique by reference to flight instruments, the performance obtained from an airplane increases noticeably. This is particularly true of modern, high performance airplanes, which are responsive to the use of correct operating airspeeds.

The use of correct power settings and climb speeds and the accurate control of headings during climbs result in a measurable increase in climb performance. The maintenance of headings and altitudes in cruising flight will definitely increase average cruising speeds.

Emergency Capability

The use of integrated flight instruction provides the student with the ability to control an airplane in flight for limited periods if outside references are lost. This ability could save the pilot's life and those of the passengers in an actual emergency.

During the conduct of integrated flight training, the flight instructor must emphasize to the students that their introduction to the use of flight instruments does not prepare them for operations in marginal or instrument weather conditions. The possible consequences, both to themselves and to others, of experiments with flight operations in weather conditions worse than those required for VFR operations before they are instrument rated, should be constantly impressed on the students.

Procedures

The conduct of integrated flight instruction is simple. The use of an airplane equipped with flight instruments and an easily demountable means of simulating instrument flight conditions, such as an extended visor cap, are needed. The student's first briefing on the function of the flight controls should include the instrument indications to be expected, as well as the outside references which should be used to control the attitude of the airplane.

Each new flight maneuver should be introduced using either outside references or instrument indications, as the instructor prefers. The student's visor should then be raised or lowered, whichever is appropriate, and the same maneuver performed by the use of the other set of references. New students, having no inhibitions about instrument flying, rapidly develop the ability to maneuver an airplane equally well by instrument or outside references. They accept naturally the fact that the manipulation of the flight controls is identical, regardless of which references are used to determine the attitude of the airplane. This practice should continue throughout the student's dual instruction for all flight maneuvers except those which require the use of ground references. To fully achieve the demonstrated benefits of this type of training, the use of visual and instrument references must be constantly integrated throughout the training. Failure to do so will lengthen the dual instruction necessary for the student to achieve the competency required for a private pilot certificate.

Precautions

During the conduct of integrated flight instruction, the instructor must be especially vigilant for other air traffic while the student is operating by instrument references. The instructor must guard against having attention diverted to the student's performance for extended periods.

At the same time, the instructor must be sure that the students develop, from the start of their training, the habit of looking for other air traffic at all times when they are not operating under simulated instrument conditions. If students are allowed to believe that the instructor assumes all responsibility for avoiding other traffic, they cannot develop the habit of keeping a constant watch, which is essential to safety. Any observed tendency of a student to enter flight maneuvers without first making a careful check for other possible air traffic must be corrected immediately.

In the earlier stages of training, students may find it easier to perform flight maneuvers by instruments than by outside references. The fact that students can perform better by reference to instruments may cause them to concentrate most of their attention on the instruments, when they should be using outside references. This must not be allowed to continue, since it will cause considerable difficulty later in training while maneuvering by reference to ground objects. This tendency will also limit vigilance for other air traffic. The instructor should carefully observe the student's performance of maneuvers during the early stages of integrated flight instruction to assure that this habit does not develop. If it is detected, the instructor should make the student concentrate on maneuvering by outside references with the gyroscopic instruments caged or covered.

During the conduct of integrated flight instruction, the instructor should make it clear that the use of instruments is being taught to prepare students to accurately monitor their own and their airplane's performance, not to qualify them for IFR operations. The instructor must avoid any indication, by word or action, that the proficiency sought is intended solely for use in difficult weather situations.

Flight Instructor Qualifications

It is essential that a flight instructor be thoroughly familiar with the functions, characteristics, and proper use of all standard flight instruments. It is also the personal responsibility of each flight instructor to main-

tain familiarity with current pilot training techniques and certification requirements. This may be done by constant use of new periodicals and technical publications, personal contacts with Federal Aviation Administration Inspectors and designated pilot examiners, and by participation in pilot and flight instructor symposiums and clinics. The application of outmoded instructional procedures, or the preparation of student pilots for obsolete certification requirements is inexcusable.

OBSTACLES TO LEARNING DURING FLIGHT INSTRUCTION

Among those obstacles which are common to flight instruction, and which have been recognized as major factors to be considered by flight instructors, are students':

1. Feeling of unfair treatment.
2. Impatience to proceed to more interesting operations.
3. Worry, or lack of interest.
4. Physical discomfort, illness, or fatigue.
5. Apathy, fostered by poor instruction.
6. Anxiety.

Students who believe that their instruction is perfunctory, or that their efforts are not conscientiously considered and evaluated, will not learn well, and their motivation will suffer no matter how intent they are on learning to fly.

UNREASONABLE DEMANDS RETARD LEARNING

Motivation will also decline when a student believes the instructor is making unreasonable demands for performance and progress. The assignment of goals which the student considers difficult, but possible, usually provides a challenge which promotes learning. The assignment of impossible goals discourages the student, diminishes effort, and retards the learning process.

Impatience is a greater deterrent to learning pilot skills than is generally recognized. With a flight student, this may take the form of a desire to make an early solo flight, or to set out on cross-country flights before the basic elements of flight have been learned.

The impatient student fails to understand the need for preliminary training and seeks only the ultimate objective without considering the means necessary to reach it. In flying an airplane, as with every complex human endeavor, it is necessary to master the basics if the whole task is to be performed competently and safely. Student impatience can be corrected by the instructor by presenting the necessary preliminary training one step at a time, with clearly stated goals for each step. The procedures and elements mastered in each step should be clearly identified in demonstrating the performance of the subsequent step.

Impatience can result from instruction keyed to the pace of a slow learner when it is applied to an apt student. It is just as important that a student be advanced to the subsequent step as soon as one goal has been attained, as it is to complete each step before the next one is undertaken. Disinterest grows rapidly when unnecessary repetition and drill are required on operations which have been learned adequately.

Worry or lack of interest has a very detrimental effect on learning. Students who are worried or emotionally upset do not learn well and derive little benefit from any practice performed. Worry or distraction may be due to students' concern about progress in the training course, or may stem from circumstances completely unrelated to their instruction. Significant emotional upsets may be due to personal problems, psychiatric disturbances, or an antipathy for the training concerned or the instructor.

Students' experiences outside their training activities affect their behavior and performance in training; the two cannot be separated. When students begin flight training, they bring with them their interests, enthusiasms, fears, and troubles. The instructor cannot be responsible for these outside diversions, but cannot ignore them because they vitally affect teaching. Instruction must be keyed to the utilization of the interests and enthusiasms students bring with them, and to diverting their attention from their worries and troubles to the learning tasks at hand. This is admittedly difficult, but must be accomplished if learning is to proceed at a normal rate.

Worries and emotional upsets which result from the flight course can be remedied. Such occurrences are usually evidence of inadequacies on the part of the course or of the instructor. The most effective cure is prevention. The instructor must be alert to see that the students understand the objectives of each step of their training, and that they know at the completion of each lesson exactly what their progress and deficiencies have been. Discouragement and emotional upsets are rare when students feel that nothing is being withheld from them or is being neglected in their training.

Physical discomfort, illness, and fatigue will materially slow the rate of learning during both classroom instruction and flight training. Students who are not completely at ease, and whose attention is diverted by discomforts such as the extremes of temperature, poor ventilation, inadequate lighting, or noise and confusion, cannot learn at a normal rate. This is true no matter how diligently they attempt to apply themselves to the learning task.

A minor illness, such as a cold, or a major illness or injury will interfere with the normal rate of learning. This is especially important to the conduct of flight instruction, because most illness adversely affects the acuteness of vision, of hearing, and of feeling which are essential to correct performance.

Airsickness can be a great deterrent to flight instruction. A student who is airsick, or bothered with incipient airsickness, is incapable of learning at a normal rate. There is no sure cure for airsickness, but resistance or immunity can be developed in a relatively short period of time. An instructional flight should be terminated as soon as incipient sickness is experienced. As the student develops immunity, flights can be increased in length until normal flight periods are practicable.

Keeping students interested and occupied during flight is a deterrent to airsickness. They are much less apt to become airsick while operating the controls themselves. Rough air and unexpected abrupt maneuvers tend to increase the chances of airsickness. Tension and apprehension apparently contribute to airsickness and should be avoided.

The detection of student fatigue is important to efficient flight instruction. This is important both in assessing a student's substandard performance early in a lesson, which may be due to inadequate rest, and also in recognizing the deterioration of performance, which results from continuing intensive concentration on a complex task. Once fatigue occurs as the result of application to a learning task, the student should be given a break in instruction and practice. Fatigue can be delayed by introducing a number of maneuvers which involve different elements and objectives.

Fatigue is the primary consideration in determining the length and frequency of flight instruction periods. The amount of training which can be absorbed by one student without incurring fatigue does not necessarily indicate the capacity of another student. Fatigue which results from training operations may be either physical or mental, or both. It is not necessarily a function of physical robustness or mental acuity. Generally speaking, complex operations tend to induce fatigue more rapidly than do simpler procedures regardless of the physical effort involved. Flight instruction should be continued only so long as the student is alert, receptive to instruction, and is performing at a level consistent with experience.

Students quickly become apathetic when they recognize that the instructor has made inadequate preparations for the instruction being given, or when the instruction appears to be deficient, contradictory, or insincere. To hold the student's interest and to maintain the motivation necessary for efficient learning, well-planned, appropriate, and accurate instruction must be provided. Nothing destroys a student's interest so quickly as an

unplanned period of instruction. Even an inexperienced student realizes immediately when the instructor has failed to prepare a

THE INSTRUCTOR SHOULD ALWAYS HAVE A PLAN

lesson. Poor preparation leads to spotty coverage, misplaced emphasis, repetition, and a complete lack of confidence on the part of the student.

Instructions may be overly explicit and so elementary as to fail to hold student interest, or they may be so general or complicated that they fail to evoke the interest necessary for effective learning. To be effective, the instructor must teach for the level of the student. The presentation must be adjusted to be meaningful to the person for whom it is intended. For example, instruction in the preflight inspection of an airplane should be presented quite differently for a student who is a skilled airplane mechanic from the instruction on the same operation for a student with no previous aeronautical experience. The inspection desired in each case is the same, but a presentation meaningful to one of these students would be inappropriate for the other.

Poor presentations of instruction may result not only from poor preparation, but also from distracting mannerisms, personal untidiness, or the appearance of irritation with the student. Creating the impression of "talking down" to the student is one of the surest ways for an instructor to lose the student's confidence and attention. Once this confidence is lost by the instructor, learning rate is unnecessarily retarded.

Anxiety may place additional burdens on the instructor. This frequently limits the student's preceptive ability and retards the development of insights.

The student must be comfortable, confident in the instructor and the airplane, and at ease, if effective learning is to occur. Providing this atmosphere for learning is one of the first and most important tasks of the instructor. Although doing so may be difficult at first, successive accomplishments of recognizable goals and the avoidance of alarming occurrences or situations will rapidly ease the student's mind. This is true of all flight students but special handling by the instructor may be required only for obvious cases.

CHAPTER XI.   PLANNING INSTRUCTIONAL ACTIVITY

Any instructional activity must be competently planned and organized if it is to proceed in an effective manner. Much of the basic planning necessary for the flight and ground instructor is provided by the knowledge and proficiency requirements of the Federal Aviation Regulations, approved school syllabi, and the various texts, manuals, and training courses available. This chapter reviews briefly the planning required of the professional flight or ground instructor as it relates to three topics: (1) *course of training*, (2) *training syllabus*, and (3) *lesson plan*.

COURSE OF TRAINING
Determination of Standards and Objectives

Before any important instruction can begin, a determination of standards and objectives is necessary. In the case of a pilot training course, the overall objective is obvious, and the minimum standards are provided by Federal Aviation Regulations and flight test guides.

The general overall objective of any pilot training course is to qualify the student to be a competent, efficient, safe pilot for the operation of specific aircraft types under stated conditions. The criteria by which we determine whether the training has been adequate are the passing of written and flight tests required by the Federal Aviation Regulations for the issuance of pilot certificates.

Conscientious instructors, however, do not limit their objectives to meeting the minimum published requirements for a pilot certificate. They establish as their objectives the training of each student to have the knowledge necessary to service an airplane properly, to maneuver and operate it accurately within its limitations, and to analyze and make prompt decisions with respect to its safe operation. This is only a partial list of general objectives, but is illustrative of the major planning which is the basis of any training endeavor.

Identification of Blocks of Learning

It is not practicable for instructors to proceed immediately toward the overall objectives they have established for a major training activity being undertaken. Training for any such complicated and involved skill as piloting an aircraft requires the development and assembly, in their proper relationships, of many segments or "blocks of learning." In this way, a student can master the segments of the overall pilot performance requirements individually and can progressively combine these with other related segments until their sum meets the final objective.

Considered from this standpoint, training is much like building a pyramid—each block of learning is an identity in itself, but the pyramid is incomplete if any one block is missing. The instructor and the student must both recognize the interrelationship of the blocks and the place of each in the total objective.

After the overall training objectives have been established, the next step is the identification of the blocks of learning which constitute the necessary parts of the total objective. Just as in building a pyramid, some blocks are submerged in the structure and never appear on the surface, but each is an integral necessary part of the structure. While identifying the blocks of learning to be assembled during the proposed training activity, the planner must examine each carefully to see that it is truly an integral part of the structure. Extraneous blocks of instruction are expensive frills, especially in flight instruction, and detract from, rather than assist in, the completion of the final objective.

The blocks of learning identified during the planning of a training activity should be progressively smaller in scope. They should represent units of learning which can be measured and evaluated—not a sequence of periods of instruction. For example, the flight training of a private pilot might be divided into the following major blocks: achievement of the skills necessary for solo, the skills necessary for solo cross-country flight, and the skills appropriate for application for a private pilot certificate. Each of these, in turn, should be broken into component blocks of learning.

The skills necessary for the first solo flight might be broken down as inflight maneuvering; airspeed control, including flight at minimum controllable airspeed, stalls, and descents at approach speed; maneuvering by ground references; normal and crosswind takeoffs and landings; maximum performance operations; etc. Each of these, in turn, must be subdivided to produce effective lesson plans for each period of instruction.

As seen from the illustration cited, the possibility for breaking down and categorizing training objectives is infinite. For practical planning, the test for a useful size of a minimum block of learning is whether it contains sufficient learning to: (1) provide a challenge for the student, (2) promise a reasonable return in accomplishment for the training effort necessary, and (3) provide measurable objectives.

As these blocks of learning are completed and the student's performance of each confirmed to be at an acceptable level, the related blocks will be combined to form larger segments of the total training objective. For example, acceptable performance of airspeed management, maneuvering by ground references, inflight maneuvering, and radio communications may be combined to provide the capability of flying a traffic pattern at an airport with a control tower. In this manner, the use of a properly planned training syllabus makes it possible for the instructor to direct each period of instruction toward the completion of blocks of learning, which are in turn combined with others to lead toward the overall objective.

TRAINING SYLLABUS

The form of the syllabus may vary, but it is always in the form of an abstract or digest of the course of training. It consists of the blocks of learning to be completed in the most efficient order.

The instructor may develop a training syllabus; however, there are available many tried and proven syllabi which may be used. These are found in various training manuals, approved school syllabi, and in publications available from industry.

Each approved training course conducted by a certificated pilot school is given in strict accordance with a training syllabus specifically approved by the Federal Aviation Administration. Compliance with the appropriate approved syllabus is a condition for graduation from such courses. A student who has not been trained in accordance with the pertinent syllabus is not eligible for certification as an approved school graudate.

Any practical training syllabus must be flexible, and should be used primarily as a guide. The order of training can and should be altered, when necessary, to suit the progress of the student and the demands of special circumstances. In departing from the order prescribed by the syllabus, however, it is the responsibility of the instructor to consider the relationships of the blocks of learning affected. It is often preferable to skip to a completely different part of the syllabus when the conduct of a scheduled lesson is impossible, rather than proceeding to the next block, which may be predicated completely on skills to be developed during the lesson which is being postponed.

Sample Private Pilot (Airplane) Ground Training Syllabus

Each lesson of the sample private pilot (airplane) ground training syllabus which follows sets forth a unit of ground school instruction. Neither the time nor the number of ground school periods to be devoted to each lesson is specified. The sequence in which the sample lessons are listed is not necessarily the most desirable one to use in all training situations and may be varied as desired. Each lesson includes an *objective*, *content*, and *completion standards*.

LESSON NO. 1

OBJECTIVE. To develop the student's knowledge with regard to the definitions and abbreviations in Part 1 and the appropriate regulatory requirements of Part 61 of the Federal Aviation Regulations.

CONTENT.

1. Airplane Registration and Airworthiness Certificates.

2. FAR, Part 1—Definitions and abbreviations important to a private pilot.

3. FAR, Part 61.
   a. Requirements for certificates and ratings.
   b. Duration of pilot certificates.
   c. Medical certificate requirements.
   d. Written tests.
   e. Flight tests.
   f. Pilot logbooks.
   g. Recency of experience (including biennial flight review).
   h. Private pilot privileges and limitations.

COMPLETION STANDARDS. The lesson will have been successfully completed when, by an oral test, the student displays a working knowledge of the appropriate portions of FAR Part 1 and Part 61, and demonstrates the ability to locate and use information in these rules.

LESSON NO. 2

OBJECTIVE. To develop the student's knowledge of the pertinent regulatory requirements of Part 91 of the Federal Aviation Regulations and the accident reporting rules of the National Transportation Safety Board as they relate to private pilot operations.

CONTENT.

1. FAR, Part 91.
   a. General operating and flight rules.
   b. VFR requirements.
   c. IFR requirements (familiarization).
   d. Maintenance, preventive maintenance, and alterations.
   e. Familiarization with Subpart D.

2. National Transportation Safety Board Procedural Regulations, Part 830—Notification and Reporting of Accidents.

COMPLETION STANDARDS. The lesson will have been successfully completed when, by an oral test, the student demonstrates the ability to locate and use information in the appropriate rule as related to private pilot operations.

LESSON NO. 3

OBJECTIVE. To develop the student's knowledge of the Airman's Information Manual as it relates to VFR operations and to develop competence in using the Advisory Circular System.

CONTENT.

1. Airman's Information Manual as it relates to:
   a. Air Navigation Radio Aids.
   b. Airports and Air Navigation Lighting and Marking aids.
   c. Airspace.
   d. Air Traffic Control.
   e. Services Available to Pilots.
   f. Airport Operations.
   g. Emergency Procedures.
   h. Good Operating Practices.
   i. Airport Directory (legend).
   j. Airport Facility Directory (legend).
   k. Graphic Notices and Supplemental Data.
2. FAA Advisory Circular System—Series 00, 20, 60, 70, 90, 150, and 170 (familiarization).

COMPLETION STANDARDS. The lesson will have been successfully completed when, by an oral test and demonstration, the student displays a basic knowledge of appropriate Parts of the Airman's Information Manual and the FAA Advisory Circular System.

LESSON NO. 4

OBJECTIVE. To develop the student's knowledge of the operation of aircraft radios, the use of proper radio phraseology with respect to air traffic control facilities, and to develop competence in the use of the slide rule face of the flight computer and aeronautical charts in planning a VFR cross-country flight.

CONTENT.

1. Radio communications.
   a. Operation of radio communications equipment.
   b. Ground control.
   c. Tower.
   d. ATIS.
   e. Flight service station.
   f. UNICOM.
   g. Technique and phraseology.
2. ATC light signals.
3. Flight computer—slide rule face.
   a. Time.
   b. Speed.
   c. Distance.
   d. Fuel consumption.
4. VFR navigation.
   a. Aeronautical charts.
   b. Measurement of courses.
   c. Pilotage.
   d. Dead reckoning.

COMPLETION STANDARDS. The lesson will have been successfully completed when, by an oral test and demonstration, the student displays a basic knowledge of radio communications, ATC facilities, and aeronautical charts, and is able to use the flight computer to solve elementary VFR navigation problems.

LESSON NO. 5

OBJECTIVE. To further develop the student's knowledge of pilotage, dead reckoning, and radio navigation.

CONTENT.

1. VFR navigation.
   a. Pilotage.
   b. Dead reckoning.
2. Operation of the navigational radio equipment.
   a. VOR.
   b. ADF.
   c. Use of radio aids.
3. Flight computer—wind face.
   a. Determination of wind correction angle and true heading.
   b. Determination of groundspeed.
4. Flight computer—slide rule face.
   a. Review time, speed, and distance problems.
   b. Review fuel consumption problems.

COMPLETION STANDARDS. The lesson will have been successfully completed when, by an oral test and demonstration, the student displays a basic knowledge of VFR navigation and the use of radio aids. The student should be able to solve fundamental and advanced problems on the flight computer.

LESSON NO. 6

OBJECTIVE. To review Lesson 5 and thereby improve the student's competence in VFR navigation procedures; to introduce advanced VFR radio navigational problems; to develop the student's knowledge of emergency procedures with respect to VFR cross-country flying; and to introduce flight planning.

CONTENT.

1. Review of Lesson 5.
2. Use of ADF.
3. Radar.
4. Use of VOR, intercepting and maintaining radials.
5. Emergency procedures.
   a. Diversion to an alternate.
   b. Lost procedures, including the use of radar and DF instructions.
   c. Inflight emergencies, including emergency landings.
6. Transponder.
7. DME.
8. Flight planning.

COMPLETION STANDARDS. The lesson will have been successfully completed when, by an oral test and demonstration, the student displays a working knowledge of advanced VFR radio navigational procedures, cross-country emergency procedures, and can accurately plan and plot a VFR cross-country flight.

LESSON NO. 7

OBJECTIVE. To further develop the student's competence in flight planning and to acquaint the student with the medical factors related to flight and general safety precautions.

CONTENT.

1. Flight planning.
2. Medical factors related to flight.
   a. Fatigue.
   b. Hypoxia.
   c. Hyperventilation.
   d. Alcohol.
   e. Drugs.
   f. Vertigo.
   g. Carbon monoxide.
3. General safety.
   a. Ground handling of aircraft.
   b. Fire—on the ground and in the air.
   c. Collision avoidance precautions.
   d. Wake turbulence avoidance.

COMPLETION STANDARDS. The lesson will have been successfully completed when, by an oral test, the student displays a basic knowledge of flight planning, the medical factors related to flight, and general safety procedures.

LESSON NO. 8

OBJECTIVE. To develop the student's knowledge of the fundamentals of weather, as associated with the operation of aircraft.

CONTENT.

1. Atmospheric layers.
2. Pressure.
3. Circulation.
4. Temperature and moisture.
5. Stability and lapse rate.
6. Turbulence.
7. Clouds.
8. Airmasses.
9. Fronts.
10. Aircraft icing.
11. Thunderstorms.

COMPLETION STANDARDS. The lesson will have been successfully completed when, by an oral test, the student demonstrates a fundamental knowledge of aviation weather.

LESSON NO. 9

OBJECTIVE. To develop the student's ability to interpret and use weather charts, reports, forecasts, and broadcasts; and to develop the student's knowledge of the procedure for obtaining weather briefings.

CONTENT.

1. Review Lesson 8.
2. Weather charts.
   a. Weather depiction charts.
   b. Surface prognostic charts.
3. Aviation weather reports.
   a. Hourly sequence reports.
   b. Special surface reports.
   c. Pilot reports.
   d. Radar reports.
4. Aviation weather broadcasts.
   a. Transcribed weather broadcasts.
   b. Inflight weather advisories.
5. Weather briefings.
6. Review requirements of regulations for VFR flight.
7. Aviation weather forecasts.
   a. Area forecasts.
   b. Terminal forecasts.
   c. Winds aloft forecasts and reports.
   d. Route forecasts.

COMPLETION STANDARDS. The lesson will have been successfully completed when, by an oral test and demonstration, the student displays the ability to interpret and use weather charts, reports, forecasts, and broadcasts, and can obtain and understand a weather briefing.

LESSON NO. 10

OBJECTIVE. To further develop the student's knowledge of aviation weather through a review of Lessons 8 and 9; to develop the student's knowledge of Greenwich time; and to develop the student's ability to recognize various weather conditions.

CONTENT.

1. Review of Lessons 8 and 9.
2. Greenwich time.
3. Weather recognition.

COMPLETION STANDARDS. The lesson will have been successfully completed when, by an oral test, the student displays a working knowledge of Greenwich time, and a knowl-

edge of how critical weather situations can be recognized both from the ground and during flight.

LESSON NO. 11

OBJECTIVE. To develop the student's knowledge of airplane structures, propellers. engines, systems, and the magnetic compass.

CONTENT.

1. Airplane structures.
   a. Construction features.
   b. Flight control systems.
   c. Rigging.
2. Propellers.
   a. Fixed pitch.
   b. Controllable.
3. Reciprocating airplane engines.
   a. Construction features.
   b. Principle of operation—four stroke cycle.
   c. Fuel system, including carburetors and fuel injectors.
   d. Lubrication system.
   e. Ignition system.
   f. Engine instruments.
   g. Operating limitations.
   h. Malfunctions and remedial actions.
4. Airplane hydraulic system.
   a. Principle of hydraulics.
   b. Use of hydraulics in airplanes.
   c. Construction features of a simple airplane hydraulic system.
   d. Retractable landing gear and flaps.
   e. Malfunctions and remedial actions.
5. Airplane electrial system.
   a. Fundamentals of electricity.
   b. Operation of airplane electrical power system units.
   c. Electrically operated flight instruments.
   d. Retractable landing gear.
   e. Flaps.
   f. Fuses and circuit breakers.
   g. Malfunctions and remedial actions.
6. Pitot-static system and instruments.
   a. Airspeed indicator, including markings.
   b. Altimeter.
   c. Vertical-speed indicator.

7. Vacuum system and instruments.
   a. Attitude indicator.
   b. Heading indicator.
   c. Turn and slip indicator.
8. Magnetic compass.
   a. Errors.
   b. Use in flight.

COMPLETION STANDARDS. The lesson will have been successfully completed when, by an oral test, the student displays a basic understanding of airplane structures, engines, systems, and instruments.

LESSON NO. 12

OBJECTIVE. To develop the student's knowledge of basic aerodynamics.

CONTENT.

1. Forces acting on an airplane in flight.
   a. Lift.
   b. Weight.
   c. Thrust.
   d. Drag.
2. Airfoils.
   a. Angle of incidence.
   b. Angle of attack.
   c. Bernoulli's Principle.
   d. Newton's Laws.
3. Factors affecting lift and drag.
   a. Wing area.
   b. Airfoil shape.
   c. Angle of attack.
   d. Airspeed.
   e. Air density.
4. Function of the controls.
   a. Axes of rotation—longitudinal, lateral, and vertical.
   b. Primary controls—ailerons, elevators, and rudder.
   c. Secondary controls—trim tabs.
   d. Flaps and other high-lift devices.
5. Stability.
   a. Static stability.
   b. Dynamic stability.
6. Loads and load factors.
   a. Effect of bank angle on stall speed.
   b. Effect of turbulence on load factor.
   c. Effect of speed on load factor.
   d. Effect of load factor on stall speed.

7. Torque.
   a. Gyroscopic reaction.
   b. Asymmetrical loading of propeller ("P" factor).
   c. Slipstream rotation.
   d. Torque reaction.

COMPLETION STANDARDS. The lesson will have been successfully completed when, by an oral test, the student displays an understanding of basic aerodynamics.

LESSON NO. 13

OBJECTIVE. To develop the student's knowledge of the fundamental flight maneuvers.

CONTENT.

1. Straight-and-level flight.
   a. Pitch, bank, and yaw.
   b. Trim.
   c. Integrated use of outside references and flight instruments.
2. Level turns.
   a. Forces acting in a turn.
   b. Aileron drag and coordination.
   c. Speed of roll.
   d. Slips and skids.
   e. Integrated use of outside references and flight instruments.
3. Climbs and climbing turns.
   a. Best rate-of-climb airspeed.
   b. Best angle-of-climb airspeed.
   c. Torque and coordination.
   d. Trim.
4. Glides and gliding turns.
   a. Effect of high lift devices.
   b. Most efficient glide speed.
   c. Coordination.
   d. Trim.
5. Descents with power.
   a. Power settings and airspeeds.
   b. Trim.

COMPLETION STANDARDS. The lesson will have been successfully completed when, by an oral test, the student displays a basic understanding of the fundamental flight maneuvers.

LESSON NO. 14

OBJECTIVE. To develop the student's ability to properly use Pilot's Operating Handbooks and FAA Approved Airplane Flight Manuals; to develop the student's ability to perform basic weight and balance computations; and to develop the student's understanding of fundamental flight training maneuvers.

CONTENT.

1. Use of data in Pilot's Operating Handbook or FAA Approved Airplane Flight Manual.
   a. Takeoff and landing distances.
   b. Fuel consumption and related charts.
   c. Maximum range power settings.
   d. Maximum endurance power settings.
2. Weight and balance.
   a. Terms and definitions.
   b. Effects of adverse balance.
   c. Finding loaded weight.
   d. Finding center of gravity—when weight is added or removed—when weight is shifted.
3. Maneuvering at minimum controllable airspeed.
4. Stalls.
   a. Theory of stalls.
   b. Imminent stalls—power-on and power-off.
   c. Full stalls—power-on and power-off.
5. Flight maneuvering by reference to ground objects.
   a. "S" turns across a road.
   b. Rectangular course.
   c. Eights along a road.
   d. Eights across a road.
   e. Turns around a point.
   f. Eights around pylons.

COMPLETION STANDARDS. The lesson will have been successfully completed when, by an oral test and demonstration, the student displays a basic knowledge of Pilot's Operating Handbooks and FAA Approved Airplane Flight Manuals; when the student is able to perform basic weight and balance computations; and when the student has a working knowledge of the performance of fundamental flight training maneuvers.

LESSON NO. 15

OBJECTIVE. To develop the student's knowledge of fundamental flight maneuvers and attitude instrument flying.

CONTENT.

1. Review Lesson 14.
2. Takeoffs and landings.
   a. Normal and crosswind takeoffs and landings.
   b. Soft field takeoffs and landings.
   c. Short field takeoffs and landings.
   d. Go-arounds or rejected landings.
3. Introduction to attitude instrument flying. Maneuvering by reference to flight instruments—pitch, power, bank, and trim control in the performance of basic flight maneuvers.
   a. Straight-and-level flight.
   b. Turns.
   c. Climbs.
   d. Descents.
   e. Recovery from unusual attitudes.

COMPLETION STANDARDS. The lesson will have been successfully completed when, by an oral test, the student displays a basic knowledge of the performance of takeoffs and landings under various conditions, and an understanding of the performance of basic maneuvers by reference to flight instruments.

LESSON NO. 16

OBJECTIVE. To develop the student's knowledge of the fundamentals of night flying.

CONTENT.

1. Night flying—general.
   a. Requirements of regulations.
   b. Preparation.
   c. Equipment.
   d. Night vision.
   e. Airport lighting.
   f. Orientation.
   g. VFR navigation.
   h. Weather factors.
2. Partial or complete power failure.
   a. Sample situations.
   b. Recommended courses of action.

3. Systems and equipment malfunctions.

   a. Sample situations.

   b. Recommended courses of action.

COMPLETION STANDARDS. The lesson will have been successfully completed when, by an oral test, the student displays a working knowledge of the fundamentals of night flying.

Sample Private Pilot (Airplane) Flight Training Syllabus

The sample private pilot (airplane) flight training syllabus which appears on the following pages is illustrative of content and organization. It is not necessarily the most desirable syllabus to use in all training situations; however, instruction in the procedures and maneuvers listed here are considered to be most effective in the development of competence in the *pilot operations* required on the private pilot (airplane) flight test.

It should be noted that each lesson prescribes a unit of flight training, not a specified period of instruction or flight time. Each lesson also includes an *objective, content,* and *completion standards.* The student must have at least the instruction required by the Federal Aviation Regulations before the first solo and the first solo cross-country flights, and the flight experience prescribed for a private pilot certificate at the completion of the syllabus.

The notation "(VR and IR)" is used to indicate maneuvers which should be performed by both visual references and instrument references during the conduct of integrated flight instruction.

Throughout the student's flight training, the instructor should emphasize collision and wake turbulence avoidance procedures.

LESSON NO. 1—DUAL

OBJECTIVE. To familiarize the student with the training airplane, its servicing, its operating characteristics, cabin controls, instruments, systems, preflight procedures, use of checklists, and safety precautions to be followed; to acquaint the student with the sensations of flight and the effect and use of controls; and to familiarize the student with the local flying area and airport.

CONTENT.

1. Preflight discussion.

2. Introduction.

   a. Airplane servicing.

   b. Purpose of preflight checks.

   c. Visual inspection.

   d. Importance of using a checklist.

   e. Engine starting procedure.

   f. Radio communications procedures.

   g. Taxiing.

   h. Pretakeoff checklist.

   i. Takeoff.

   j. Traffic pattern departure, climb-out, and level-off.

   k. Effect and use of controls (VR and IR).

   l. Straight-and-level flight (VR and IR).

   m. Medium bank turns (VR and IR).

   n. Local flying area familiarization.

   o. Collision avoidance.

   p. Wake turbulence avoidance.

   q. Traffic pattern entry, approach, landing, and parking.

   r. Ground safety.

3. Postflight critique and preview of next lesson.

COMPLETION STANDARDS. The lesson will have been successfully completed when the student understands how to service the airplane, the use of a checklist for the visual inspection, starting procedure, and engine run-up; displays a knowledge of the effect and use of controls; and has a reasonable familiarity with the local flying area and airport.

LESSON NO. 2—DUAL

OBJECTIVE. To develop the student's skill in the performance of the four basic flight maneuvers (climbs, descents, turns, and straight-and-level flight).

CONTENT.

1. Preflight discussion.

2. Review.

   a. Airplane servicing.

   b. Visual inspection.

   c. Engine starting procedure.

   d. Radio communications procedures.

e. Taxiing.

f. Pretakeoff checklist.

g. Takeoff.

h. Traffic pattern departure.

i. Straight-and-level flight (VR and IR).

j. Medium bank turns (VR and IR).

k. Traffic pattern entry, approach, landing, and parking.

3. Introduction.

a. Climbs and climbing turns (VR and IR).

b. Glides and gliding turns (VR and IR).

c. Torque effect.

d. Level-off from climbs and glides (VR and IR).

4. Postflight critique and preview of next lesson.

COMPLETION STANDARDS. The lesson will have been successfully completed when the student can perform, with minimum assistance from the instructor, climbs, straight-and-level flight, turns, and glides. During straight-and-level flight the student should, with minimum instructor assistance, be able to maintain altitude within ±100 feet, airspeed within ±10 knots, and heading within ±10° of that assigned.

LESSON NO. 3—DUAL

OBJECTIVE. To review lessons One and Two; to develop the student's proficiency in the performance of the basic flight maneuvers; and to introduce maneuvering at minimum controllable airspeed and power-off stalls.

CONTENT.

1. Preflight discussion.

2. Review.

a. Use of checklist.

b. Engine starting procedure.

c. Radio communications procedures.

d. Takeoff.

e. Traffic pattern departure.

f. Climbs and climbing turns (VR and IR).

g. Straight-and-level flight (VR and IR).

h. Medium bank turns (VR and IR).

i. Glides and gliding turns (VR and IR).

j. Level-off procedures (VR and IR).

k. Traffic pattern and landing.

3. Introduction.

a. Maneuvering at minimum controllable airspeed (VR and IR).

b. Power-off stalls (imminent and full) (VR and IR).

c. Descents and descending turns, with power (VR and IR).

4. Postflight critique and preview of next lesson.

COMPLETION STANDARDS. The lesson will have been successfully completed when the student can display reasonable proficiency in the performance of the four basic flight maneuvers, and perform with minimum assistance, flight at minimum controllable airspeed. During this and subsequent flight lessons, the student should be able to perform the visual inspection, starting procedure, radio communications, taxiing, pretakeoff check, parking, and shut-down procedure without assistance. During climbs, level flight, turns, glides, and maneuvering at minimum controllable airspeed the student should, with minimum instructor assistance, be able to maintain assigned airspeed within ±10 knots. The student should also, with minimum instructor assistance, be able to maintain assigned altitude within ±100 feet and assigned heading within ±10°.

LESSON NO. 4—DUAL

OBJECTIVE. To review previous lessons, thereby increasing the student's competence in the performance of fundamental flight maneuvers; and to introduce power-on stalls, rectangular course, S-turns across a road, eights along a road, and elementary emergency landings.

CONTENT.

1. Preflight discussion.

2. Review.

a. Takeoff.

b. Traffic pattern departure.

c. Climbs and climbing turns (VR and IR).

d. Straight-and-level flight and medium bank turns (VR and IR).

e. Maneuvering at minimum controllable airspeed (VR and IR).

f. Power-off stalls (imminent and full) (VR and IR).

g. Glides and gliding turns (VR and IR).

h. Descents and descending turns, with power (VR and IR).

i. Level-off procedures (VR and IR).

j. Traffic pattern and landing.

3. Introduction.

a. Power-on stalls (imminent and full) (VR and IR).

b. Rectangular course.

c. S-turns across a road.

d. Eights along a road and eights across a road.

e. Elementary emergency landings.

4. Postflight critique and preview of next lesson.

COMPLETION STANDARDS. The lesson will have been successfully completed when the student is competent to perform, with minimum instructor assistance, the procedures and maneuvers given during previous lessons. The student should achieve the ability to recognize stall indications and make safe prompt recoveries. The student should maintain assigned airspeed within ±10 knots, assigned altitude within ±100 feet, and assigned heading within ±10°, and display a basic knowledge of elementary emergency landings.

LESSON NO. 5—DUAL

OBJECTIVE. To review previous lessons, with emphasis on maneuvering by reference to ground objects. To develop the student's ability to perform climbs at best rate and best angle, crosswind takeoffs and landings; and to introduce emergency procedures, changes of airspeed and configuration, turns around a point, and eights around pylons.

CONTENT.

1. Preflight discussion.

2. Review.

a. Takeoff.

b. Climbs and climbing turns (VR and IR).

c. Maneuvering at minimum controllable airspeed (VR and IR).

d. Power-off and power-on stalls (imminent and full).

e. Rectangular course.

f. S-turns across a road.

g. Eights along a road.

h. Elementary emergency landings.

i. Traffic pattern and landing.

3. Introduction.

a. Crosswind takeoffs and landings.

b. Climb at best rate (VR and IR).

c. Climb at best angle (VR and IR).

d. Emergency procedures.

e. Change of airspeed and configuration (VR and IR).

f. Turns around a point.

g. Eights around pylons.

4. Postflight critique and preview of next lesson.

COMPLETION STANDARDS. The lesson will have been successfully completed when the student can recognize imminent and full stalls and make prompt effective recoveries, perform ground reference maneuvers with reasonably accurate wind drift corrections and good coordination, and has a proper concept of crosswind technique during takeoffs and landings. The student should have a working knowledge of emergency procedures, and be able to perform them with minimum assistance. During ground reference maneuvers, the student should maintain airspeed within ±10 knots, altitude within ±100 feet, and heading within ±10° of that desired.

LESSON NO. 6—DUAL

OBJECTIVE. To review previous lessons; to develop the student's ability to perform slips, accelerated stalls, cross-control stalls, and advanced emergency landings; to improve the student's proficiency in normal and crosswind takeoffs and landings; and to introduce balked takeoffs and go-arounds (rejected landings).

CONTENT.

1. Preflight discussion.

2. Review.

a. Normal and crosswind takeoffs.

b. Climbs at best rate and best angle (VR and IR).

c. Power-off stalls (imminent and full) (VR and IR).

d. Power-on stalls (imminent and full) (VR and IR).

e. Change of airspeed and configuration (VR and IR).

f. Turns around a point.

g. Eights around pylons.

h. Emergency procedures.

i. Normal and crosswind landings.

3. Introduction.

a. Balked takeoffs.

b. Accelerated stalls.

c. Cross-control stalls.

d. 180° and 360° gliding approaches.

e. Advanced emergency landings.

f. Side slips and forward slips.

g. Go-arounds (rejected landings).

4. Postflight critique and preview of next lesson.

COMPLETION STANDARDS. The lesson will have been successfully completed when the student can perform stall recoveries smoothly and promptly with a minimum loss of altitude, is able to make unassisted normal and crosswind takeoffs and landings, and can plan and fly emergency landing patterns with accuracy and consistency. The student should be able to execute balked takeoffs and go-arounds (rejected landings) without assistance, and should maintain assigned airspeed within ±10 knots, assigned altitude within ±100 feet, and assigned heading within ±10°.

LESSON NO. 7—DUAL

OBJECTIVE. To review previous lessons. To further develop the student's competence in takeoffs, traffic patterns, and landings through concentrated practice. To develop the student's ability to use slips during landing approaches and improve the ability to perform go-arounds (rejected landings).

CONTENT.

1. Preflight discussion.

2. Review.

a. Normal and crosswind takeoffs.

b. Normal and crosswind landings (touch-and-go and full-stop).

c. Forward slips.

d. Go-arounds (rejected landings).

e. 180° and 360° gliding approaches.

f. Advanced emergency landings.

g. Emergency procedures.

3. Postflight critique and preview of next lesson.

COMPLETION STANDARDS. The lesson will have been successfully completed when the student can fly accurate traffic patterns and make unassisted normal and crosswind takeoffs and landings. The student should be competent in the go-around (rejected landing) procedure. During traffic patterns, the student should maintain desired airspeed within ±10 knots, desired altitude within ±100 feet, and desired heading within ±10°.

LESSON NO. 8—DUAL

OBJECTIVE. To review power-off stalls, maneuvering at minimum controllable airspeed, and advanced emergency landings. To continue to develop the student's competence in takeoffs, traffic patterns, and landings, and to improve the ability to recover from poor approaches and landings.

CONTENT

1. Preflight discussion.

2. Review.

a. Normal and crosswind takeoffs.

b. Power-off stalls (imminent and full) (VR and IR).

c. Maneuvering at minimum controllable airspeed (VR and IR).

d. Advanced emergency landings.

e. Normal and crosswind landings (touch-and-go and full-stop).

f. Go-arounds (rejected landings).

g. Recovery from poor approaches and landings.

3. Postflight critique and preview of next lesson.

COMPLETION STANDARDS. The lesson will have been successfully completed when the student can demonstrate a degree of proficiency in normal and crosswind takeoffs and landings and traffic patterns, which is considered safe for solo. The student should display sound judgment and proper techniques in recoveries from poor approaches and landings. During traffic patterns, the student should maintain desired airspeed within ±10 knots, desired altitude within ±100 feet, and desired heading within ±10°.

LESSON NO. 9—DUAL AND SOLO

OBJECTIVE. To develop the student's competence to a level which will allow the safe accomplishment of the first supervised solo in the traffic pattern.

CONTENT.

1. Preflight discussion.
2. Review.
   a. Normal and crosswind takeoffs.
   b. Normal and crosswind landings (full-stop).
   c. Go-arounds (rejected landings).
   d. Recovery from poor approaches and landings.
   e. Elementary emergency landings.
3. Introduction—first supervised solo in the traffic pattern. Three takeoffs and three full-stop landings should be performed.
4. Postflight critique and preview of next lesson.

COMPLETION STANDARDS. The lesson will have been successfully completed when the student safely accomplishes the first supervised solo in the traffic pattern.

LESSON NO. 10—DUAL AND SOLO

OBJECTIVE. To review previous lessons and to accomplish the student's second supervised solo in the traffic pattern.

CONTENT.

1. Preflight discussion.
2. Review.
   a. Takeoff and traffic departure.
   b. Climbs and climbing turns (VR and IR).
   c. Maneuvering at minimum controllable airspeed (VR and IR).
   d. Power-off stalls (imminent and full) (VR and IR).
   e. Advanced emergency landings.
   f. Traffic patterns, approaches and landings.
   g. Recovery from poor approaches and landings.
3. Introduction—second supervised solo in the traffic pattern. Three takeoffs, two touch-

and-go, and one full-stop landing should be performed.
4. Postflight critique and preview of next lesson.

COMPLETION STANDARDS. The lesson will have been successfully completed when the student demonstrates solo competence in maneuvers performed and safely accomplishes the second supervised solo in the traffic pattern.

LESSON NO. 11—DUAL AND SOLO

OBJECTIVE. To review presolo maneuvers with higher levels of proficiency required. To introduce short and soft field takeoffs, and maximum climbs; and to accomplish the student's third supervised solo in the traffic pattern.

CONTENT.

1. Preflight discussion.
2. Review.
   a. Selected presolo maneuvers (VR and IR).
   b. Takeoffs, traffic patterns, and landings.
   c. Balked takeoff.
   d. Go-around (rejected landing).
   e. Recovery from poor approach and landing.
3. Introduction.
   a. Short field takeoffs and maximum climbs.
   b. Soft field takeoffs.
   c. Third supervised solo in the traffic pattern. At least three takeoffs and landings should be performed.
4. Postflight critique and preview of next lesson.

COMPLETION STANDARDS. The lesson will have been successfully completed when the student demonstrates solo competence in the selected presolo maneuvers performed and safely accomplishes the third supervised solo in the traffic pattern. The student should be able to perform short field takeoffs, soft field takeoffs, and maximum climbs without instructor assistance.

LESSON NO. 12—DUAL

OBJECTIVE. To refamiliarize the student with the local practice area and to improve proficiency in the presolo maneuvers in preparation for local area solo practice flights. To develop the student's ability to obtain radar and DF heading instructions and to become oriented in relation to a VOR, and to "home" to a nondirectional beacon using ADF. To introduce wheel landings (tail wheel airplanes).

CONTENT.

1. Preflight discussion.
2. Review.
   a. Practice area orientation.
   b. Power-off stalls (imminent and full) (VR and IR).
   c. Power-on stalls (imminent and full) (VR and IR).
   d. Maneuvering at minimum controllable airspeed (VR and IR).
   e. Turns around a point.
   f. Eights around pylons.
   g. Crosswind takeoffs and landings.
   h. 180° and 360° gliding approaches.
   i. Advanced emergency landings.
   j. Emergency procedures.
3. Introduction.
   a. Use of radar and DF heading instructions (VR and IR).
   b. VOR orientation (VR and IR).
   c. ADF "homing" (VR and IR).
   d. Wheel landings (tailwheel airplanes).
4. Postflight critique and preview of next lesson.

COMPLETION STANDARDS. The lesson will have been successfully completed when the student demonstrates an improved performance of the presolo maneuvers, is able to determine position in the local practice area by pilotage, VOR, or ADF; and can safely perform assigned maneuvers. The student should be competent in obtaining radar and DF heading instructions and in the performance of simulated emergency landings and emergency procedures.

LESSON NO. 13—SOLO

OBJECTIVE. To develop the student's confidence and proficiency through solo practice of assigned maneuvers.

CONTENT.

1. Preflight discussion.
2. Review.
   a. Normal and/or crosswind takeoffs and landings.
   b. Power-off stalls (imminent and full).
   c. Power-on stalls (imminent and full).
   d. Maneuvering at minimum controllable airspeed.
   e. Other maneuvers specified by the instructor during the preflight discussion.
3. Postflight critique and preview of next lesson.

COMPLETION STANDARDS. The lesson will have been successfully completed when the student has accomplished the solo review and practiced the basic and precision flight maneuvers, in addition to those specified by the instructor. The student should gain confidence and improve flying technique as a result of the solo practice period.

LESSON NO. 14—DUAL

OBJECTIVE. To improve the student's proficiency in previously covered procedures and maneuvers and to review advanced emergency landings, emergency procedures, and orientation by means of VOR and/or ADF.

CONTENT.

1. Preflight discussion.
2. Review.
   a. Normal and/or crosswind takeoffs and landings.
   b. Power-off stalls (imminent and full) (VR and IR).
   c. Power-on stalls (imminent and full) (VR and IR).
   d. Maneuvering at minimum controllable airspeed (VR and IR).
   e. Accelerated stalls.
   f. Eights around pylons.
   g. Short field and soft field takeoffs and landings.
   h. Advanced emergency landings.
   i. Emergency procedures.
   j. Orientation by means of VOR and/or ADF.

3. Postflight critique and preview of next lesson.

COMPLETION STANDARDS. The lesson will have been successfully completed when the student demonstrates an increased proficiency in previously covered procedures and maneuvers. The student should be able to maintain airspeed within ±10 knots, altitude within ±100 feet, and heading within ±10° of that desired.

LESSON NO. 15—SOLO

OBJECTIVE. To further develop the student's confidence and proficiency through solo practice of assigned maneuvers.

CONTENT.

1. Preflight discussion.
2. Review.
   a. Normal and/or crosswind takeoffs and landings.
   b. Turns around a point.
   c. Eights around pylons.
   d. Other maneuvers specified by the instructor during the preflight discussion.
3. Postflight critique and preview of next lesson.

COMPLETION STANDARDS. The lesson will have been successfully completed when the student has accomplished the solo review and thereby increased proficiency and confidence.

LESSON NO. 16—DUAL

OBJECTIVE. To develop the student's ability to plan, plot, and fly a 2-hour day cross-country flight with landings at two unfamiliar airports; to develop the student's proficiency in navigating by means of pilotage, dead reckoning, VOR, and/or ADF; and to develop the ability to take proper action in emergency situations.

CONTENT.

1. Preflight discussion.
   a. Planning flight, including weather check.
   b. Plotting course.
   c. Preparing log.
   d. Filing and closing VFR flight plan.

2. Inroduction.
   a. Filing VFR flight plan.
   b. Pilotage.
   c. Dead reckoning.
   d. Tracking VOR radial and/or homing by ADF (VR and IR).
   e. Departure, en route, and arrival radio communications.
   f. Simulated diversion to an alternate airport.
   g. Unfamiliar airport procedures.
   h. Emergencies, including DF and radar heading instructions (VR and IR).
   i. Closing VFR flight plan.
3. Postflight critique and preview of next lesson.

COMPLETION STANDARDS. The lesson will have been successfully completed when, with instructor assistance, the student is able to perform the cross-country preflight planning, fly the planned course making necessary off-course corrections, and can make appropriate radio communications. The student should be competent in navigating by means of pilotage, dead reckoning, VOR, and/or ADF, and when so instructed, is able to accurately plan and fly a diversion to an alternate airport.

LESSON   NO.   17—DUAL

OBJECTIVE. To improve the student's proficiency in cross-country operations through the planning, plotting, and flying of a second dual 2-hour day cross-country flight, with landings at two unfamiliar airports. To improve the student's competence in navigating by means of pilotage, dead reckoning, VOR, and ADF; and to further develop the ability to take proper action in emergency situations.

CONTENT.

1. Preflight discussion.
   a. Planning flight, including weather check.
   b. Plotting course.
   c. Preparing log.
   d. Filing and closing VFR flight plan.
2. Review.
   a. Filing VFR flight plan.
   b. Pilotage and dead reckoning.

c. Radio navigation (VOR and/or ADF) (VR and IR).

d. Departure, en route, and arrival radio communications.

e. Simulated diversion to an alternate airport.

f. Unfamiliar airport procedures.

g. Emergencies, including DF and radar heading instructions (VR and IR).

h. Closing VFR flight plan.

3. Postflight critique and preview of next lesson.

COMPLETION STANDARDS. The lesson will have been successfully completed when the student, with minimum instructor assistance, is able to plan, plot, and fly the planned course. Estimated times of arrival should be accurate with an apparent error of not more than 10 minutes. Any off-course corrections should be accomplished accurately and promptly. The student should be able to give the instructor an accurate position report at any time without hesitation. When given a "simulated lost" situation, the student should be able to initiate and follow an apppropriate "lost procedure."

LESSON NO. 18—SOLO

OBJECTIVE. To develop the student's ability to plan, plot, and fly a 3-hour solo day cross-country flight, with landings at two unfamiliar airports, thereby improving proficiency and confidence in the conduct of future solo cross-country flights. To improve the student's proficiency in navigating by means of pilotage, dead reckoning, VOR, and/or ADF; and to increase the ability to cope with new or unexpected flight situations.

CONTENT.

1. Preflight discussion.
   a. Planning flight, including weather check.
   b. Plotting course.
   c. Preparing log.
   d. Filing and closing VFR flight plan.
   e. Procedure at unfamiliar airports.
   f. Emergencies.

2. Review.
   a. Filing VFR flight plan.

b. Pilotage.

c. Dead reckoning.

d. Radio navigation (VOR and/or ADF).

e. Departure, en route, and arrival radio communications.

f. Unfamiliar airport procedures.

g. Closing VFR flight plan.

3. Postflight critique and preview of next lesson.

COMPLETION STANDARDS. The lesson will have been successfully completed when the student is able to plan, plot, and fly the 3-hour cross-country flight as assigned by the instructor. The instructor should determine how well the flight was conducted through oral questioning.

LESSON NO. 19—DUAL AND SOLO

OBJECTIVE. To develop the student's ability to make solo night flights in the local practice area and airport traffic pattern. To familiarize the student with such aspects of night operations as: night vision, night orientation, judgment of distance, use of cockpit lights, position lights, landing lights, and night emergency procedures.

CONTENT.

1. Preflight discussion.
   a. Night vision and vertigo.
   b. Orientation in local area.
   c. Judgment of distance.
   d. Aircraft lights.
   e. Airport lights.
   f. Taxi technique.
   g. Takeoff and landing technique.
   h. Collision avoidance.
   i. Unusual attitude recovery.
   j. Emergencies.

2. Introduction.
   a. Night visual inspection.
   b. Use of cockpit lights.
   c. Taxi techniques.
   d. Takeoff and traffic departure.
   e. Area orientation.
   f. Interpretation of aircraft and airport lights.

g. Recovery from unusual attitudes (VR and IR).

h. Radio communications.

i. Traffic entry.

j. Power approaches and full-stop landings.

k. Use of landing lights.

l. Simulated electrical failure to include at least one black-out landing.

3. Postflight critique and preview of next lesson.

COMPLETION STANDARDS. The lesson will have been successfully completed when the student displays the ability to maintain orientation in the local flying area and traffic pattern, can accurately interpret aircraft and runway lights, and can competently fly the traffic pattern and perform takeoffs and landings. The student should display, through oral quizzing and demonstrations, competence in performing night emergency procedures. At least five takeoffs and landings should be accomplished.

LESSON NO. 20—DUAL

OBJECTIVE. To develop the student's ability to plan, plot, and fly a 1½-hour night cross-country flight around a triangular course with at least one landing at an unfamiliar airport. To develop the student's competence in navigating at night by means of pilotage, dead reckoning, and VOR or ADF; and to develop the student's ability to take proper action in night emergency situations.

CONTENT.

1. Preflight discussion.

   a. Planning 1½-hour night cross-country flight, including weather check.

   b. Plotting course.

   c. Preparing log.

   d. Filing and closing VFR flight plan.

2. Introduction.

   a. Filing VFR flight plan.

   b. Proper use of cockpit lights and flashlight for chart reading.

   c. Pilotage—factors peculiar to night flying.

   d. Dead reckoning.

e. Tracking VOR radial and/or homing by ADF.

f. Departure, en route, and arrival radio communications.

g. Simulated diversion to an alternate airport.

h. Emergencies, including simulated failure of electrical system, also DF and radar heading instructions.

i. Closing VFR flight plan.

3. Postflight critique and preview of next lesson.

COMPLETION STANDARDS. The lesson will have been successfully completed when, with minimum assistance from the instructor, the student is able to perform the night cross-country preflight planning, fly the planned course making necessary off-course corrections, and can make appropriate radio communications. The student should be competent in navigating by means of pilotage, dead reckoning, and VOR or ADF. The student should have a thorough knowledge of night emergency procedures.

LESSON NO. 21—SOLO

OBJECTIVE. To further develop the student's competence in cross-country operations through the planning, plotting, and flying of a second solo 3-hour day cross-country flight with landings at two unfamiliar airports. To improve the student's proficiency in navigating by means of pilotage, dead reckoning, VOR, and/or ADF; and to further increase the student's confidence and ability to properly handle unexpected flight situations.

CONTENT.

1. Preflight discussion.

   a. Planning flight, including weather check.

   b. Plotting course.

   c. Preparing log.

   d. Filing and closing VFR flight plan.

   e. Procedure at unfamiliar airports.

   f. Emergencies.

2. Review.

   a. Filing VFR flight plan.

   b. Pilotage and dead reckoning.

   c. Radio navigation (VOR and/or ADF).

d. Departure, en route, and arrival radio procedures.

e. Unfamiliar airport procedures.

f. Closing VFR flight plan.

3. Postflight critique and preview of next lesson.

COMPLETION STANDARDS. The lesson will have been successfully completed when the student is able to plan, plot, and fly the second 3-hour day cross-country flight as assigned by the instructor. The instructor should determine how well the flight was conducted through oral questioning.

LESSON NO. 22—SOLO

OBJECTIVE. To further develop the student's competence in cross-country operations through the planning, plotting, and flying of a solo 4-hour day cross-country flight, with landings at three unfamiliar airports, each of which is more than 100 nautical miles from the other airports.

CONTENT.

1. Preflight discussion.

a. Planning flight, including weather check.

b. Plotting course.

c. Preparing log.

d. Filing and closing VFR flight plan.

e. Procedure at unfamiliar airports.

f. Emergencies.

2. Review.

a. Filing VFR flight plan.

b. Pilotage and dead reckoning.

c. Radio navigation (VOR and/or ADF).

d. Departure, en route, and arrival radio communications.

e. Unfamiliar airport procedures.

f. Closing VFR flight plan.

3. Postflight critique and preview of next lesson.

COMPLETION STANDARDS. The lesson will have been successfully completed when the student is able to plan, plot, and fly the 4-hour day cross-country flight as assigned by the instructor. The instructor should determine how well the flight was conducted through oral questioning.

LESSON NO. 23—DUAL

OBJECTIVE. To develop precision in the student's performance of procedures and maneuvers covered previously with emphasis directed to stalls.

CONTENT.

1. Preflight discussion.

2. Review.

a. Power-off stalls (imminent and full) (VR and IR).

b. Power-on stalls (imminent and full) (VR and IR).

c. Maneuvering at minimum controllable airspeed (VR and IR).

d. 180° and 360° gliding approaches.

e. Advanced emergency landings.

f. Slips.

g. Crosswind takeoffs and landings.

h. Short field and soft field takeoffs and landings.

i. Emergency procedures.

3. Introduction of ASR approaches.

4. Postflight critique and preview of next lesson.

COMPLETION STANDARDS. The lesson will have been successfully completed when the student demonstrates improved performance in the various maneuvers given. The student should be able to make ASR approaches with minimum instructor assistance.

LESSON NO. 24—SOLO

OBJECTIVE. To further develop the student's competence through solo practice of assigned maneuvers. Emphasis will be directed to stalls.

CONTENT.

1. Preflight discussion.

2. Review.

a. Power-on and power-off stalls (imminent and full).

b. Maneuvering at minimum controllable airspeed.

c. Short field and soft field takeoffs and landings.

d. Other maneuvers assigned by the instructor during preflight discussion.

3. Postflight critique and preview of next lesson.

COMPLETION STANDARDS. The lesson will have been successfully completed when the student has accomplished the solo review and practiced the basic and precision flight maneuvers in addition to those specified by the instructor. The student should gain confidence and improve flying technique as a result of the solo practice period.

LESSON NO. 25—DUAL

OBJECTIVE. To develop improved performance and precision in the procedures and maneuvers covered previously with emphasis directed to ground track maneuvers.

CONTENT.

1. Preflight discussion.

2. Review.

a. Maneuvering at minimum controllable airspeed.

b. Turns around a point.

c. Eights around pylons.

d. 180° and 360° gliding approaches.

e. Advanced emergency landings.

f. Slips.

g. Crosswind takeoffs and landings.

h. Wheel landings (tail wheel airplane).

i. ASR approach.

3. Postflight critique and preview of next lesson.

COMPLETION STANDARDS. The lesson will have been successfully completed when the student demonstrates improved performance in the maneuvers given.

LESSON NO. 26—SOLO

OBJECTIVE. To further develop the student's competence through solo practice of assigned maneuvers. Emphasis will be directed to ground track maneuvers.

CONTENT.

1. Preflight discussion.

2. Review.

a. Turns around a point.

b. Eights around pylons.

c. Short and soft field takeoffs and landings.

d. Wheel landings (tail wheel airplanes).

e. Other maneuvers assigned by the instructor during the preflight discussion.

3. Postflight critique and preview of next lesson.

COMPLETION STANDARDS. The lesson will have been successfully completed when the student has accomplished the solo review. The student should gain proficiency in the ground track and other maneuvers assigned by the instructor.

LESSON NO. 27—SOLO

OBJECTIVE. To improve the student's proficiency in the pilot operations required on the private pilot (airplane) flight check.

CONTENT.

1. Preflight discussion.

2. Review.

a. Ground track maneuvers.

b. Power-on and power-off stalls (imminent and full).

c. Maneuvering at minimum controllable airspeed.

d. Crosswind takeoffs and landings.

e. Other maneuvers assigned by the instructor during the preflight discussion.

3. Postflight critique and preview of next lesson.

COMPLETION STANDARDS. The lesson will have been successfully completed when the student has gained proficiency in the procedures and maneuvers assigned by the instructor.

LESSON NO. 28—DUAL

OBJECTIVE. To evaluate the student's performance of the procedures and maneuvers necessary to conduct flight operations as a private pilot.

CONTENT.

1. Preflight discussion.

2. Review.
   a. Power-on and power-off stalls (imminent and full).
   b. Maneuvering at minimum controllable airspeed.
   c. Ground track maneuvers.
   d. 180° and 360° gliding approaches.
   e. Advanced emergency landings.
   f. Short field and soft field takeoffs and landings.
   g. Crosswind takeoffs and landings.
   h. Straight-and-level flight, turns, climbs, descents, and recovery from unusual attitudes by reference to flight instruments.
   i. Tracking VOR radial and homing by ADF (VR and IR).
   j. Use of radar and DF heading instructions (VR and IR).
   k. ASR approach (VR and IR).
   l. Emergency operations.

COMPLETION STANDARDS. The lesson will have been successfully completed when the student satisfactorily performs the procedures and maneuvers selected to show competence in the pilot operations listed in the Private Pilot (Airplane) Flight Test Guide.

NOTE: Before signing a student's flight-test recommendation, it is the responsibility of the flight instructor to see that all the aeronautical experience requirements for a private pilot certificate are met.

LESSON PLAN

A lesson plan is an organized outline or "blueprint" for a single instructional period and should be prepared in written form for each ground school and flight period, regardless of the instructor's experience. A lesson plan should be developed to show specific knowledge and/or skills to be taught. It is a necessary guide for the instructor in that it tells *what to do*, in *what order to do it*, and *what procedure to use* in teaching the material of the lesson.

A so-called "mental outline" of a lesson is *not* a lesson plan. A lesson plan must be put into writing. Another instructor should be able to take the lesson plan and know what to do in conducting the same period of instruction. When placed in writing, the lesson plan can be analyzed from the standpoint of adequacy and completeness.

Purpose of the Lesson Plan

Lesson plans are designed to assure that each student receives the best possible instruction under the existing conditions. Lesson plans help instructors keep a constant check on their own activity, as well as that of their students. The development of lesson plans by instructors signifies, in effect, that they have taught the lessons to themselves prior to attempting to teach the lessons to students. An adequate lesson plan, when properly used, should:

1. Assure a wise selection of material and the elimination of unimportant details.
2. Make certain that due consideration is given to each part of the lesson.
3. Aid the instructor in presenting the material in a suitable sequence for efficient learning.
4. Provide an outline of the teaching procedure to be used.
5. Serve as a means of relating the lesson to the objectives of the course of training.
6. Give the inexperienced instructor confidence.
7. Promote uniformity of instruction regardless of the instructor or the date on which the lesson is given.

Characteristics of a Well-Planned Lesson

1. *Unity.* Each lesson should be a unified segment of instruction. A lesson is concerned with certain limited objectives which are stated in terms of desired student learning outcomes. All teaching procedures and materials should be selected to attain these objectives.
2. *Content.* Each lesson should contain new material. However, the new facts, principles, procedures, or skills should be related to the lesson previously presented. A short review of earlier lessons is usually necessary, particularly in flight training.
3. *Scope.* Each lesson should be reasonable in scope. A person can master only a few principles or skills at a time, the number

depending on complexity. Presenting too much material in a lesson results in confusion; presenting too little material results in inefficiency.

4. *Practicality.* Each lesson should be planned in terms of the conditions under which the training is to be conducted. Lesson plans conducted in an airplane or ground trainer will differ from those conducted in a classroom. Also, the kinds and quantities of instructional aids available have a great influence on lesson planning and instructional procedures.

5. *Relation to Course of Training.* Each lesson should be planned and taught so that its relation to the course objectives are clear to each student. For example, a lesson on short field takeoffs and landings should be related to both the certification and safety objectives of the course of training.

6. *Instructional Steps.* Every lesson, when adequately developed, falls logically into the four steps of the teaching process; i.e., preparation, presentation, application, and review and evaluation.

How to Use a Lesson Plan Properly

1. *Be Familiar With the Lesson Plan.* The instructor should study each step of the plan and should be thoroughly familiar with as much information related to the subject as possible.

2. *Use the Lesson Plan as a Guide.* The lesson plan is an outline for conducting an instructional period. It assures that pertinent materials are at hand and that the presentation is accomplished with order and unity. Having a plan prevents the instructor from "getting off the track," omitting essential points, and introducing irrelevant material. Students have a right to expect an instructor to give the same attention to teaching that they give to learning. The most certain means of achieving teaching success is to have a carefully thought-out lesson plan.

3. *The Lesson Plan is not a Substitute for Thinking.* Instructors should always know more than they have time to teach.

The lesson plan is a framework or skeleton; the instructor should fill it out with as many relevant examples and practical applications as possible.

4. *Adapt the Lesson Plan to the Class or Student.* In teaching a ground school period, the instructor may find that the procedures outlined in the lesson plan are not leading to the desired results. In this situation, the instructor should change the approach. There is no certain way of predicting the reactions of different groups of students. An approach which has been successful with one group may not be equally successful with another.

A lesson plan for an instructional flight period should be appropriate to the background, flight experience, and ability of the particular student. A rigidly prepared lesson plan should *not* be used for an instructional flight because each student requires a slightly different approach. A lesson plan may have to be modified considerably during flight, due to deficiencies in the student's knowledge or poor mastery of elements essential to the effective completion of the lesson. In some cases, the entire lesson plan may have to be abandoned in favor of review.

5. *Revise the Lesson Plan Periodically.* After a lesson plan has been prepared for a ground school period, a continuous revision will be necessary. This is true for a number of reasons; e.g., availability or nonavailability of instructional aids; changes in regulations, new manuals and textbooks; changes in the state-of-the-art; etc.

Lesson Plan Items

Any lesson plan, whether it is for a ground school period or an instructional flight, should contain the following items:

1. *Lesson objective.* The objective of the lesson should be clearly stated in terms of desired student learning outcomes. The objective is the reason for the lesson—what the instructor expects the student to know or do at the completion of the lesson.

The objective for a ground school period on "maneuvering by reference to flight instruments" could be, "To develop the student's understanding of attitude instrument flying as related to straight-and-level flight, climbs and descents, and recovery from unusual attitudes." The objective for an instructional flight period on "ground reference maneuvers" could be, "To develop the student's skill in planning and following a pattern over the ground compensating for wind drift at varying angles."

2. *Elements involved.* This is a statement of the elements of knowledge and skill necessary for the fulfillment of the lesson objective. This may include both elements previously learned and those to be introduced during this lesson. A statement of the elements of a ground school lesson on "maneuvering by reference to flight instruments" should include: (a) straight-and-level flight, (b) turns, (c) climbs and descents, and (d) recovery from unusual attitudes.

The elements of an instructional flight period on "ground reference maneuvers" could be: (a) use of ground references to control path, (b) observation and control of wind effect, and (c) control of airplane attitude, altitude, and heading.

3. *Schedule.* The instructor should estimate the amount of time to be spent on a particular ground school lesson, and also the approximate time to be devoted to the presentation of the elements of that lesson. For example, the time to be devoted to a ground school lesson on "maneuvering by reference to flight instruments" could be 90 minutes, with approximately the following time periods being used to present each of the elements: (a) straight-and-level flight—25 minutes, (b) turns—25 minutes, (c) climbs and descents—25 minutes, and (d) recovery from unusual attitudes—15 minutes.

An example of the approximate time to be devoted to the presentation and practice of the elements of a 90-minute instructional flight period on "ground reference maneuvers" could be: (a) preflight instruction—10 minutes, (b) instructor demonstrations—25 minutes, (c) student practice—45 minutes, and (d) postflight critique—10 minutes.

4. *Equipment.* This includes all instructional materials and training aids required to teach the lesson. For a ground school period, such items as films, slides, mockups, charts, computers, and reference materials should be included. For example, the equipment for a ground school period on "maneuvering by reference to flight instruments" could include the following: (a) an instrument panel mockup, (b) a copy of the FAA Instrument Flying Handbook, AC 61-27B, (c) selected slides on instrument flying, and (d) chalkboard and chalk.

For an instructional flight period on "ground reference maneuvers," the equipment should include at least: (a) a chalkboard for preflight discussion, (b) a copy of the FAA Flight Training Handbook, AC 61-21, and (c) an IFR visor for maneuvers reviewed.

5. *Instructor's actions.* This is a statement of the instructor's proposed procedures for presenting the elements of knowledge and performance involved in the lesson. Utilizing a combination of the lecture and the demonstration-performance methods, the instructor's actions during a ground school period on "maneuvering by reference to flight instruments" could be somewhat as follows: (a) discusses objective, (b) discusses concept of attitude instrument flying, (c) discusses and demonstrates straight-and-level flight from the standpoint of pitch, bank, power control, and trim, using an instrument panel mockup or chalkboard, (d) discusses and demonstrates turns from the standpoint of pitch, bank, power control, and trim, using an instrument panel mockup or chalkboard, (e) discusses and demonstrates climbs and descents from the standpoint of pitch, bank, power control, and trim, using an instrument panel mockup or chalkboard, (f) discusses and demonstrates recovery from unusual atti-

tudes, (g) assigns individual students the task of describing, and demonstrating, by means of an instrument panel mock-up or chalkboard, the control of an airplane by reference to flight instruments, and (h) critiques student presentation.

The instructor's action during an instructional flight period on "ground reference maneuvers" could be: (a) discusses objective, (b) diagrams "S" turns, eights along a road, and rectangular course on chalkboard, (c) demonstrates following a road and coaches student practice, (d) demonstrates "S" turns and coaches student practice, (e) demonstrates eights along a road and coaches student practice, (f) demonstrates rectangular course and coaches student practice, and (g) conducts postflight critique.

6. *Student's actions.* This is a statement of desired student responses to instruction. The student's actions during a ground school lesson on "maneuvering by reference to flight instruments" could be: (a) discusses objective, (b) listens, takes notes, and asks pertinent questions as the instructor lectures and demonstrates, (c) visualizes instrument maneuvers as the instructor lectures and demonstrates, (d) presents maneuvers, and (e) responds to questions posed by the instructor.

The student's actions during an instructional flight period on "ground reference maneuvers" could be: (a) discusses objective, (b) asks pertinent ques-

tions during preflight briefing, (c) at instructor's direction, reviews and practices power-off stalls and flight at minimum controllable airspeed, (d) performs ground reference maneuvers as directed by instructor, (e) asks pertinent questions both during flight and the postflight critique, and (f) responds to questions posed by the instructor.

7. *Completion standards.* This is the evaluation basis for determining how well the student has met the objective of the lesson in terms of knowledge and skill. For a ground school lesson on "maneuvering by reference to flight instruments," the evaluation may be accomplished by oral quizzing or by means of a short written test.

The evaluation at the end of an instructional flight period on "ground reference maneuvers" could be made from the standpoint of coordination, division of attention, orientation, proper wind drift correction, and accuracy in the maintenance of headings, altitude, and airspeed.

A sample lesson plan for a ground school period on "maneuvering by reference to flight instruments" appears on page 100. The "Instructor's Actions" are expanded and detailed on page 101. They may be further expanded as required by the individual instructor.

A sample lesson plan for an instructional flight period on "ground reference maneuvers" appears on page 140.

LESSON <u>MANEUVERING BY REFERENCE TO FLIGHT INSTRUMENTS</u> STUDENT _____ DATE____

OBJECTIVE
- TO DEVELOP THE STUDENT'S UNDERSTANDING OF ATTITUDE INSTRUMENT FLYING AS RELATED TO STRAIGHT-AND-LEVEL FLIGHT, TURNS, CLIMBS AND DESCENTS, AND RECOVERY FROM UNUSUAL ATTITUDES

ELEMENTS
- STRAIGHT-AND-LEVEL FLIGHT
- TURNS
- CLIMBS AND DESCENTS
- RECOVERY FROM UNUSUAL ATTITUDES

SCHEDULE
- STRAIGHT-AND-LEVEL FLIGHT   : 25
- TURNS   : 25
- CLIMBS AND DESCENTS   : 25
- RECOVERY FROM UNUSUAL ATTITUDES   : 15

EQUIPMENT
- INSTRUMENT PANEL MOCKUP
- FAA INSTRUMENT FLYING HANDBOOK
- SELECTED SLIDES ON INSTRUMENT FLYING
- CHALKBOARD AND CHALK

INSTRUCTOR'S ACTIONS
- DISCUSS LESSON <u>OBJECTIVE</u>
- DISCUSS CONCEPT OF ATTITUDE INSTRUMENT FLYING
- DISCUSS, AND BY MEANS OF INSTRUMENT PANEL MOCKUP OR CHALKBOARD, DEMONSTRATE STRAIGHT-AND-LEVEL FLIGHT, TURNS, CLIMBS AND DESCENTS AND UNUSUAL ATTITUDE RECOVERIES
- ASSIGN INDIVIDUAL STUDENTS TASK OF DE-SCRIBING, AND DEMONSTRATING BY MEANS OF INSTRUMENT PANEL MOCKUP OR CHALK-BOARD, THE CONTROL OF AN AIRPLANE BY REFERENCE TO FLIGHT INSTRUMENTS
- CRITIQUE STUDENT PRESENTATION AND ASK QUESTIONS

STUDENT'S ACTIONS
- DISCUSS LESSON OBJECTIVE
- LISTEN, TAKE NOTES, ASK PERTINENT QUESTIONS
- VISUALIZE INSTRUMENT MANEUVERS
- PRESENT MANEUVERS AND RESPOND TO INSTRUCTOR'S QUESTIONS

COMPLETION STANDARDS
- THE STUDENT SHOULD DEMONSTRATE, BY MEANS OF AN ORAL QUIZ OR WRITTEN TEST, THAT HE HAS AN UNDERSTANDING OF THE CONCEPT OF ATTITUDE INSTRUMENT FLYING AND OF THE PERFORMANCE OF BASIC FLIGHT MANEUVERS BY REFERENCE TO FLIGHT INSTRUMENTS

SAMPLE LESSON PLAN FOR A 90-MINUTE GROUND SCHOOL PERIOD

INSTRUCTIONAL AID	OUTLINE	NOTES
SLIDES ON INSTRUMENT FLYING	1. INTRODUCTION	1. ATTENTION--MAKE A STATEMENT OR ASK A QUESTION THAT RELATES LESSON TO STUDENT GOAL OF BECOMING A PROFICIENT INSTRUMENT PILOT. REVIEW PREVIOUS MATERIAL ON ATTITUDE INSTRUMENT FLYING AND GIVE TIE-IN BETWEEN THIS LESSON AND PREVIOUS LESSONS. 2. MOTIVATION--PROVIDE STUDENTS REASONS FOR NEEDING TO LEARN BASIC INSTRUMENT FLIGHT TECHNIQUE. 3. OVERVIEW--DISCUSS LESSON OBJECTIVE AND KEY IDEAS TO BE PRESENTED.
INSTRUMENT PANEL MOCKUP CHALKBOARD SLIDES ON INSTRUMENT FLYING FAA INSTRUMENT FLYING HANDBOOK	2. DEVELOPMENT	1. DISCUSS CONCEPT OF ATTITUDE INSTRUMENT FLYING. 2. PRESENT STRAIGHT-AND-LEVEL FLIGHT ON MOCKUP FROM STANDPOINT OF PITCH, BANK, POWER, AND TRIM CONTROL. 3. PRESENT TURNS ON MOCKUP FROM STANDPOINT OF PITCH, BANK, POWER, AND TRIM CONTROL. 4. PRESENT CLIMBS AND DESCENTS ON MOCKUP FROM STANDPOINT OF PITCH, BANK, POWER, AND TRIM CONTROL. 5. PRESENT RECOVERY FROM UNUSUAL ATTITUDES ON MOCKUP. 6. ASSIGN INDIVIDUAL STUDENTS TO PRESENT INSTRUMENT MANEUVERS ON MOCKUP MONITOR STUDENT PRESENTATION AND MAKE APPROPRIATE COMMENTS.
FAA INSTRUMENT FLYING HANDBOOK	3. CONCLUSION	1. RETRACE IMPORTANT POINTS RELATED TO ELEMENTS OF KNOWLEDGE PRESENTED AND RELATE THEM TO THE LESSON OBJECTIVE. 2. DETERMINE WHETHER OR NOT STUDENTS HAVE MET OBJECTIVE OF LESSON BY SHORT ORAL QUIZ OR WRITTEN TEST. 3. ASSIGN STUDENTS TO STUDY CHAPTER V OF THE FAA INSTRUMENT FLYING HANDBOOK AS IT RELATES TO MAGNETIC COMPASS, TURNS TO PREDETERMINED HEADINGS AND TIMED TURNS. GIVE TIE-IN BETWEEN THIS LESSON AND NEXT LESSON.

"INSTRUCTOR'S ACTIONS" EXPANDED AND DETAILED

LESSON GROUND REFERENCE MANEUVERS **STUDENT** _____ **DATE** _____

OBJECTIVE
- TO DEVELOP THE STUDENT'S SKILL IN PLANNING AND FOLLOWING A PATTERN OVER THE GROUND COMPENSATING FOR WIND DRIFT AT VARYING ANGLES

ELEMENTS
- USE OF GROUND REFERENCES TO CONTROL PATH
- OBSERVATION AND CONTROL OF WIND EFFECT
- CONTROL OF AIRPLANE ATTITUDE, ALTITUDE, AND HEADING

SCHEDULE
- PREFLIGHT DISCUSSION : 10
- INSTRUCTOR DEMONSTRATIONS : 25
- STUDENT PRACTICE : 45
- POSTFLIGHT CRITIQUE : 10

EQUIPMENT
- CHALKBOARD FOR PREFLIGHT DISCUSSION
- IFR VISOR FOR MANEUVERS REVIEWED

INSTRUCTOR'S ACTIONS
- PREFLIGHT—DISCUSS LESSON OBJECTIVE. DIAGRAM "S" TURNS, EIGHTS ALONG A ROAD, AND RECTANGULAR COURSE ON CHALKBOARD

- INFLIGHT—DEMONSTRATE ELEMENTS. DEMONSTRATE FOLLOWING A ROAD, "S" TURNS, EIGHTS ALONG A ROAD, AND RECTANGULAR COURSE. COACH STUDENT PRACTICE

- POSTFLIGHT—CRITIQUE STUDENT PERFORMANCE AND MAKE STUDY ASSIGNMENT

STUDENT'S ACTIONS
- PREFLIGHT—DISCUSS LESSON OBJECTIVE AND RESOLVE QUESTIONS

- INFLIGHT—REVIEW PREVIOUS MANEUVERS INCLUDING POWER-OFF STALLS AND FLIGHT AT MINIMUM CONTROLLABLE AIRSPEED. PERFORM EACH NEW MANEUVER AS DIRECTED.

- POSTFLIGHT—ASK PERTINENT QUESTIONS

COMPLETION STANDARDS
- STUDENT SHOULD DEMONSTRATE COMPETENCY IN MAINTAINING ORIENTATION, AIRSPEED WITHIN 10 KNOTS, ALTITUDE WITHIN 100 FEET, AND HEADINGS WITHIN 10 DEGREES, AND IN MAKING PROPER CORRECTION FOR WIND DRIFT.

SAMPLE LESSON PLAN FOR A 90—MINUTE INSTRUCTIONAL FLIGHT PERIOD

APPENDIX C
GROUND SCHOOL COURSE SUGGESTIONS

The purpose of this appendix is to suggest ideas concerning marketing, organization, and presentation of ground schools for the private pilot knowledge test. I appreciate any comments or suggestions you may have after reading this material, and so will other aviation professionals when I incorporate this information into subsequent editions. Please jot down notes on the last page of this book and send these to me at your convenience. Thank you.

RATIONALE FOR CONDUCTING A GROUND SCHOOL

1. **Aid to the industry.** Although some flight schools are financially sound, general aviation (which includes flight instruction) is faring poorly in most areas of the country. The market can be developed, but only with the realistic expectation that ground schools by themselves will not generate large profits. A ground school is generally a labor of love.

2. **Professional updating.** Obtaining your flight and/or ground instructor certificate will keep you up to date on the FARs and all other academic areas of flight. Additionally, teaching will challenge you to learn and understand a wide variety of material.

3. **Market entry.** Many flight instructors use ground schools as a source of student pilots.

4. **Public service.** Many flight and/or ground instructors feel that they can provide ground schools to Civil Air Patrol (CAP) chapters, high school classes, etc., as a public service to young people.

5. **Personal employment.** Obtaining your flight and/or ground instructor certificate can result in part-time work at FBOs, community colleges, and adult education programs.

POTENTIAL SPONSORS OF GROUND SCHOOLS

1. **Community colleges.** Call your local junior college and ask if a ground school is offered. Ask what division it is in and call the Dean or Director to indicate your interest in teaching the ground school. While talking to the Dean or Director, you should obtain a course outline, as well as information on the cost and class schedule. The college may already have an instructor, but you should make your interest in teaching known in case there should be an opening.

   a. Send me the Dean or Director's name and address and your own name and address. I will send him/her a complimentary copy of *Private Pilot and Recreational Pilot FAA Written Exam* and explain that it was at your suggestion. I will reiterate your interest in presenting a ground school.

2. **Local high school adult education centers.** Call all local high schools for more information.

3. **FBOs.** Inquire at your local airport, or check the Yellow Pages.

4. **Civil Air Patrol units.** Inquire at your local armed forces recruiting or training station for the name and telephone number of local CAP unit commanders (see the U.S. Government section of your telephone book).

MARKETING GROUND SCHOOLS

The objective is to contact new students if you are beginning a new ground school and to increase enrollment if you are associated with an existing ground school. The following are only a few suggestions.

1. **Classified ads in local newspapers.** Ads usually cost only a few dollars a day for a brief description that might read:

   "Private Pilot Ground School. 6 weeks in length, Tuesday and Thursday evenings, 7:00-9:00 p.m. Offered at (course location). Tuition, books, etc., $(your price). Call (instructor or sponsor name) at (phone number) after 7 p.m."

2. **Radio ads.** Call your local radio station and pay for an advertisement or, preferably, have it broadcast as a public service announcement. Provide the same information stated in the sample ad above.

3. **Posters.** Prepare posters and provide a telephone number, again with the above information. Post it at your local community college, university, airport, in stores, etc.

GROUND SCHOOL COURSE ORGANIZATION

Of course, we hope you will use *Pilot Handbook* and *Private Pilot and Recreational Pilot FAA Written Exam*. Based on that presumption, it is probably easiest to follow our chapter organization, which is the same in both books, so you can use them together.

Chapter 1 • Airplanes and Aerodynamics
Chapter 2 • Airplane Instruments, Engines, and Systems
Chapter 3 • Airports, Air Traffic Control, and Airspace
Chapter 4 • Federal Aviation Regulations
Chapter 5 • Airplane Performance and Weight and Balance
Chapter 6 • Aeromedical Factors
Chapter 7 • Aviation Weather
Chapter 8 • Aviation Weather Services
Chapter 9 • Navigation: Charts, Publications, Flight Computers
Chapter 10 • Navigation Systems
Chapter 11 • Cross-Country Flying

Note that both books can be purchased for $27.90 retail, or at a discount if ordered in quantity. For instance, you may purchase four or more books and *FAA Test Prep* diskettes ($30 retail) at a 40% discount by prepaying. Thus, you could package the books and software at $40-$50 or include them in the cost of the ground school. Other purchase options are also available, including having your students order directly from us. To place an order or to obtain additional information, call us at (800) 87-GLEIM.

You will probably have a different number of class sessions than 11, which may necessitate combining chapters for various classes. Even if you have 11 sessions, you may want to combine certain chapters and spend more time on other chapters. For example, if you have a 6-week program that meets for 10 sessions, you might want to combine Chapters 9, 10, and 11. Additionally, you can easily cover the Introduction in Session 1 and still use a good part of the session to get into Chapter 1. Then spend another entire meeting to finish Chapter 1.

In any event, you may wish to reserve 15 or 20 minutes at the end of each session for an overview and introduction of the material to be covered in the next session. That will help your students to study for the next session and help them understand it.

COURSE SYLLABUS AND HANDOUTS

1. At the beginning of the course, you should hand out an outline of the material to be covered in the course. It should show the meeting times, quiz schedule, and reading assignments for each session.

2. A suggested syllabus for a 9-week class that meets for 3 hours one night per week is presented on the following page.

    a. Undoubtedly you will have to change the scheduling of topics. The topics have been overlapped so that you can talk about the same topic during two periods, i.e., double exposure. Introducing the topic the week before provides 3 weeks' coverage, which may be useful to your students.

3. Another ground school syllabus (16 lessons) is provided in Chapter XI, Planning Instructional Activity, of *Aviation Instructor's Handbook*, which is reprinted in Appendix B of this book beginning on page 108. You should refer to that also.

4. Of course, the 30 modules grouped in six chapters in this book will be helpful to you as general background in preparing and presenting your ground school.

OTHER TEXTBOOKS

You should have Gleim's *Aviation Weather and Weather Services* and *FAA Test Prep* and access to a number of competitor ground school books as a source of discussion, ideas, etc. Additionally, you will presumably have the FAA's *Pilot Handbook of Aeronautical Knowledge*, recent copies of the FARs and the *Aeronautical Information Manual*, and your FAA *Flight Training Handbook*.

Use these as sources of information and show the FAA books to your students. Pass the books around so they may see the books that are referred to in questions, explanations, and/or outlines.

ENROLLMENT PROCEDURES

1. You should list the students and their telephone numbers in the event the classes need to be changed, rescheduled, etc.

    a. Note the form and date of their payment.

2. As students enroll, you can sell them a book (or give it to them if they buy the book as part of the ground school course).

3. If you have a syllabus ready, give it to them and encourage them to do some study in advance.

SAMPLE COURSE SYLLABUS

COURSE SYLLABUS

Jonesville Community College
Evening Education Course 1121

Tuesday evenings, 7:00 - 10:00 p.m.
North Campus, Building C, Room 171

PRIVATE PILOT GROUND SCHOOL
Summer Term A, 199X
June 1 - July 27

INSTRUCTOR: Mr. Harold Gray, AGI
Office: (111) 555-5252
Home: (111) 555-2525

COURSE OBJECTIVE: Learn the material required by the FAA for the private pilot knowledge test (airplane) with the objective of each student passing the test.

CLASSROOM PROCEDURE: Lecture and guided discussion.

1. Each class will begin with a review and questions from the last class (approximately 5-15 minutes).

2. Next, there will be a brief overview and core concepts for the current evening's assignment, followed by class discussion and questions.

3. When appropriate, after the class break, an in-class quiz will be administered, self-graded, and analyzed through class discussion.

4. The last 15-30 minutes of each class session will be directed toward an overview and discussion of the next class's assignment.

5. Visual aids and handouts will be used as appropriate.

REQUIRED TEXT: *Private Pilot and Recreational Pilot FAA Written Exam*, by Irvin N. Gleim.

RECOMMENDED TEXT: *Pilot Handbook*, by Irvin N. Gleim.

These texts are available in the College Bookstore on the North Campus, which is open until 8:00 p.m. each Tuesday.

SCHEDULE

Class	Date	PPWE* Chapters	Topic
1	June 1	Introduction, 1	Introduction, Aerodynamic Theory
2	June 8	1, 2	Aerodynamics and Airplane Systems
3	June 15	2, 3	Airplane Systems, Airports, ATC
4	June 22	3, 4	Airspace, FARs
5	June 29	4, 5	FARs, Airplane Performance
6	July 6	5, 6	Weight and Balance, Aeromedical Factors
7	July 13	7, 8	Aviation Weather and Weather Services
8	July 20	9, 10, 11	Navigation, Cross-Country Flight
9	July 27		Review for pilot knowledge test

* PPWE = *Private Pilot and Recreational Pilot FAA Written Exam*

You may photocopy this syllabus and change it in any way you like.

4. With respect to requiring or recommending *Pilot Handbook* and *Aviation Weather and Weather Services*, you should experiment:

   a. Put one of each on reserve.

   b. Get one copy of each and pass them around to the class; indicate they can purchase another one from you, a local FBO, a bookstore, or by calling Gleim Publications, Inc.

   c. Alternatively, have them order the book using our standard mail order brochure (let us know how many brochures you would like).

5. Note that you may wish to encourage each person who enrolls or even inquires about the program to invite friends to take the course with him/her. The idea is to build enrollment by enthusiasm and interest in aviation.

THE FIRST CLASS SESSION

1. Preliminaries

   a. Arrive early with a supply of books, handouts, and your lecture notes for the first lecture.
   b. Begin by enrolling students who show up at the last minute.
   c. Go over the roll and pass out the syllabus.
   d. Stop and introduce yourself.

2. Student-Instructor Interaction

   a. Tell the students about your background, the origination of the course, your reasons for teaching, and other personal anecdotes.

   b. Tell the class that you need to learn more about them.

      1) Ask people to introduce themselves.

      2) Unless the class is too large, make notes on your roster to individualize participants and help you learn their names.

      3) Ask them why they are taking the course, if they have any flying experience, if they know anyone else who flies, if they have ever flown before in a small aircraft, etc.

   c. Such interaction breaks the ice, not only to let students get to know you and each other, but also for you to get to know them.

3. Discussion of Course Objective (FAA Private Pilot Knowledge Test)

   a. Display *Private Pilot and Recreational Pilot FAA Written Exam*.

   b. Point out that the textbook has the FAA questions reorganized by topic with answer explanations next to them.

   c. Indicate that the areas tested on the exam will be the topics specified on your syllabus (course outline), that the test will be only 60 questions, and that the students need to get only 42 questions correct to pass.

      1) This will be very easy because they will have gone over all possible test questions during your course (all of which appear in *Private Pilot and Recreational Pilot FAA Written Exam*), as well as additional material to help them learn how to fly safely.

   d. Explain the content of *Private Pilot and Recreational Pilot FAA Written Exam*.

      1) Explain that the Introduction is the current topic of discussion.
      2) Show them the organization of Chapters 1 through 11.

         a) Each chapter begins with an outline, module by module (topic by topic).

> b) Following the outlines are questions and answer explanations organized in the same modules in the same order.
>
> c) Thus, the students are able to study and try to learn the material before they answer the questions. This format provides an extra level of reinforcement as they study the material.

LECTURE PRESENTATION

1. There are many ways to present a lecture, and you should use the method with which you feel most comfortable. The best method for you will be the best method for your students.

2. One approach to keep in mind is the idea of hitting the high points or key concepts.

   a. What are the basic or major concepts within any topic? These are generally outlined at the opening of each chapter in *Private Pilot and Recreational Pilot FAA Written Exam*.

   b. To amplify these concepts and provide additional discussion, consult *Pilot Handbook*, after which you can use additional examples from other textbooks, including the FAA/government textbooks.

3. A major objective of your lecture presentation is to make it interactive: the students must respond to you and participate.

   a. Learning is **not** a one-way communication from you to your students.

   b. You need to ask questions of individual students and of the class as a whole so that they can react and commit to an answer (silently or orally), and then get immediate feedback about the accuracy of their responses.

4. Another approach is to have them work examples, e.g., provide them with a calculation and ask them to determine the answer.

   a. You could present a series of questions from the FAA written test (current or earlier test), take away the alternative answers, and have them work through a couple of exercises.

   b. You might also put these on overhead projectors.

5. Preclass preparation is very important. You should consult the lesson plan discussed in Appendix B of this book and review Chapter 5, Teaching Methods, beginning on page 45.

VISUAL AIDS

1. Visual aids include small model airplanes, film strips, slides, blackboard presentations, overhead projector pictures, etc.

2. You can bring items to class and pass them around, such as other textbooks and operating manuals from airplanes.

3. Experiment with visual aids. Use them as attention getters or to break the pace of the normal presentation.

COURSE EVALUATIONS

1. At the end of the course, but before the session set aside for the FAA written test, you should administer a course evaluation.

   a. Your objective is to gain feedback from your students about how the course can be improved in several aspects, including:

      1) Course organization
      2) Textbook(s)
      3) Lecture presentation
      4) Physical facilities

b.   Let the students know that you are seeking constructive criticism across many areas.

c.   Tell them that you do not want to make them ill at ease, so you are going to ask one member (tell them who) to hold the evaluations until the course is over.

d.   If the course is for grade credit, the evaluations should be held until after you have turned in the grades.

2.   Please feel free to photocopy and modify the course evaluation illustrated below. Note that you should leave the back blank for additional written comments.

3.   Remember that, at the conclusion of the last class session prior to your students' taking the FAA pilot knowledge test, you need to complete the Instructor Certification Form at the back of *Private Pilot and Recreational Pilot FAA Written Exam* for each student.

Date _____

(NAME OF COURSE)
GROUND SCHOOL EVALUATION FORM

This Ground School is being presented to aid you in your preparation for the FAA knowledge test. Please help us by answering the following questions, keeping in mind our objective: to help you prepare for the FAA knowledge test. Please check one response for each line. Return the completed form to the person designated to hold the evaluations until the completion of the last class (or after grades have been turned in).

Instructor	Excellent	Good	Adequate	Poor
1. Instructor presentation of material	—	—	—	—
2. Instructor knowledge of subject	—	—	—	—
3. Allocation of time to topics	—	—	—	—
4. Use of slides, boards, visual aids, etc.	—	—	—	—
5. Use of handouts, problems, etc.	—	—	—	—
6. Overall rating of instructor	—	—	—	—
Other questions				
7. Classroom comfort	—	—	—	—
8. Progress of course as a whole	—	—	—	—
9. Outlines in *Private Pilot and Recreational Pilot FAA Written Exam*	—	—	—	—
10. Answer explanations in *Private Pilot and Recreational Pilot FAA Written Exam*	—	—	—	—
11. Overall rating of *Private Pilot and Recreational Pilot FAA Written Exam*	—	—	—	—

12. **Other comments.** Please explain "poor" responses and make any other suggestions you feel may be relevant in the space provided below and on the back of this sheet. **Thank you.**

HELPING YOUR STUDENTS SELECT A COMPUTER TESTING CENTER

1.   Since most computer testing centers have limited seating, it is unlikely that you will be able to have all of your students take the test at the same time and place.

a.   Thus, you will need to help your students in the selection of a computer testing center.

2.   Call each testing service to determine if any discounts are being offered and the payment policy. Explain your class situation (number of students, etc.)

a.   Some students may not have a credit card, so they need to select a computer testing center that will accept a check or cash at the time of the test.

      1)   Some computer testing services may require that a check or money order be sent before the student can take the test.

   b.   Make yourself available to assist your students as necessary.

3.   Provide your students with the telephone numbers of the following computer testing services and the results of your inquiries.

        CATS   (800) 947-4228
        LASERGRADE (800) 211-2754
        SYLVAN   (800) 274-1900

4.   Discuss the examination process and demonstrate testing procedures by using Gleim's *FAA Test Prep* software.

5.   You are required to maintain a record of each person for whom you sign a certification for a pilot knowledge test, including the kind of test, date of test, and the test result (FAR 61.189).

   a.   An efficient way of obtaining test results is to preaddress and stamp one postcard for each student (include the student's name on the card) and explain why you need these returned.

      1)   Hand them out on the exam day.
      2)   Ask students to mail their numerical scores to you.
      3)   List the student scores on your roster as they come in the mail.
      4)   Call any individuals who have not submitted cards.

   b.   You can use these pass rates in future advertising.

AN ALTERNATIVE APPROACH: EXPANDING YOUR MARKET

1.   You may wish to broaden your ground school course so that it appeals to aviation enthusiasts interested in doing more than passing the FAA private pilot (airplane) knowledge test. If so, you need to

   a.   Diversify your marketing plan and advertisements.
   b.   Edit the suggested syllabus (make it more general).
   c.   Prepare fewer class assignments focused on the FAA pilot knowledge test.

2.   Can you prepare student pilots for the FAA pilot knowledge test **and** provide a general-interest aviation course?

   a.   Many ground schools are so directed, especially at community colleges where a considerable number of enrollees do not take the FAA pilot knowledge test.

   b.   One approach is to emphasize discussion of FAA test questions at the end (optional part) of each class; e.g., in a 100-minute class.

      1)   The last 30 minutes might be restricted to discussion of FAA questions in *Private Pilot and Recreational Pilot FAA Written Exam*.

      2)   The first 70 minutes would involve lecture discussion.

   c.   Occasional questions might be discussed, but the emphasis would be on learning about airplanes, weather, and navigation rather than passing the FAA pilot knowledge test.

   d.   In such a course, *Pilot Handbook* would be the required text instead of *Private Pilot and Recreational Pilot FAA Written Exam*, which can serve as the optional text.

3.   With these general guidelines, we trust you will take the plunge and **start your class** (or at least begin to prepare for it) **right now**! It is fun, and it provides a valuable service -- teaching new aviation enthusiasts to **ENJOY FLYING -- SAFELY!**

AUTHOR'S RECOMMENDATION

The Experimental Aircraft Association, Inc. is a very successful and effective nonprofit organization that represents and serves those of us interested in flying, in general, and in sport aviation, in particular. I personally invite you to enjoy becoming a member:

$35 for a 1-year membership
$20 per year for individuals under 19 years old
Family membership available for $45 per year

Membership includes the monthly magazine *Sport Aviation*.

Write to: Experimental Aircraft Association, Inc.
P.O. Box 3086
Oshkosh, Wisconsin 54903

Or call: (414) 426-4800
(800) 564-6322

The annual EAA Oshkosh Fly-in is an unbelievable aviation spectacular with over 10,000 airplanes at one airport! Virtually everything aviation-oriented you can imagine! Plan to spend at least 1 day (not everything can be seen in a day) in Oshkosh (100 miles northwest of Milwaukee).

Convention dates:
1998 -- July 29 through August 4
1999 -- July 22 through August 2

* *

The National Association of Flight Instructors (NAFI) is a nonprofit organization dedicated to raising and maintaining the professional standing of the flight instructor in the aviation community. Members accept the responsibility to practice their profession according to the highest ethical standards. I personally invite you to become a member:

Active - Certificated flight instructors (civilian and military)
Initial membership = $35
Annual renewal = $30

Associate - Individuals and organizations in support of professional flight education
Initial membership and annual renewal = $100

Membership includes the bimonthly *NAFI Foundation Newsletter,* an accidental death and dismemberment policy, and representation with the FAA in Washington.

Write to: National Association of Flight Instructors
EAA Aviation Center
P.O. Box 3086
Oshkosh, WI 54903-3086

Or call: (800) 843-3612

CROSS-REFERENCES TO THE FAA PILOT KNOWLEDGE TEST QUESTION NUMBERS

Pages 141 and 142 contain the FAA fundamentals of instructing question numbers from the flight/ground instructor knowledge test bank. The questions are numbered 6001 to 6160. To the right of each FAA question number, we have added the FAA's subject matter knowledge code (refer to page 10 in Chapter 1 for a complete listing and description of each). To the right of the subject matter knowledge code, we have listed our answer and our chapter and question number. For example, the FAA's question 6001 is cross-referenced to the FAA's subject matter knowledge code H20, *Aviation Instructor's Handbook*, Chapter I, The Learning Process." The correct answer is A, and the question appears with answer explanations in our book under 2-1, which means it is reproduced in Chapter 2 as question 1.

The first line of each of our answer explanations in Chapters 2 through 7 contains

1. The correct answer
2. The FAA question number
3. A reference for the answer explanation, e.g., *AIH Chap I*.

Thus, our question numbers are cross-referenced throughout this book to the FAA question numbers, and these two pages cross-reference the FAA question numbers back to this book.

FAA Q. No.	FAA Subject Code	Gleim Answer	Gleim Chap/ Q. No.	FAA Q. No.	FAA Subject Code	Gleim Answer	Gleim Chap/ Q. No.	FAA Q. No.	FAA Subject Code	Gleim Answer	Gleim Chap/ Q. No.
6001	H20	A	2-1	6023	H20	B	4-5	6045	H21	C	3-3
6002	H20	C	2-2	6024	H20	C	4-9	6046	H21	B	3-9
6003	H20	C	2-3	6025	H20	B	4-4	6047	H21	A	3-5
6004	H20	B	2-4	6026	H20	A	4-6	6048	H21	B	3-6
6005	H20	A	2-6	6027	H20	A	2-28	6049	H21	B	3-8
6006	H20	A	2-7	6028	H20	B	2-29	6050	H21	A	3-7
6007	H20	C	2-5	6029	H20	C	2-31	6051	H21	B	3-10
6008	H20	C	2-9	6030	H20	A	2-30	6052	H21	B	7-8
6009	H20	B	2-10	6031	H20	B	2-32	6053	H21	A	4-7
6010	H20	A	2-8	6032	H20	C	6-26	6054	H21	A	6-22
6011	H20	A	2-11	6033	H20	B	2-33	6055	H21	A	4-21
6012	H20	A	2-13	6034	H20	C	2-23	6056	H22	B	4-11
6013	H20	C	2-19	6035	H20	C	2-22	6057	H22	C	4-14
6014	H20	A	2-14	6036	H20	A	2-21	6058	H22	C	4-13
6015	H20	A	2-12	6037	H20	B	2-24	6059	H22	B	4-12
6016	H20	C	3-1	6038	H20	C	2-26	6060	H22	B	4-15
6017	H20	A	2-17	6039	H20	B	2-25	6061	H22	C	4-19
6018	H20	A	3-2	6040	H20	A	2-27	6062	H22	C	4-18
6019	H20	A	2-15	6041	H21	B	4-1	6063	H22	C	4-16
6020	H20	A	2-20	6042	H21	A	4-2	6064	H22	C	4-17
6021	H20	B	2-18	6043	H21	C	4-3	6065	H23	A	6-6
6022	H20	B	4-8	6044	H21	C	3-4	6066	H23	C	5-15

FAA Q. No.	FAA Subject Code	Gleim Answer	Gleim Chap/Q. No.	FAA Q. No.	FAA Subject Code	Gleim Answer	Gleim Chap/Q. No.	FAA Q. No.	FAA Subject Code	Gleim Answer	Gleim Chap/Q. No.
6067	H23	B	7-30	6107	H26	C	7-27	6147	H32	B	6-2
6068	H23	A	5-1	6108	H26	B	7-28	6148	H32	C	6-13
6069	H23	A	7-29	6109	H26	B	7-26	6149	H32	C	6-5
6070	H23	A	7-1	6110	H26	A	7-21	6150	H32	C	6-21
6071	H24	A	6-9	6111	H26	A	7-17	6151	H32	A	6-24
6072	H24	C	6-8	6112	H26	C	7-16	6152	H32	C	6-23
6073	H24	B	6-7	6113	H26	B	7-18	6153	H32	B	6-12
6074	H24	B	6-11	6114	H26	C	7-22	6154	H32	B	6-14
6075	H24	A	6-10	6115	H26	B	7-19	6155	H32	A	6-15
6076	H24	C	5-5	6116	H26	C	7-20	6156	H32	C	6-20
6077	H24	C	5-4	6117	H26	B	7-23	6157	H32	C	6-18
6078	H24	B	5-6	6118	H26	B	7-31	6158	H32	A	6-16
6079	H24	A	5-2	6119	H27	B	6-27	6159	H32	B	6-17
6080	H24	A	5-8	6120	H27	B	6-29	6160	H32	C	6-19
6081	H24	B	5-7	6121	H27	A	6-30				
6082	H24	B	5-3	6122	H27	C	6-28				
6083	H24	B	5-10	6123	H30	A	4-20				
6084	H24	C	5-14	6124	H30	A	4-10				
6085	H24	A	5-9	6125	H30	A	3-18				
6086	H24	B	5-12	6126	H30	C	3-17				
6087	H24	A	5-11	6127	H30	C	4-23				
6088	H24	C	5-13	6128	H30	B	5-25				
6089	H24	C	5-16	6129	H30	B	5-24				
6090	H24	B	5-18	6130	H30	B	3-11				
6091	H24	B	5-17	6131	H30	B	3-13				
6092	H25	B	7-3	6132	H30	A	3-14				
6093	H25	C	7-7	6133	H30	B	3-12				
6094	H25	C	7-2	6134	H31	C	5-19				
6095	H25	C	7-4	6135	H31	C	5-21				
6096	H25	B	7-5	6136	H31	A	5-20				
6097	H25	C	7-6	6137	H31	C	5-22				
6098	H26	A	7-10	6138	H31	A	5-23				
6099	H26	B	7-11	6139	H31	B	3-16				
6100	H26	A	7-9	6140	H31	B	3-15				
6101	H26	A	7-13	6141	H31	A	6-25				
6102	H26	B	7-14	6142	H31	C	4-22				
6103	H26	A	7-12	6143	H31	A	2-16				
6104	H26	A	7-15	6144	H32	A	6-1				
6105	H26	C	7-25	6145	H32	B	6-4				
6106	H26	A	7-24	6146	H32	C	6-3				

INSTRUCTOR CERTIFICATION FORM
FUNDAMENTALS OF INSTRUCTING KNOWLEDGE TEST

Name: _____

I certify that I have reviewed the above individual's preparation for the FAA Fundamentals of Instructing (FOI) knowledge test [covering the topics specified in FAR 61.185(a)(1) and 61.213(a)(3)] using the *Fundamentals of Instructing FAA Written Exam* book and/or software by Irvin N. Gleim and find him/her competent to pass the FOI knowledge test.

| Signed | Date | Name | CFI Number | Expiration Date |

* *

INSTRUCTOR CERTIFICATION FORM
FLIGHT INSTRUCTOR KNOWLEDGE TEST

Name: _____

I certify that I have reviewed the above individual's preparation for the FAA Flight Instructor -- Airplane knowledge test [covering the topics specified in FAR 61.185(a)(2)] using the *Flight Instructor FAA Written Exam* book and/or software by Irvin N. Gleim and find him/her competent to pass the knowledge test.

| Signed | Date | Name | CFI Number | Expiration Date |

* *

INSTRUCTOR CERTIFICATION FORM
GROUND INSTRUCTOR -- ADVANCED KNOWLEDGE TEST

Name: _____

I certify that I have reviewed the above individual's preparation for the FAA Basic/Advanced Ground Instructor knowledge test [covering the topics specified in FAR 61.213(a)(4)(i) or (ii)] using the *Ground Instructor FAA Written Exam* book and/or software by Irvin N. Gleim and find him/her competent to pass the knowledge test.

| Signed | Date | Name | CFI Number | Expiration Date |

USE GLEIM'S *FAA TEST PREP* --
A POWERFUL TOOL IN THE
GLEIM KNOWLEDGE TRANSFER SYSTEM

Give yourself the competitive edge! Because all of the FAA's "written" tests have been converted to computer testing, Gleim has developed software specifically designed to prepare you for the computerized pilot knowledge test.

➡ *FAATP* emulates the computer testing vendor of your choice -- CATS, LaserGrade, Sylvan, or AvTEST. You will be completely familiar with the computer testing system you will be using.

➡ *FAATP* has two interactive modes: "Study" and "Test." Study mode permits you to select questions from specific sources, e.g., Gleim modules, questions that you missed from the last session, etc. You can also determine the order of the questions (Gleim or random), and you can randomize the order of the answer choices for each question.

➡ *FAATP* precludes you from looking at the answers before you commit to an answer and provides the actual testing environment. This is a major difference from the book.

➡ *FAATP* contains the well-known Gleim answer explanations which are intuitively appealing and easy to understand.

➡ *FAATP* maintains a history of your proficiency in each topic. This enables you to focus your study only on topics that need additional study.

➡ *FAATP* is the most versatile and complete software available. Only $30 per test.

GLEIM'S NEW
E-MAIL UPDATE SERVICE

update@gleim.com

our message to Gleim must include (in the subject or body) the acronym
r your book or software, followed by the edition-printing for books and
rsion for software. The edition-printing is indicated on the book's spine.
e software version is indicated on the diskette label.

	Written Exam		Practical Test Prep
	Book	Software	Book
Private Pilot	PPWE	FAATP PP	PPPT
Instrument Pilot	IPWE	FAATP IP	IPPT
Commercial Pilot	CPWE	FAATP CP	CPPT
Flight/Ground Instructor	FIGI	FAATP FIGI	FIPT
Fundamentals of Instructing	FOI	FAATP FOI	
Airline Transport Pilot	ATP	FAATP ATP	

	Reference Book
Pilot Handbook	PH
Aviation Weather and Weather Services	AWWS

For **Fundamentals of Instructing,** sixth edition-fifth printing:

> To: update@gleim.com
> From: your e-mail address
> Subject: FOI 6-5

For **FAA Test Prep** software, FOI, version 2.5:

> To: update@gleim.com
> From: your e-mail address
> Subject: FAATP FOI 2-5

**E
X
A
M
P
L
E
S**

**IT
ONLY
TAKES
A
MINUTE**

ou do not have e-mail, have a friend send e-mail to us and print our response for you.

LESSON:

STUDENT: _____   **DATE:** _____

OBJECTIVE

ELEMENTS

SCHEDULE

EQUIPMENT

INSTRUCTOR'S ACTIONS

STUDENT'S ACTIONS

COMPLETION STANDARDS

PILOT KNOWLEDGE (WRITTEN EXAM) BOOKS AND SOFTWARE

Before pilots take their FAA pilot knowledge tests, they want to understand the answer to every FAA test question. Gleim's pilot knowledge test books are widely used because they help pilots learn and understand exactly what they need to know to do well on the FAA pilot knowledge test.

Gleim's books contain all of the FAA's airplane questions (nonairplane questions are excluded). We have unscrambled the questions appearing in the FAA Pilot Knowledge Test Bank and organized them into logical topics. Answer explanations are provided next to each question. Each of our chapters opens with a brief, user-friendly outline of exactly what you need to know to pass the test. Information not directly tested is omitted to expedite your passing. This additional information can be found in our reference books and practical test prep/flight maneuver books described below.

Gleim's **FAA Test Prep** software will get you off to a fast and successful start. Use **FAA Test Prep** in conjunction with the appropriate Gleim book to emulate all of the major computer testing centers.

PRIVATE PILOT AND RECREATIONAL PILOT FAA WRITTEN EXAM ($13.95)

The FAA's pilot knowledge test for the private pilot certificate consists of 60 questions out of the 711 questions in our book. Also, the FAA's pilot knowledge test for the recreational pilot certificate consists of 50 questions from this book.

INSTRUMENT PILOT FAA WRITTEN EXAM ($16.95)

The FAA's pilot knowledge test consists of 60 questions out of the 900 questions in our book. Also, anyone who wishes to become an instrument-rated flight instructor (CFII) or an instrument ground instructor (IGI) must take the FAA's pilot knowledge test of 50 questions from this book.

COMMERCIAL PILOT FAA WRITTEN EXAM ($14.95)

The FAA's pilot knowledge test consists of 100 questions out of the 565 questions in our book.

FUNDAMENTALS OF INSTRUCTING FAA WRITTEN EXAM ($9.95)

The FAA's pilot knowledge test consists of 50 questions out of the 160 questions in our book. This test is required for any person to become a flight instructor or ground instructor. The test needs to be taken only once. For example, if someone is already a flight instructor and wants to become a ground instructor, taking the FOI test a second time is not required.

FLIGHT/GROUND INSTRUCTOR FAA WRITTEN EXAM ($14.95)

The FAA's flight instructor knowledge test consists of 100 questions out of the 833 questions in our book. This book is to be used for the Flight Instructor--Airplane (FIA), Basic Ground Instructor (BGI), and the Advanced Ground Instructor (AGI) knowledge tests.

AIRLINE TRANSPORT PILOT FAA WRITTEN EXAM ($26.95)

The FAA's pilot knowledge test consists of 80 questions each for the ATP Part 121, ATP Part 135, and the flight dispatcher certificate. This difficult FAA pilot knowledge test is now made simple by Gleim. As with Gleim's other written test books, studying for the ATP will now be a learning and understanding experience rather than a memorization marathon -- at a lower cost and with higher test scores and less frustration!!

REFERENCE AND PRACTICAL TEST PREP/FLIGHT MANEUVER BOOKS

Our Practical Test Prep and Flight Maneuvers books are designed to replace the FAA Practical Test Standards reprint booklets which are universally used by pilots preparing for the practical test. These books will help prepare pilots for FAA practical tests as much as the Gleim written exam books help prepare pilots for FAA pilot knowledge tests. Each task, objective, concept, requirement, etc., in the FAA's practical test standards is explained, analyzed, illustrated, and interpreted so pilots will be totally conversant with all aspects of their practical tests.

Private Pilot Practical Test Prep and Flight Maneuvers	360 pages	($16.95)
Instrument Pilot Practical Test Prep and Flight Maneuvers	288 pages	($17.95)
Commercial Pilot Practical Test Prep and Flight Maneuvers	304 pages	($14.95)
Flight Instructor Practical Test Prep and Flight Maneuvers	544 pages	($17.95)

PILOT HANDBOOK ($13.95)

A complete pilot ground school text in outline format with many diagrams for ease in understanding. This book is used in preparation for private, commercial, and flight instructor certificates and the instrument rating. A complete, detailed index makes it more useful and saves time. It contains a special section on biennial flight reviews.

AVIATION WEATHER AND WEATHER SERVICES ($18.95)

This is a complete rewrite of the FAA's Aviation Weather 00-6A and Aviation Weather Services 00-45D into a single easy-to-understand book complete with all of the maps, diagrams, charts, and pictures that appear in the current FAA books. Accordingly, pilots who wish to learn and understand the subject matter in these FAA books can do it much more easily and effectively with this book.

148

INDEX

ABBREVIATIONS AND ACRONYMS
IN
FUNDAMENTALS OF INSTRUCTING

AC	Advisory Circular
AC Form	Airman Certification Form (i.e., AC Form 8080-2)
ADF	automatic direction finder
AGI	Advanced Ground Instructor
AIH	Aviation Instructor's Handbook
APS	Accident Prevention Specialist
ASR	Airport Surveillance Radar
ATC	Air Traffic Control
ATIS	Automatic Terminal Information Service
ATP	Airline Transport Pilot
BGI	Basic Ground Instructor
CAP	Civil Air Patrol
CFI	Certificated Flight Instructor
DF	direction finding
DME	distance measuring equipment
DUAT	Direct User Access Terminal
EAA	Experimental Aircraft Association
FAA	Federal Aviation Administration
FAR	Federal Aviation Regulation
FBO	Fixed-Base Operator
FOI	Fundamentals of Instructing
FSDO	Flight Standards District Office
GADO	General Aviation District Office (now called FSDO)
IFR	instrument flight rules
IGI	Instrument Ground Instructor
IMC	Instrument Meteorological Conditions
IR	instrument reference
NAFI	National Association of Flight Instructors
VFR	visual flight rules
VMC	Visual Meteorological Conditions
VOR	VHF omnidirectional range
VR	visual reference

Please forward your suggestions, corrections, and comments to **Irvin N. Gleim • c/o Gleim Publications, Inc. • P.O. Box 12848 • University Station • Gainesville, Florida • 32604** for inclusion in the next edition of *Fundamentals of Instructing FAA Written Exam*. Please include your name and address on the back of this page so we can properly thank you for your interest. Also, please refer to both the page number and the FAA question number for each item.

1. _____

2. _____

3. _____

4. _____

5. _____

6. _____

7. _____

8. _____

9. _____

10. _____

11. _____

12. _____

13. _____

14. _____

15. _____

16. _____

17. _____

Name:	_____
Address:	_____
City/State/Zip:	_____
Telephone:	Home: _____ Work: _____ Fax: _____
E-mail:	_____